CONTENTS   W9-CQZ-640

Institutional Research: Decision Support in Higher Education

Forward

During the past four to five decades, institutional research has become a significant administrative support function on most postsecondary campuses in the United States. The growth and importance of institutional research in higher education has occurred in response to increased external demands for accountability and a recognition on the part of campus leaders that effective planning and decision making require the analysis and consideration of reliable institutional input data, productivity data, and comparative data. Regardless of whether institutional research is an "art" to be practiced or a "science" to be defined and refined, each institutional researcher tends to define institutional research in terms of what he or she is paid to do at his or her specific campus, and these campus specific activities are the focus of discussions in our publications and at our conferences. The fact is, that there is no consensus definition (or single reality) of what institutional research is across all campuses or systems. As our campuses have reacted to the ever-changing demands and challenges of our society, and as technology has enhanced our capacity to access and analyze greater volumes of data, institutional research has been, and continues to be, a dynamic profession; and discussions about institutional research over time have reflected the changing and expanding nature of the profession. This volume is designed to continue this discussion.

The Association's Forum track structure, familiar to most institutional research professionals, is the framework used to organize the discussion in this book. Using a familiar structure is consistent with a growing body of knowledge about an individual's or organization's understanding or knowing. This body of knowledge emphasizes the role of having a mental or conceptual model that structures or puts into perspective various information. The creation and refinement of mental models enhances and sustains learning, both for individuals and organizations. Peter Senge emphasizes that "the discipline of managing mental models - surfacing, testing, and improving our internal pictures of how the world works - promises to be a major breakthrough for building learning organizations." (p. 174) This is reinforced by the recent National Research Council publication, How People Learn, (2000) where the organization of knowledge is a factor of adaptive expertise and experts' "knowledge is not simply a list of facts and formulas that are relevant to their domain; instead their knowledge is organized around core concepts or 'big ideas' that guide their thinking about their domains."

The structure of knowledge that has served to organize the Association's Forums for many years provides a conceptual model of institutional research that guided the development of this volume. The genesis of this structure was a number of collegial discussions and the analysis of empirical evidence that categorized what we do in the practice of institutional research. The outcomes of these discussions and analyses were incorporated into a track structure for a Forum in the late 1980's. The boundaries of the tracks have never been precise nor have their definitions been static. *

It is important to use a conceptual model, even if it reflects a point-in-time, in order to pursue the development of knowledge as defined above. Having a conceptual model allows us to look at the "completeness" of our professional knowledge and to reflect on what we know and what we do not know. In addition, it allows us to communicate the state of our activities and abilities as required by our code of ethics and professional practices. A recent issue of the AIR Professional File (Volkwein and Volkwein) used this same structure to organize and assess the content of the Association's publications.

Without the sense of a cogent structure we are doomed to the continued level of novice or at best an expert at applying existing knowledge. However, with appropriate conceptual knowledge and the meta-cognition that comes from learning more about our conceptual models, we can fit our uncertainties into our individual models and move to higher levels in the creative application of this new knowledge. We can communicate to others our knowledge, whether it is at the level of a deterministic science controlled by laws and principles or an art to be practiced as the craft we have developed over the past half century. In either case, we can continue our own personal mastery and growth.

This volume has been prepared with such intent. It is intended that this volume be a marker on the way to continued learning and the application of our professional knowledge, skills, and abilities. It contains a great deal of useful information about institutional research, its theoretical framework, practice, tools, and contribution to the management of higher education. This information is provided within a conceptual framework for thinking about the conduct of institutional research - the seven content tracks of the 2001 AIR Forum.

These seven tracks reflect the general content areas that in general define the activities of the profession and provide the chapter structure of this volume. Writing to the descriptions of the individual tracts, the authors of each chapter provide a description and discussion of the status of institutional research at this point-in-time. They have provided a "marker" in the continuum of the development of the profession. This marker reflects the status of the profession after the first four or five decades of its existence as a recognized administrative function in higher education

As editor of this volume, I want to thank the authors for the time and effort they have put into sharing their knowledge (conceptual models) of institutional research. I believe that they have outlined the current status of the profession, how it is practiced and why. In working with these individuals to create a holistic conceptual model of institutional research, my mental model of the profession has expanded. My hope is that your mental model(s) of institutional research will be impacted in the same way.

Richard D. Howard

Consistent with the changing nature of the practice of institutional research, the track structure for the 2002 Forum will change to reflect new or expanded roles that institutional research professionals are facing on their campuses.

References

National Research Council. (2000). How people learn, No. 36. Washington, DC: National Academy Press

Senge, P. M. (1990). The fifth discipline: The art and practice of the learning organization. New York, NY: Doubleday.

Volkwein, J. & Volkwein, V. (1997). IR for IR-indispensable resources for institutional researchers: An analysis of AIR publications topics since 1974. The AIR Professional File. Tallahassee, FL: Association for Institutional Research.

CHAPTER 1: ENROLLMENT MANAGEMENT AND STUDENT AFFAIRS

Authors: Rick Kroc and Gary Hanson

This chapter focuses on undergraduate and graduate participants in postsecondary education. Topics include enrollment planning and projections, recruitment and retention, student needs assessment, student profiles, and student financial aid.

THE ENROLLMENT MANAGEMENT DOMAIN

Introduction

When asked to define enrollment management, many college faculty and administrators will point toward the admissions office and say, "it's what those admissions folks do—get us the students." While this is clearly part of managing college enrollments, much more is at stake. Writers and practitioners have proposed several more comprehensive definitions.

- Kemerer, Baldridge and Green (1982) suggest that enrollment management is both a process and a series of activities that involve the entire campus.

- Hossler, Bean and Associates (1990, p. 5) observe: "Organized by strategic planning and supported by institutional research, enrollment management activities concern student college choice, transition to college, student attrition and retention, and student outcomes. These processes are studied to guide institutional practices in the areas of new student recruitment and financial aid, student support services, curriculum, and other academic areas that affect enrollments, student persistence, and student outcomes from college."

- Clagett (1992) describes enrollment management as "the coordinated effort of a college or university to influence the size and characteristics of the institution's student body," and suggests that institutional research is an essential component of the process.

Enrollment management for the purpose of this chapter is defined as an institutional research and planning function that examines and seeks to manage the flow of students to, through, and from college. We have viewed the enterprise chronologically, from the time a student becomes a prospect to the time they exit or become an alumnus. Two primary domains, student recruitment and student flow, have been identified, partly because colleges tend to organize their offices and resources somewhat separately around these areas and partly

1

because much of the writing about enrollment management has considered recruitment and retention separately. We have used the term "student flow" rather than retention to make the case for widening that domain somewhat. Student recruitment has been divided into the educational pipeline (marketing and recruitment), enrollment projections, enrollment yield, and financial aid. In the student flow domain, areas and issues include student retention theories, influences on student retention (including academic preparation, the curriculum, campus climate, and academic support programs), and alumni.

Assessment of student learning, which is considered more extensively in chapter 2 should be an integral part of enrollment management. The increased emphasis on assessment on many campuses enriches our understanding of students, providing the opportunity to widen and deepen our discussion of student retention. It is partly because of this that we have labeled our second domain student flow rather than retention, broadening it to include areas where information gained from student assessment may prove helpful. Where relevant, then, we have linked assessment issues to enrollment management, but refer readers to the assessment chapter for more detailed information about this important topic. Enrollment management can be done without assessment of student learning, but the conversation is more productive if information from an active assessment program informs the process.

In addition to exploring many of the important enrollment management issues, this chapter considers how colleges can best address enrollment needs and how institutional researchers can help. How should we organize for enrollment management? What technical skills are needed? How do we collect and organize the data? How can we best communicate results? This chapter has two goals:

- To provide a richer understanding of the important enrollment management issues; and
- To help campuses and institutional researchers move from reacting to enrollments to managing them.

A Brief History

Enrollment management in the United States may have started with parchment paper, a quill pen, and an inkpot. Concern with attracting, admitting and graduating students began shortly after the Pilgrims arrived. Harvard College was established in 1636 by vote of the Great and General Court of Massachusetts Bay and nine students were admitted for tutelage under a single master. Ever since, colleges have been concerned with managing their enrollment.

The early history of higher education is laced with stories of recurring cycles where rapid college expansion was followed by severe enrollment declines, and the eventual demise of certain colleges. For example, Cohen (1998) reports that between 1790 and 1860 more than 500 colleges were established, but less than half of them stayed in existence. In 1840 the census showed that there were 173 colleges that shared 16,233 students or an average of only 93 students per college. Cohen (1998) asks what kind of faculty could be supported by 93 or fewer students. Colleges failed primarily because students did not enroll. Decreased enrollment created a financial hardship that colleges found difficult to overcome. As a result, each college had to promise something to attract students, and the era of brochures and catalogs, active recruiting, and enrollment management came into being. Because colleges and universities relied on a continual stream of students to and through the institution, enrollment management became a critical issue for institutional survival.

In the very early years, the president dominated the college. The president recruited students, admitted them, taught them, and conferred the degrees. Later, as college enrollments increased, the student enrollment management responsibility was transferred from the president to other faculty, and eventually to specialized administrators. As colleges and universities increased in number, administrative complexity, and sheer size, the management of student enrollment became a full-time administrative responsibility. Initially, the enrollment management function focused on student recruitment and was often placed in an admissions or registrar's office for administrative convenience. Enrollment management maintained a focus on the "recruitment" of students until the mid-1980s.

When governing boards, state legislators and tax payers became concerned with how many of their sons and daughters were completing college, increased pressure was placed on institutions of higher education to not only recruit students to the front door, but to make sure they earned their degrees in a timely fashion. With increasing external pressure, more and more institutions created high-level administrative positions such as the vice president for enrollment management. Today, the enrollment management function starts with student outreach programs that begin in middle school or earlier, and continues through to the graduation of students from masters and doctoral degree granting institutions.

STUDENT RECRUITMENT

The Educational Pipeline

Student recruitment begins with asking two important questions: "Who do we want to educate?" and "Who is available?" Defining who to educate is a product of your institution's mission and goals, but these goals must be moderated with an understanding of how many students exist in the potential pipeline. Student recruitment is an expensive business and pursuing enrollment goals beyond the available pipeline can be frustrating and a waste of precious institutional resources. Understanding the pipeline and how to reach those students will lead to more effective practice. The purpose of this section is to help define and understand educational pipelines that will result in effective student recruitment. The end goal is to identify, attract, enroll, and graduate students.

While the pipeline of potential students may vary from one institution to the next, defining the boundaries of the educational pipeline for your institution is an important task for effective student recruitment. To define these boundaries for the educational pipeline, it is important to ask, "What are the defining characteristics of the students we want to recruit?" For example, the educational pipeline for a community college may be defined in terms of the numbers of students who live and work within a three-county area, the number who are more than 25 years old, and the number who want vocational training in the high technology industries. A private liberal arts college may define their educational pipeline as high school graduates with SAT test scores above 1200 who reside within a five-state area. A large public research university may define their educational pipeline relative to two student populations—graduate and undergraduate students. The graduate student pipeline may be a mix of U.S. citizens and international students with GRE scores greater than 1400, while the undergraduate pipeline may be those state residents who graduate in the top 10% of their high school and obtained SAT scores greater than 1000.

As these examples suggest, the educational pipeline first must be defined in terms of those student characteristics your institution finds most important. The next step is to identify data sources that summarize how many pre-college students with those characteristics exist in the pipeline; that is, who is available. This process starts with a broad global picture of who is "in" the higher education educational pipeline. For example, if an institution recruits a traditional age population of college students, this broad picture of the pipeline may be defined in terms of the number of students who graduate from high school in your state for a given year. This picture is far too broad and includes too many students for effective recruitment strategies to be implemented at most institutions. Hence, a more refined definition of the recruitment pool is needed. This broad picture may be refined in terms of many other characteristics, but we will examine two for purposes of illustration.

Assume an institution values both multicultural diversity and high academic merit. If this institution is a four-year college or university it can refine the pipeline definition further by examining the number of students, by ethnicity, who take college admissions tests. The admissions policy of an institution may be used to further refine the definition of the educational pipeline by determining the number of students who "qualify" for admission to the institution. The pool of available students changes as each criteria is added to the definition. The more precisely the characteristics are defined, the smaller the potential applicant pool becomes. Chart 1.1 illustrates this point.

The educational pipeline for Hispanic students in this state shows that while more than 54,000 students graduated from high school, less than 34,000 planned to attend college and only 13,500 submitted an SAT test score to a four-year college or university. Of those who submitted test scores, less than

Chart 1.1
Hispanic Student Pipeline

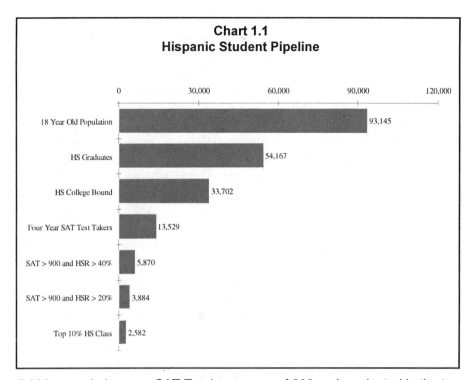

5,900 earned above an SAT Total test score of 900 and graduated in the top 40% of their high school class. Even fewer (less than 4,000) earned a test score above 900 and graduated in the top 20% of their class. Of the students who submitted test scores, only about 2,500 graduated in the top 10% of their high school graduating class. As the criteria used to define the educational pipeline are more clearly defined, the pipeline shrinks to extraordinarily small numbers. If the goal is to recruit academically able Hispanic students within this state, then the pipeline is not the 54,000 high school graduates, but is much more likely to be the 4,000 students who graduated in the top 20% of their high school class with SAT scores greater than 900. Yet, these numbers provide valuable insight to the institution about the number of students in the potential applicant pool. If the numbers become too small, the criteria need to be changed. Changing the admissions policy, expanding the geographical area, or changing the characteristics that define the educational pipeline may be needed. Understanding the educational pipeline and being able to compile data and present it to others involved in the student recruitment process is essential for the institutional research professional.

Understanding Student Choice

Understanding how students chose a college is an important aspect of recruiting students. Hossler, Schmitz and Vespar (1999) provide a useful, empirically-based description of this process in their recent book, *Going to*

College. Here the IR professional may assist the institution in several ways. One way is to conduct marketing studies that determine what factors influenced students to apply, become admitted, and enroll at the institution. Commercial instruments, like the Admitted Student Questionnaire (College Board, 1999), or locally developed instruments may be used. A second way is to identify databases and software analysis tools that facilitate the institution's ability to locate, recruit, and attract students in the pipeline. Both college admissions services (College Board and The American College Testing Program) provide access to data and sell lists of students who meet specific educational criteria. In addition, software tools like The College Board Enrollment Planning Service or ACT's Enrollment Information Service provide a more sophisticated way to identify, contact, and track students during the recruiting and admissions process. IR professionals are often asked to evaluate and implement these tracking tools. A third way IR offices become involved in recruiting students is to be asked to generate a trend analysis of the profiles of this year's applicants to identify trends in the gain or loss of students with certain characteristics. A fourth way the IR office may become involved is to analyze data on a post-hoc basis after the recruitment year is over. For example, Hanson, Norman and Williams (1998) use a student information system to study the characteristics of students who were successfully recruited, admitted and enrolled with the profile of students who chose not to apply or those who chose not to enroll. Because institutional image plays an important role in the college choice process, IR professionals frequently provide institutional data to college ranking services such as *U.S. News and World Report*, *Peterson's Guide*, and *The College Blue Book*. These institutional data provide a basis of comparison for students and families to make informed decisions. Finally, the IR office may be asked to provide benchmark data about student and parental perceptions of the institution's image with data from other institutions.

Enrollment Projections

Projecting college enrollments can be a difficult, even perilous, activity. The stakes can be high in terms of budgetary, facilities planning, and instructional concerns, yet projections are often not as accurate as hoped or expected. Before engaging in this process, several questions should be addressed:

- What are the needs?
- What are the dimensions of the analysis (variables and levels of analysis)?
- What is the time horizon?
- What methodology should be used?
- How should qualitative and quantitative input into the model be balanced?

The Needs

A thorough grasp of the needs and context for enrollment projections is essential to successfully completing the project. Often, the budget process of the institution drives the need for projections, so an understanding of the sometimes Byzantine budgetary processes and their timing is critical. In addition, the need to identify instructors and classroom space may drive the need for projections, as may the needs of the admissions and financial aid offices to organize their recruitment efforts around projections of potential enrollment demand. Strategic planning and facilities management committees also need to consider enrollment forecasts in their deliberations. Although budget needs typically require some kind of full-time equivalent (FTE) calculation, it is usually best to project headcount enrollment, since most other needs call for headcount figures, and FTE is not always well understood, particularly by the press and public. Budget issues can usually be addressed by converting headcount to FTE using historical ratios to model any changes in the proportion of part-time students.

The Dimensions

Both current and anticipated needs will drive decisions about the particular levels of analysis and the variables to be included in enrollment projections. Levels may range from the major or department, to statewide or even national projections. Colleges within universities often have considerable autonomy, hence forecasting at this level may be useful. Branch campuses, which have increasingly emerged as strategies for meeting enrollment needs, may also merit consideration. Linking campus projections (usually done at the individual college or university), with statewide forecasts (often done at a central office) can be a challenging but important task. Recently, many campuses have begun grappling with technology-delivered education as an enrollment strategy. This emerging trend also provides a considerable forecasting challenge. Scenario development (described below) may provide a better method for addressing some of these less predictable aspects of enrollment planning.

After deciding on the broader levels of the analysis, variables within each level need to be identified. Likely candidates may include graduate/ undergraduate, tuition domicile (critical for budgeting), ethnicity, class level, new/ continuing, and academic preparation. A careful consideration of the needs will minimize errors made in identifying levels and variables.

Time Horizon

Useful distinctions can be made between short-term and long-term projections. Budgeting, instructional planning, and student recruitment activities generally need two- to three-year projections. Strategic planning and facilities management require longer term thinking, often 10 years or more into the future. A variety of quantitative methods can produce reasonably accurate results for projecting enrollments when the time horizon is only a few years, but these same methods can be disappointingly inaccurate over a longer term for several reasons. First, changes in trend lines are much more probable over a longer period of time—linear trends change direction or become non-linear, for example.

Second, small biases in parameter estimates will be magnified considerably over a 10-15 year span. Third, influences that are difficult to model or predict are more likely to occur over a longer time interval. Such influences might include economic, political, technological or social changes. In one southwestern state, some rather extensive quantitative attempts to model long-term demand for enrollment at public universities and community colleges have proved unsuccessful and have been abandoned. Alternative strategies, including scenario development, are being considered.

Methods

A variety of quantitative methods can be used for projecting enrollments. Brinkman and McIntyre (1997) compare and contrast many of these methods, providing useful descriptions of strengths and weaknesses. One useful method will be briefly described here. This approach first separates enrollment into two components: continuing and new students.

Continuing students are projected using Markov chain methodology, which estimates the conditional probabilities of students returning from one year to the next. This can be done using a spreadsheet, but depends on having unit record data that is used to determine whether previous years' students returned for subsequent years. Last year's first-time freshmen, for example, may still be freshmen this year, may have become sophomores, may have left the institution, may have become non-degree students, etc. Having historical information about these rates allows the researcher to estimate future probabilities. Changes in retention and graduation rates and in time-to-graduation can be usefully modeled using this method.

New student enrollment can be more difficult to estimate. For institutions primarily dependent on high school graduates, historic yield rates applied to Western Interstate Commission on Higher Education (WICHE) projections of high school graduates (http://www.wiche.edu/pubs/pubs.htm) can be valuable. At four-year institutions, community college projections can be helpful for estimating numbers of transfer students. Out-of-state students may be constrained by policy. Graduate students can be very difficult to estimate— historic trends and comparisons with peer institutions may be helpful. The sum of the continuing and new students, then, becomes the total projected headcount enrollment. Table 1.1 shows an example of this approach. The top section of the table calculates the number of current students (fall 2000) who are projected to continue into the subsequent fall (fall 2001), based on a ten-year history of progression rates. The bottom section combines this calculation of the number of continuing students with estimates of the expected number of new students, to arrive at the total projected fall 2001 enrollment.

As discussed in the previous section, quantitative approaches may have limited utility for long-term projections. Scenario development, a more qualitative alternative, can provide a much richer sense of long-term possibilities. Scenarios are designed to be a planning tool that develops a set (usually 3-5) of plausible future stories or scenes that a linear projection of the past may not anticipate. A scenario "describes a situation in common terms that represents what might happen in the future. It is not a prediction, but a way of putting a lot of ideas and possibilities together" (Caldwell, 1999). These are not simply someone's momentary visions, but are based on a solid understanding of social, technological, environmental, economic, and political issues (Morrison, 1992). At the University of Michigan, Velleman (1996) has developed four interesting scenarios that illustrate this approach (http://www.si.umich.edu/V2010/matrix.html).

Balancing Quantitative and Qualitative Approaches

Although quantitative methods can be accurate and useful, particularly for short-term projections, they may often be improved by incorporating other, more subjective information. A change in financial aid packaging or in admissions requirements, for example, may have effects on enrollment that are difficult to model. It can be very valuable to have an enrollment management committee to add their expert judgment to the initial quantitative modeling. These informed judgments add critical information regarding why and how much enrollments may deviate from the projections. For presentation, a preamble describing issues that may affect enrollments (including estimates of their magnitude) might be added to a projection spreadsheet.

As previously discussed, long-term quantitative forecasts often badly miss the mark. In Arizona, the university system is considering using quantitative methods for short-term projections and scenario planning for long-term forecasts, appropriately blending qualitative and quantitative methods. The short-term projections provide the type of solid quantitative extrapolations that many administrators seek, while thoughtfully crafted scenarios can enrich and focus long-term planning discussions in creative, important ways.

Enrollment Yield

Understanding yield rates is one of the most critical issues associated with the recruitment and admissions process. "Yield rates" refer to ratios among the numbers of students who apply, are admitted, and enroll at an institution. Of particular importance is monitoring yield rates over time to detect possible trends, as well as the characteristics of those who applied, were admitted, and ultimately enrolled. Faculty and administrators need this information to project class enrollment and to understand the nature of the preparation level or readiness for college instruction. Admissions offices need this information to target more carefully their recruitment activities and to better allocate their resources to maximize the yield rates for a given activity or combination of activities. Institutional research offices may assume an important role in analyzing, interpreting and disseminating the information that informs these considerations.

The analysis of yield rates involves a comparison of those who applied, were admitted, and enrolled with those who did not. It should also include comparing trends from the current year with previous years, often using three-,

Table 1.1
Fall 2001 Projected Enrollment

Projected Fall 2001 Enrollment of Students Continuing from Fall 2000						
Actual Fall 2000 Enrollment		New Fresh	Other Fresh	Soph	Junior	Senior
New Freshmen	5694	1	678	3197	344	17
	100%	0.02%	11.91%	56.14%	6.04%	0.30%
Other Freshmen	900	0	24	437	104	4
	100%	0.00%	2.62%	48.58%	11.54%	0.42%
Sophomores	5279	0	0	730	3230	318
	100%	0.00%	0.00%	13.83%	61.18%	6.03%
Juniors	5777	0	0	1	764	3938
	100%	0.00%	0.00%	0.02%	13.23%	68.16%
Seniors	7909	0	0	0	0	2839
	100%	0.00%	0.00%	0.00%	0.00%	35.89%
Undergrad unclassified	6	0	0	0	0	0
	100%	0.00%	0.00%	0.00%	2.38%	0.00%
Undergrad non-degree	839	7	0	10	0	32
	100%	0.84%	0.12%	1.2%	1.8%	3.84%
Undergrad Total	**26404**	**8**	**702**	**4375**	**4442**	**7148**
	100%	**0.03%**	**2.55%**	**16.18%**	**17.06%**	**26.92%**
New First Professional	322	0	0	0	0	0
	100%	0.00%	0.00%	0.00%	0.00%	0.00%
Continuing First Prof.	787	0	0	0	0	0
	100%	0.00%	0.00%	0.00%	0.00%	0.00%
New Graduate	1449	0	0	0	0	0
	100%	0.00%	0.00%	0.00%	0.00%	0.00%
Continuing Graduate	4507	0	0	0	0	6
	100%	0.00%	0.00%	0.00%	0.00%	0.13%
Graduate non-degree	1019	1	0	0	0	9
	100%	0.09%	0.00%	0.00%	0.00%	0.93%
Grad/Prof. Total	**8084**	**1**	**0**	**0**	**0**	**15**
	100%	**0.01%**	**0.00%**	**0.00%**	**0.00%**	**0.19%**
Total Enrollment	**34488**	**9**	**702**	**4375**	**4442**	**7163**
	100%	**0.03%**	**2.03%**	**12.69%**	**12.88%**	**20.77%**

	Total Projected Enrollment (Continuing Plus New) Total Projected Fall 2000 Enrollment (Continuing Plus New)				
	New Fresh	Other Fresh	Soph	Junior	Senior
Continuing	9	702	4375	4442	7163
New Freshmen (Prior Year Act+100)	5,523				
New Transfers (Prior Year Act +50)	292	61	704	715	286
% New Transfers	14.07%	2.94%	33.88%	34.39%	13.79%
New First Professional					
New Grads (Prior year Act +50)					
Other	0	171	331	573	606
Total	5825	934	5,410	5,730	8,055

Table 1.1 Continued
Fall 2001 Projected Enrollment

	Projected Fall 2001 Enrollment of Students Continuing from Fall 2000							
Actual Fall 2000 Enrollment	UG Uncl.	UG NDS	New 1st Prof.	Cont. 1st Prof.	New Grad	Cont. Grad.	Grad. NDS	TOTAL
New Freshmen	5694	0	0	0	0	0	0	0	4237
	100%	0.00%	0.00%	0.00%	0.00%	0.00%	0.00%	0.00%	74.41%
Other Freshmen	900	0	2	0	0	0	0	0	570
	100%	0.00%	0.21%	0.00%	0.00%	0.00%	0.00%	0.00%	63.38%
Sophomores	5279	0	8	5	0	0	0	0	4291
	100%	0.00%	0.15%	0.09%	0.00%	0.00%	0.00%	0.00%	81.29%
Juniors	5777	0	24	9	0	6	0	1	4744
	100%	0.00%	0.42%	0.16%	0.00%	0.11%	0.00%	0.02%	82.12%
Seniors	7909	0	106	66	0	129	20	89	3249
	100%	0.00%	1.34%	0.84%	0.00%	1.63%	0.25%	1.13%	41.08%
Undergrad unclassified	6	0	0	0	0	0	0	0	0
	100%	2.38%	0.00%	0.00%	0.00%	0.00%	0.00%	0.00%	4.76%
Undergrad non-degree	839	0	155	0	0	0	5	0	237
	100%	0.12%	18.49%	0.36%	0.00%	0.48%	0.60%	0.36%	28.21%
Undergrad Total	**26404**	**0**	**295**	**80**	**0**	**135**	**5**	**91**	**17329**
	100%	**0.01%**	**1.13%**	**0.32%**	**0.00%**	**0.54%**	**0.02%**	**0.34%**	**65.63%**
New First Professional	322	0	0	1	221	4	2	0	227
	100%	0.00%	0.00%	0.23%	68.6%	1.16%	0.47%	0.00%	70.46%
Continuing First Prof.	787	0	0	0	473	2	2	0	477
	100%	0.00%	0.00%	0.00%	60.08%	0.25%	0.25%	0.00%	60.58%
New Graduate	1449	0	1	3	3	3	1201	5	1217
	100%	0.00%	0.07%	0.22%	0.22%	0.22%	82.87%	0.36%	83.96%
Continuing Graduate	4507	0	0	4	1	5	2944	21	2980
	100%	0.00%	0.00%	0.09%	0.02%	0.11%	65.31%	0.47%	66.13%
Graduate non-degree	1019	0	3	9	0	87	101	207	416
	100%	0.00%	0.28%	0.84%	0.00%	8.49%	9.89%	20.34%	40.86%
Grad/Prof. Total	**8084**	**0**	**4**	**17**	**698**	**100**	**4249**	**234**	**5317**
	100%	**0.00%**	**0.05%**	**0.20%**	**8.63%**	**1.24%**	**52.56%**	**2.89%**	**65.77%**
Total Enrollment	**34488**	**0**	**299**	**97**	**698**	**236**	**4254**	**324**	**22598**
	100%	**0.00%**	**0.87%**	**0.28%**	**2.02%**	**0.68%**	**12.33%**	**0.94%**	**65.52%**

	Total Projected Enrollment (Continuing Plus New) Total Projected Fall 2000 Enrollment (Continuing Plus New)							
	UG Unc.	UG NDS	New Prof.	Cont. Prof.	New Grad.	Cont. Grad.	Grad. NDS	Row Total
Continuing	0	299	97	698	236	4254	324	22598
New Freshmen (Prior Year Act+100)								5,523
New Transfers (Prior Year Act +50)	1	4	15	0	0	0	0	2,078
% New Transfers	0.05%	0.19%	0.70%	0.00%	0.00%	0.00%	0.00%	100.00%
New First Professional			220					220
New Grads (Prior year Act +50)					1,251			1,251
Other	3	526	0	11	0	323	668	3,212
Total	4	829	332	709	1,487	4,577	992	**34883**

five- or 10-year rolling averages. To accomplish these analyses, student tracking systems that capture student behavior during the recruitment, admission, and matriculation stages of college enrollment must be established. These tracking systems may be developed locally or purchased from commercial vendors.

At the heart of these tracking systems is the ability to capture information about how, when, and for what purpose students interacted with various offices on campus. It is important to make these tracking systems accessible to a variety of stakeholders, because the admissions office, the financial aid office, and a wide range of academic departments are involved in the recruitment and admissions process. Data warehousing and data mining software may be used to answer specific individual faculty and staff queries, but the development and maintenance of these tracking systems may fall within the institutional research office.

A few brief examples may illustrate the nature and scope of student tracking systems and the kinds of data they yield that will help various campus administrators make informed decisions about the recruitment and admissions process. The table below (Table 1.2) shows a typical database report summarizing the number of students who applied and were admitted from a given week during the 1998-99 admissions year, compared with the same week from the 1997-98 admissions year. This table shows a demographic profile that includes gender, ethnicity, and state residency for those who applied and were admitted. These data can be summarized within specific academic units for any week throughout the current year (or for any previous year) by making simple changes in the command line for the query. Similar tables may be generated for transfer students or students admitted under special admissions policies and procedures.

Using this information, the recruiting office can determine whether their efforts need to be increased, maintained, or decreased in order to meet their enrollment targets.

Table 1.2
Freshman Counts by School

COMMAND: 01	SCHOOL: $		YYS: 999		WEEK: 125		MAJOR: 99999	
		MEN		WOMEN		SEX UNKNOWN		ANGLO
	APPS	ADMITS	APPS	ADMITS	APPS	ADMITS	APPS	ADMITS
999	9162	3337	9081	3467	19	8	10698	4194
989	8157	3116	8226	3307	25	3	9894	4005
989 TOTAL	8178	3160	8238	3309	9969		9969	4079
		BLACK		HISPANIC		ASIAN		INDIAN
	APPS	ADMITS	APPS	ADMITS	APPS	ADMITS	APPS	ADMITS
999	970	248	2686	921	2581	1169	83	25
989	621	175	2250	845	2438	1079	90	33
989 TOTAL	633	195	2267	859	2450	1083	90	33
		IN STATE		OUT OF STATE		FOREIGN		TOTAL
	APPS	ADMITS	APPS	ADMITS	APPS	ADMITS	APPS	ADMITS
999	14778	6258	2317	319	1167	235	18262	6812
989	13233	5767	2255	430	920	229	16408	6426
989 TOTAL	13275	5829	2243	425	918	215	16436	6469

Note: The first row in each comparison shows the current week's application and admitted numbers, the second row shows the same week the previous year, and the third row shows the total numbers for the previous year.

Another way to examine enrollment yield is to compare the number of students who applied, were admitted, and enrolled across several years. This trend analysis provides an important context for evaluating the effectiveness of recruitment activities or changes in admissions policy. If the number of applications either declines or increases several years in a row, significant changes in the educational pipeline for your institution may be evident.

Similar changes across multiple student "target" groups will inform campus administrators about changes in the pipeline or the effectiveness of various recruiting activities aimed at these student groups. Two indicators are important to monitor. The "admit yield rate" is the percentage of applicants who were admitted. This indicator is a function of institutional admissions policy. Changing the admissions policy will change the "admit yield rate." The second indicator is the "enrollment yield rate." This indicator is the percentage of admitted students who enroll, and is a function of the students' decisions to enroll at your institution or to attend another institution.

The chart below (Chart 1.2) summarizes these two indicators for a period of ten years at one institution. The chart shows clear evidence of a change in the "admit yield rate" for 1989. During the prior year, the enrollment at this institution exceeded the institution's capacity to teach and administer the campus services to students so a change was initiated for the 1989 year. The trend in the enrollment yield fluctuated across the ten years, and reflects relatively small changes in the "attractiveness" of the institution to students. These two indicators may be used to monitor the admissions policy and the enrollment behavior for many different target populations of students.

Note: The "admit yield" represents the percentage of applicants admitted. The "enroll yield rate" represents the percentage of admitted students who enrolled.

Chart 1.2
A 10-Year History of Admit and Enroll Yeild Rates

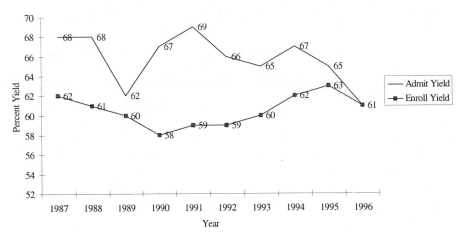

While these relatively small percentage changes across years may not seem significant, the practical implications are important. Even a 1% change in an entering class of 6,000 students will mean a difference of 60 students, the equivalent of two sections of freshman English or Math for which a department chair had not planned.

Financial Aid

As college costs have risen in recent years, financial aid has become a critical aspect of enrollment management. Both colleges and students are increasingly dependent on "discounting" tuition and fees by using financial aid resources. Although private colleges have been grappling with aid issues for many years, public institutions often find themselves in unfamiliar territory as their dependence on student aid escalates. The National Commission on the Cost of Higher Education (1998) clarifies some of the confusing terminology, provides a framework for many of the critical issues, and makes 42 recommendations related to costs, prices, and student aid. This report is a good point of embarkation for the financial aid researcher.

As federal and state subsidies have decreased, financial aid administrators have moved from being processors of government aid to being key players in their college marketing, admissions, and enrollment planning programs. In this more complex environment, though, colleges and universities often find themselves lacking data and policy analyses to support their decisions. Institutional researchers are increasingly being asked to enter the fray and fill this void.

Understanding the Issues and Data

Close collaboration with the financial aid office is essential to successful enrollment management. Financial aid is a large, complex area. Without a thorough understanding of the aid landscape, research in this area is perilous. Aid studies are often at the intersection of enrollment, local aid policies, federal policies, politics, and economics. Navigating this minefield can best be accomplished with frequent consultation with staff in the financial aid office. Aid packaging, for example, is a complex process that needs to be understood before the researcher can expect to assess the impact of aid on enrollment.

Reflective of the complex processes, financial aid data can be difficult to work with. Disentangling data about students, dollars, aid types, and need assessment can be tricky and time-consuming. In addition, federal policy requirements further complicate the data—and the National Center for Education Statistics (NCES) may soon be requiring new information about student aid and prices. Of all the enrollment management areas, financial aid provides the greatest challenges with regard to the retrieval and analysis of data, as well as the complexity of issues.

A number of questions can help guide the analyst exploring this area:

- What is your college's student financial aid policy?
- Who determines it?
- How well integrated are admissions and aid policies?
- What types of aid are available?
- How do students qualify?
- How is aid packaged?
- How and when are students offered aid?
- How is it disbursed?
- How are gift aid, loans and employment balanced in aid packaging?
- How are the recruitment and retention functions of aid balanced?
- What are some of the basic aid statistics reported by the aid office?
- How many students receive aid? New students? Continuing students?
- How many receive gift aid? Loans? Employment?
- How many receive need-based aid? How many show unmet need?
- How much aid is disbursed? What is the net tuition revenue?
- What is the price of attendance?
- What is the level of student indebtedness?
- How do these statistics vary by student subgroup?
- What are the trends over time?

Sources of Information

For the institutional researcher investigating student financial aid, several sources provide valuable information. The *New Directions for Institutional Research* series has published *Researching Student Aid: Creating an Action Agenda* (Voorhees, ed., 1997), while the National Association of Student Financial Aid Administrators has published *Student Aid Research: A Manual for Aid Administrators* (Davis, ed., 1997). These two publications include important background information about financial aid issues and suggest useful approaches for research studies. They also discuss national databases that may be valuable to the analyst. In addition, the Postsecondary Education Opportunity newsletter (published monthly by Tom Mortenson) addresses critical aid, funding, and access issues, often providing useful comparative data for all 50 states. Finally, the National Association of State Student Aid and Grant Programs sponsors an annual conference focused entirely on student aid research. This conference provides cutting-edge research presentations and access to a national network of financial aid researchers.

Some National Concerns

The price of attendance. Understanding the interplay between financial aid and college prices, especially tuition, is fundamentally important. Pressure to raise tuition at public institutions has increased as state appropriations have declined. This has caused close examinations of tuition policies in many states. Could the high tuition/high aid policies that have been successful at many private colleges be implemented in the public sector (Griswold and Marine, 1996)? Are there better alternatives (Stampen and Layzell, 1997)? Examining the elasticity of tuition and calculating Student Price Response Coefficients have become increasingly relevant. Leslie and Brinkman (1993) and Heller (1997) are essential sources for background on this topic. It is important to remember that the sweep of aid packaging is wider than tuition. It also includes room and board, books, and other expenses. Analysts need to understand how the total price of attendance is calculated and how aid packaging incorporates this broader picture at their institution.

Government policies. The impact of federal and state policies on financial aid is extensive. The ability of colleges to attract and enroll low-income students using Pell Grants has declined in recent years as a result of insufficient funding. The Tax Relief Act has established tax credits for middle-income families, which will affect enrollments. Many states have established prepaid tuition plans for their residents. Recent court rulings about affirmative action have forced changes in race-based financial aid. Although these policies are not within the control of an institution, some modeling—or at least speculation—about their impact on enrollment is warranted. Mortenson's Postsecondary Opportunity Newsletter is a useful source for both ideas and data in this area.

Leveraging and recruitment. Financial aid leveraging has become more fashionable as competition for students and tuition increases. Colleges want to know how much aid it will take to recruit a student with certain demographic and academic background characteristics. A number of consulting firms offer their services, often at considerable expense, to help colleges mine and analyze their data to this end. Part of the dilemma involves difficult decisions about the distribution of aid between needy students and academically meritorious students. The struggle to provide access and ensure quality can be difficult for many colleges. The analysts can help by producing yield analyses that examine the intersection of aid, income level, academic background, and yield. Finally, many aid offices spend most of their efforts and money on recruitment, often leaving little for retention. Students can find themselves with a reasonable initial aid award that they are unable to renew because the criteria are extraordinarily high. A comprehensive enrollment management program should evaluate the flow of students from recruitment to withdrawal or graduation to ensure that students who are initially attracted to the college do not leave because aid has been reduced or withdrawn after the first semester or year.

Indebtedness. The rapid escalation of student loans and indebtedness has been well documented. The proceedings from a national symposium, *Student Loan Debt: Problems and Prospects* (Institute for Higher Education Policy, 1998) are a useful source of information about the issue. The balance between gift aid (grants, scholarships, waivers), loans, and employment is important to monitor. Even if gift aid is increasing in absolute dollars, its proportion of the price of attendance may be dropping while the proportion met by loans is increasing. A similar increase may be taking place with unmet need, which families and students must find a way to pay. And when these proportions are translated into absolute dollars, which is what matters to students and their families, the increase may be even more rapid. We may quickly be approaching limits of sacrifice and indebtedness beyond which families may be unwilling to go. Careful analysis of this issue may help colleges find better strategies to deal with increasing costs and prices. The value of a college education is certainly diminished if a graduate's quality of life suffers under the burden of enormous debts.

STUDENT FLOW

Theories of Student Retention

Understanding why students leave college is a critical component of enrollment management. Colleges and universities spend a considerable amount of time and money recruiting and admitting students only to have them leave before graduating. In a national study, the freshman-to-sophomore dropout rate across all colleges in the United States was 25.9% (American College Testing, 2000). Attrition also occurs at other points in student's academic lives, and it is a recurring annual phenomenon. Early departure has negative economic and psychological implications for both the departing student and the campus community they are leaving behind. Theories and models of departure can be helpful in studying the process of early departure. In this section, we will review some of the primary theories and models that can help institutional researchers understand why students leave college early and inform their efforts to design policies and programs that help students stay enrolled until graduation.

A Little History

Efforts to explain why students depart college have evolved through three stages: (1) descriptive, (2) comparative, and (3) theoretical. Terenzini (1982) has referred to the earliest efforts at departure research as *autopsy studies*. Students who had already left college were asked to describe the factors that influenced their decision to leave. The results were presented in a descriptive analysis of what students had reported, and that analysis typically contained a long list of reasons for leaving. Students were rarely studied in the process of withdrawing, and very little was known about the students who persisted. Moreover, the institution's responsibility for student attrition was rarely examined. The focus of these early studies was solely on students who had left.

The second stage of study, the comparative stage, was marked by studies of both departing and persisting students. Better understanding was gained of the departure process through matching the pre-college demographic characteristics of those who persisted with the characteristics of those who departed early. Attention was focused in this way on both the factors that most contributed to persistence and those that most contributed to departure. While these efforts yielded valuable data, they raised as many questions as they resolved. The need to relate the findings from this second stage of institutional research led to the development of the early student retention models and theories. The next section will briefly outline some of the major theoretical attempts to explain how and why students leave college.

Models of Student Departure

Models of student attrition may be organized into three types. The most dominant type consists of the *interactionist* models (Milem and Berger, 1997). The second type, *naturalistic* models, relies upon the qualitative analyses typified by Seymour and Hewitt (1997). The third type has been referred to as *systems* models (Ruddock, Hanson, & Moss, 1999). A brief explanation of these models should provide guidance for designing, implementing and interpreting studies of student departure.

Early theories of student retention were based on the student's interaction with the college, most notably with other students and faculty (Astin, 1968; Bean, 1980; Pascarella, 1985; Spady, 1970; Tinto, 1975, 1987). These theories are called interactionist theories of student departure because they examined how a student's interaction with the college over time led to the integration of that student into the academic and social life of the college community. Interaction models go beyond describing differences between leavers and stayers and offer an explanation of how these differences arise within the context of a specific institution (Tinto, 1987).

One of the earliest attempts to formulate a theory to explain why students left college (Spady, 1970) was based on Durkheim's (1951, 1961) sociological theory of suicide. Durkheim proposed that personal friendship and shared group values would reduce suicide. By analogy, Spady (1970) suggested the same factors would help reduce student dropout. He suggested that the decision to leave college was made over time and that the student's personal background and preparation would influence how the student interacted socially with other students. Students who were successfully integrated into the social life of the institution were more likely to stay; those who did not were more likely to leave. Tinto (1975, 1987) incorporated the work of Spady into a more refined theory and proposed that students bring with them to college a set of personal dispositions and intentions, influenced by family background and academic preparation, that shape their initial goals and commitment to graduate from the institution. These initial goals and commitments change as the student experiences college over time. He or she is more likely to stay and graduate when the student experiences satisfying and rewarding encounters with the

18

informal and formal academic and social systems within the institution. When the interaction of the student with the institution is negative, academic and social integration do not occur. The student then modifies his or her goal and commitment to the institution and withdraws. This basic notion of how well the student becomes integrated into the social and academic environment of the institution, often referred to as the "fit," underlies nearly all of the interaction models of Astin (1993), Bean & Metzner (1985) and Tinto (1987). Implicit in the interactionist models of student departure is that to improve retention we must help students adjust to the existing institutional environment. Rarely is the focus on changing the institution to better fit the student.

Naturalistic models use qualitative methods to understand why students leave college. The primary difference between the naturalistic approach and the interactionist approach is that the naturalistic approach pays greater attention to the environment as a cause of attrition rather than some weakness or deficiency of the student. The study by Seymour and Hewitt (1997) illustrates a classic naturalistic methodology for examining the factors contributing to student departure. They asked female and minority students who left science, engineering, and math-related college majors in seven colleges and universities to identify the institutional factors that contributed to their departure decisions. All of the students who departed left in good academic standing and were capable of completing the curriculum but chose instead to transfer to another major. The authors found that many of the "causes" of student attrition were embedded in the institutional culture and were evident in faculty attitudes. Women and minority students who departed found a climate that was unfriendly, impersonal, and task oriented far beyond their expectations. A rigid faculty culture that based learning on lectures and passive learning contributed to student attrition as well.

The third school of thought is based on systems thinking and looks at both student and institutional "causes" of attrition. While the systems models may look much like the interactionist models, there is an important but subtle difference. The systems models look at how student and institutional factors contribute to attrition, whereas the interactionist models look at the student as a primary source within an institutional context. Consequently, to improve the retention rate, not only is educational programming offered to the student, but a careful examination of institutional policies, procedures and practices come under scrutiny in the systems models. The figure below (Figure 1.1) shows the multitude of possible factors in a systems model proposed by Ruddock, Hanson and Mss (1999). Not only are the traditional student variables, like admissions test scores, high school rank, sex, or ethnicity used in the model, but student service and academic support program participation, grading practices, academic policy, structured learning opportunities, and faculty attitudes are considered possible contributors to student retention.

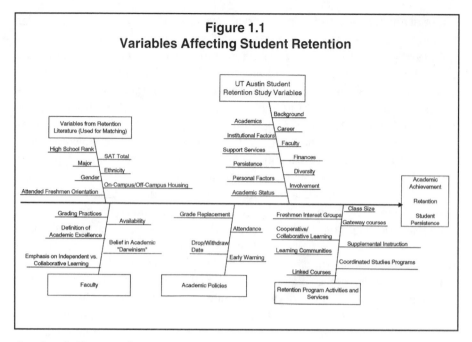

Figure 1.1
Variables Affecting Student Retention

Academic Preparation

Indicators of academic preparation have been used in two ways to facilitate enrollment management decisions regarding student flow into and through college. First, indicators of academic preparation have been used to select students for admission to college. Second, these measures have been used to place students into appropriate levels of a college curriculum. The selection and placement uses are very different and we must understand the strengths and weakness of each use.

Selecting Students

At the very heart of enrollment management is the identification, recruitment, and admission of qualified students. Who is a "qualified" student? The answer may be found in the mission statement of every campus. Each institution seeks to attract the best possible students from within their educational pipeline, and the characteristics used to define the pipeline also become the basis for defining who is qualified to attend. Indicators of academic preparation are used to sort, select and admit students at some colleges and universities while at other institutions they are not. Whether to consider the academic preparation of students in the enrollment management process depends on several issues. First, does an institution need to be selective? Can it afford to admit all students who apply, or does it need to limit the number who enroll? If it needs to limit enrollment, on what basis are students selected? How much emphasis should be placed on measures of academic preparation relative to other student characteristics such as age, gender, leadership ability, socioeconomic status, ability-to-pay, or racial/ethnic background?

Historically, two measures of academic preparation have been used in making selection decisions. First, colleges and universities use measures of academic performance in high school such as relative class rank or average grade point average over a selected number of courses. Second, they use standardized measures of academic ability such as the Scholastic Ability Test (SAT) or the American College Testing Program (ACT) tests to supplement measures of high school performance. More recently, Adelman (1999) suggested that we re-conceptualize the academic resources students bring with them to college and recommended that indicators of the quality of the high school curriculum and the students' level of "engagement" in the curriculum be used, as well.

Indicators of high school academic performance are useful because they summarize the student's academic performance over several years and many classes. They are not subject to daily fluctuations in performance level. Rather, they reflect how consistently a student has achieved in a given school setting over a long period of time. Assuming students apply similar levels of effort in college, high school academic performance represents a good estimate of how well that student may perform at similar tasks in the future. However, measures of high school performance have been criticized and their usefulness questioned because of grade inflation within high schools. Astin, et.al. (1997), for example, reports that among freshmen entering college during the late 1960s, "C" grades outnumbered "A" grades by better than two to one, but by 1996 the "A" grades outnumbered "C" grades by better than two to one. If all students applying to a college or university have an A or A- high school grade point average, the usefulness of this information to rank students relative to their high school performance is diminished.

Standardized tests of ability were developed to help admissions office directors select students for colleges and universities with more student applicants than places available. These tests were designed to reflect the abilities students would need to succeed in college, primarily verbal and math reasoning. The assumption underlying the use of these tests was that students with higher scores were better prepared for college than students with lower scores. By taking students with higher test scores, the college was selecting students with a better chance for success. Not all students with similar levels of academic preparation, however, obtain similar standardized scores. While exposure to a given high school curriculum influences the performance on the test, other factors such as gender, race, and socioeconomic status also influence how well students score on standardized tests. Consequently, the tests have been criticized as biased. Most colleges and universities currently use these standardized tests in combination with other factors to reduce the possible consequences of bias.

Did We Select the "Right" Students?

Do measures of academic preparation enable colleges to select the "best" students? The answer is a mix of good news and bad news. The good news is that both measures of high school performance and standardized test scores are related in significant ways to the academic performance of students in college (ACT, 2000b). In fact, over the last 50 years, high school performance and standardized test scores typically account for about 25% to 40% of the variance in college grades. These measures consistently do better than almost any other indicator of student preparation. The bad news is that academic performance is only one of the ways to define our "best" students. There is much that these measures do not tell us about the nature of college student success.

The research literature shows that high school rank or high school grade point average in combination with a standardized test score consistently do the best job of predicting college grade point average and retention during the first year. They do not, however, work as well predicting subsequent academic performance. They also do a relatively poor job of predicting who will graduate after four, five or six years. Nor do these measures predict important student measures of success as leadership ability, writing ability, analytical thinking, or the ability to work as a team member.

Placing Students

Enrollment managers first select students for college and then must place them into the "right" level of a particular course. Students with insufficient preparation for a given course will struggle in that course and may perform poorly or fail. Students who are over-qualified for a given course will not be challenged by that course and may feel they have wasted their time and money. They consequently may leave dissatisfied. None of these students will benefit, and both the institution and students lose. Measures of academic preparation are used widely for placing students into courses. Often, the same measures are used both to select and to place students. While students may have sufficiently high test scores and/or high school rank/GPA to be admitted to a given institution, they may not meet the faculty standards for the preparation needed to benefit from instruction in a particular course. Hence, more appropriate measures of academic preparation are needed to make these placement decisions for enrollment managers.

Historically, achievement tests, rather than the standardized admissions tests, have been used to place students into the appropriate level of course work in college. The achievement tests have been used because the content is most closely tied to the content of the courses in the college curriculum. Local faculty may construct these achievement tests, or the institution may purchase commercial tests. In some institutions, the college admissions test such as ACT or SAT are used as a proxy measure that closely approximates what will be taught in the curriculum. The SAT Mathematics test, for example, measures students' mathematical reasoning abilities. The content may contain a sufficient number of items similar to the kinds of mathematical problems students encounter in their first mathematics course. Similarly, the ACT tests in English, Mathematics, Science, and Social Studies may be used to place students in related coursework.

The effectiveness with which measures of academic preparation can help us to place students appropriately can be evaluated using three indicators. First, how many of the students we expect to pass their courses do so? Second, how many of the students that we judged to be "ready" for a particular course fail the course? Finally, how many of the students we judged to be under-prepared could have successfully completed a more difficult course without taking the prerequisite course? The first question addresses the success rate. The second question is relatively easy to answer because the failures are so evident. The third question is more difficult to answer, but the consequences of making a mistake are lower. In the first case, students did what we expected, but the students in the second case may never make it to a higher level course. In the third case, students will surely enroll in the appropriate level of course eventually, but will have wasted time and money getting there.

When enrollment managers fail to place students into the appropriate level of beginning coursework, two outcomes are possible. First, students fail their coursework or leave the class because they are either under- or over-prepared. Second, faculty are irritated with students who are not prepared for the difficulty level of the course, or the students are bored and remain unchallenged for the length of the semester. In either case, the flow of students from the entry-level course to higher-level courses and eventual graduation is diminished.

Other Academic Assets

When standardized tests were first used for admissions and placement, the college student population was less diverse than we find it today. In addition, the high school curriculum completed by those pursuing college was more closely related to the college curriculum. Students today, however, are more diverse in their level of preparation and fewer of them who pursue college have completed a "college-prep" curriculum. Consequently, we find that the traditional standardized tests used for admissions and placement may not tell us as much as we need to know. Adelman (1999) argues that the best indicators of academic performance and eventual graduation from college for today's college students are the intensity and the patterns of coursework completed in high school rather than measures of high school grade point average, high school rank, or standardized admissions and placement tests. He found that those students who were more actively engaged in demanding math, science, English, and foreign language courses in high school were more successful. Completing demanding courses in several subjects was more important than receiving a high grade or class rank in less difficult courses.

In addition to better understanding the rigor and the intensity of involvement with demanding high school course work, we should also examine other indicators of accomplishment that students bring with them to college. College faculty want students who can write and they want students with increasingly higher levels of computer literacy. Business and industry leaders want students who can work together in teams, show leadership initiative, and can work with others from diverse backgrounds. To meet these demands, our definition of academic preparation must expand beyond our traditional measures of high school performance and standardized test scores. We must broaden our definition of success and look for ways to not only recruit a diverse student body, but to educate those diverse students so all of them complete college with a broader education than we now provide.

The Curriculum

The curriculum is at the heart of the student college experience. A comprehensive program of enrollment management research logically should include a systematic examination of the impact of the curriculum, yet this is not often done. In this chapter, we have used the term student flow rather than retention to expand the enrollment management domain to include such studies. Two relatively recent developments make this appropriate and timely. First, the growth of student assessment and accountability has focused increasing attention on the student experience. Assessment forces us to think about the context of the student experience—from the student's perspective. Accountability has focused attention not only on retention, but also on such issues as time-to-graduation and the number of credit hours earned. Second, improvements in data administration and technology permit easier retrieval and analysis of curricular data. In the past, these obstacles were sometimes insurmountable. Prying the data out of operational systems not designed for this type of work, combined with the difficulty of processing the massive amount of data that was needed, made these studies nearly impossible to complete in a timely manner. Immensely improved administrative systems and data warehouses, coupled with much higher speed computers, have brought these analyses within easier reach. For these reasons, curricular studies are likely to become a much more common part of the enrollment management landscape.

Types of Studies

Conversations with faculty and academic administrators can be a particularly useful way to identify the curricular studies that would be most valuable to an institution. We will briefly discuss several such areas of study. First, analyzing the impact of gatekeeping or gateway courses on student progress can result in valuable information and stimulate useful campus discussion. These are the key courses, often with high failure rates, that control the flow of lower division students into higher levels of study. There are a number of issues to be addressed about these courses, including the number and characteristics of students who fail, the impact of failure on retention, the impact of performance in these courses on subsequent courses, and trends over time.

24

Useful indices have been developed to assess the efficiency and effectiveness of gateway courses (Andrade, 1999). Also, the materials from panel presentations at the 1998 and 1999 Association for Institutional Research (AIR) Annual Forums are available at http://www.airweb.org. These materials include data from five universities and also illustrate some strategies for analyzing the data.

Closely related to gateway course studies are analyses of grading practices. Some institutions have found that course grade distributions in gateway courses have not changed over a period of years even though student high school preparation may have markedly improved (Hanson, Norman & Caillouet, 1998). Moreover, the failure rate in individual course sections may vary greatly, even after controlling for initial preparation. On the other hand, institutions are also greatly concerned about grade inflation and about courses where all students receive grades of "A," partly as a result of the public scrutiny of athletic eligibility. Examining grading practices and patterns can be a perilous pursuit because the analysis may raise questions about the validity of faculty assessment of students. Diplomacy may be more important than analytic expertise in this arena.

Academic advising and choice of a major have also become topics of increasing importance. At large public Research I universities, a recent study (Kroc, et al. 1997) determined that 72% of those students who initially chose a major changed that major before they graduated. In light of legislative and governing board concerns about students taking too many credit hours and too much time to graduate, as well as student complaints about inadequate advising, such studies will continue to develop.

Course availability is another issue that generates controversy and concern. Once exclusively the domain of the registrar's office, institutional researchers are increasingly being asked to determine the problem areas. It can be difficult to disentangle this issue. As an example, students' unwillingness to take classes early in the morning or on Fridays can easily masquerade as course availability problems.

Ewell (1996) uses the term "behavioral curriculum" to distinguish how students actually navigate the curriculum as opposed to what we ask and expect them to do. Behavioral curriculum issues offer fruitful territory for curricular studies. Interrupting attendance or taking courses out of sequence are examples of behaviors that may adversely affect grades and retention. Another example is taking the relevant math course too far in advance of a science course. The institutional researcher needs to engage the faculty and others with curricular responsibilities in conversation to determine the areas most in need of study.

The link between student outcomes assessment and enrollment management should be particularly strong in the area of student flow through the curriculum. A good assessment program not only provides valuable data, including other dependent variables to use for research studies, but will also have established a feedback loop where assessment results are used to inform faculty and to improve the curriculum. Developing collaborative research in this area can be fruitful if another office is responsible for student assessment.

Data Management

The majority of curricular studies can best be constructed as longitudinal analyses of particular undergraduate student cohorts. Students entering as first-time freshmen are a good place to start, particularly because the diverse academic backgrounds of transfer students make the curricular progress of these students more difficult to analyze. The core of the database needs to be all of the courses and grades for each student in every enrolled term, including post-census date withdrawals, incompletes, and other non-standard grades. In addition, high school achievement data, demographic background, and ancillary academic data (major, degree type and date, term and cumulative GPAs, etc.) need to be included. Because it can be awkward to add data to the database after it has been originally created, it is best to anticipate as many questions as possible and incorporate the required data at the beginning. Data warehouses and data marts have the potential to facilitate curricular studies by increasing the ease and flexibility of data retrieval.

Having an Impact

More than in most institutional research and enrollment management areas, working closely with faculty is essential when studying curricular issues. Support may also be available from deans' offices and from the curriculum and advising committees that are present on most campuses. As mentioned earlier, studies (course grades, for example) that pertain to individual courses and instructors can be particularly delicate. In many cases, the department is the right "unit of analysis." Math departments, for example, teach many gateway courses. Making presentations across campus to initiate a conversation about curricular issues can help illuminate issues as well as sharpen and extend the analysis. As researchers, we need to listen if we are to understand the complexities and earn the respect of the academic community.

Campus Climate

The assessment of campus climate is an important function for institutional researchers (Bauer, 1998). Increasingly, administrators want to monitor what students think about the campus atmosphere. Is the campus a warm and friendly place? Are students turned off because of bureaucratic nightmares? Are there campus environments that facilitate student learning? Are there campus climates that negate student learning? The assessment of campus climate is all about discovering the nature of the relationship students have with their campus. Students may learn more and graduate at a higher rate when there is a positive relationship. They may leave when the campus interferes with learning or with the social life of students. What are the issues associated with the assessment of campus climate, and what should institutional researchers be doing about it? What does campus climate have to do with enrollment management?

The assessment of campus climate is important because attitudes about the institutional climate may influence enrollment behavior at three critical points in time. First, institutional image attracts or repels students early in the college choice process. A positive image brings the institution into the field of choice for students, while a negative image or no image eliminates the institution even before the student begins the decision-making process. Second, students' perceptions of the campus climate also influence their specific choice. Typically, students narrow their college choice to a small, select list of colleges or universities. The institutional climate and the institution's reputation are critical factors when making their final choice. Numerous studies have documented the importance of campus climate and institutional image as important determinants of college choice (Pascarella & Terenzini, 1991). Once students arrive on campus, the day-to-day campus climate sets the boundaries of attachment or involvement the student has with the institution. The student will be more likely to leave if the campus climate interferes with the bond he or she makes with the institution. On the other hand, when students find the campus climate attractive, the bond strengthens, the student develops a level of commitment to the institution, and he or she will be more likely to stay. Student retention theory suggests that the level of social integration is a key factor in whether or not students persist or leave (Tinto, 1997). Students' willingness to persist will vary by the way that campus climate facilitates or hinders the extent to which students become involved in both the academic and social milieu of the campus.

What is Campus Climate?

The term "campus climate" has been used in a variety of ways by numerous authors. Campus climate typically refers to the perceptions individuals hold about the campus environment. Campus climate may include perceptions about the "feel" or "mood" of the campus. Boyer (1990) describes six primary dimensions of campus climate: purposeful, open, just, disciplined, caring and celebrative. He maintains that these dimensions define important characteristics of the collegiate environment and that the ways in which students perceive them make a difference in how welcoming they find the campus. Kuh et al. (1991) also identify significant dimensions of the campus climate that define whether an institution is considered an "involving" college. These authors note that "involving" colleges take advantage of both the physical and psychological environments. For example, colleges can take advantage of their physical setting, create a human-scale institution and provide a variety of opportunities for involvement. Positive psychological climates can be created by providing personal space, reducing student anonymity, and providing multiple student sub-communities for involvement. A series of studies at The University of Minnesota, (Harrold, 1990, 1995, 1998), more pragmatically defines the perceptions students hold about the mood or feel of the campus. In those studies, students were asked to rate the institution on friendliness, social inclusiveness, respectfulness, racism, sexism, competitiveness, and homophobia.

Campus climate can also be defined in terms of how students experience the campus. Did students participate in discussions with faculty or other students about topics related to sexism, racism, spirituality, or diversity? Did they encounter coursework, write papers, or participate in extracurricular activities that helped define the campus climate along these important dimensions? What students do can be a powerful determinant in shaping their perceptions. Consequently, experience is an important element of the campus climate.

Finally, campus climate can also be defined in terms of how much effort the campus invests in creating the climate. The institution can create opportunities for a positive campus climate, or they can pursue other priorities. A campus audit will quickly identify the extent to which the institution is vested in changing, modifying, or improving the campus climate versus maintaining the status quo. Does the institution provide workshops for faculty and students to deal with harsh aspects of the climate? Does the institution respond quickly and effectively when difficulty among student or faculty groups erupts? Does the institution reward students, faculty, and staff for creating opportunities for building a positive campus climate? Institutional response is a critical dimension of campus climate and should be considered when conducting an institutional audit.

How Do We Assess It?

Assessing campus climate can be accomplished using several modes of inquiry and different methodological techniques. The assessment of campus climate may begin with selecting a model or theory that helps define the dimensions you wish to assess. For example, it may be helpful to start with the Boyer (1991) dimensions and assess student, faculty, and staff perceptions of the campus climate. Several previous attempts by Harrold and Skousen (1990, 1995, 1998) and Hanson, Ouimet, and Williams (1997) have described the campus climates of two large public research universities using Boyer's model. Other surveys of students' perceptions have assessed important dimensions of campus climate.

Another way to assess campus climate is to identify the critical issues that mold it. These issues often come in the form of "isms" that lead to negative campus environments. The ways in which students perceive the climate with respect to racism, sexism, homophobia, or ageism provide institutions with very specific information about critical issues or "hot spots" for institutional response.

It may be advisable to pursue a different paradigm of inquiry if one is just starting to assess campus climate at an institution in order to identify the important defining issues on campus. This can be accomplished through a qualitative study using individual or group interviews or focus groups. One example of this mode of inquiry by Seymour and Hewitt (1997) studies the classroom climates that facilitated or hindered women and minority students' pursuit of science, mathematics, and engineering majors in college. They found significant examples of hostile environments that discouraged students from continuing their studies in these majors, as well as positive environments that "pulled" students in other directions.

Conducting a campus audit of how an institution responds to negative events that shape the climate or the extent to which they create and foster positive events is another way to initiate your assessment activities. These audits can be conducted by either an internal committee or by an external team. These audits may focus on a particular issue or they may examine general dimensions of your institution's response to programs and activities that shape the campus climate. The value of this assessment approach is that recommendations for improving or changing the campus climate may be directly related to the findings of the audit.

What Do We Do with the Results?

It is important when conducting campus climate assessments to link perceptions, attitudes, and behaviors to enrollment behavior. For example, do students who have more positive perceptions of the campus persist and graduate at higher rates than students who have negative perceptions? Do students who participate in programmatic activities or classroom assignments designed to improve campus climate persist and graduate at higher rates than students who do not participate? Without linking the assessment of campus climate to enrollment behaviors, it would be difficult to justify the time and money spent on conducting the assessment. Consequently, the institutional research office may be asked to combine survey data with institutional records to make these important linkages.

Once important observations about campus climate perceptions and behavior are linked to enrollment outcomes such as retention and graduation rate, the institutional research office may be asked to make recommendations for improving the campus climate in ways that increase graduation and decrease attrition. Knowing how campus climate influences enrollment behavior of students is an important step in understanding the flow of students through the college. More will be learned about how campus climate influences special subgroups of students as these studies are conducted. It is possible, for example, that particular elements of the campus climate influence women to persist more than men. The way the institution responds to a negative racial incident may have a dramatic impact on whether minority students consider the institution as an attractive choice at which to enroll and graduate or whether they eliminate it from further consideration at the point of college choice decision or retention decisions.

Academic and Student Support Programs

Higher education institutions spend considerable time and money over and beyond the cost of classroom instruction to improve student learning. These additional services take place in academic and student affairs offices in the form of academic tutoring, supplemental instruction, retention programming, and a wide variety of programs aimed at helping students socially integrate into campus life. Because the investment of time and money is substantial, colleges and universities often ask institutional researchers to evaluate the effectiveness of these programs. What is involved and how can it be determined whether these academic and student support services contribute to student learning and success?

The Issues

The variety of academic and student support services across colleges and universities is phenomenal. Presenting a single evaluation model would be folly, hence we will discuss the issues involved in evaluating these programs and present the advantages and disadvantages associated with a number of evaluation strategies. The evaluation issues can be discussed in the context of two broad sets of questions. We can evaluate the effectiveness in achieving the program's goals and objectives through summative evaluation. We may also evaluate the process by which the program was delivered via formative evaluation. Here, then, are two sets of questions that define the issues.

Process questions:

1. Were elements of the program delivered as intended?
2. Did the target group of students attend?
3. Were students satisfied with the delivery of the program?
4. What improvements could be made to the program process?

Outcome questions:

1. Does the program provide an added benefit over and above what the student brings to college in the way of academic preparation and readiness to learn?
2. Do students who participate earn higher grades, return more frequently and graduate at higher rates than students who do not participate?
3. How can we isolate the "effect" of a single program within the context of all the other academic activities in which the student participates?
4. Does the program contribute to the broader mission of the institution [e.g. the improvement in institutional graduation rates]?

Were the Elements of the Program Delivered as Designed?

Every program is designed with a set of intended components that must be delivered if the program is to be successful. All too often some, but not all, program components are delivered, especially if the program is coordinated by multiple individuals or across many points in time. Variations in organization, timing, and discussion during a program may cause some aspects of the program to be deleted or slighted in some way. To evaluate whether or not program components are delivered, as intended, written specifications of the program must be shared with all the individuals responsible for delivering the program, as well as with the institutional researcher conducting the evaluation. In addition, as the program is implemented, data must be collected from program participants to assess their perceptions regarding what they received. External observers may be used to monitor and assess how the program unfolds. Using information from the program participants and the external observer, judgments may be made regarding the extent to which the program was implemented according to the written specifications. Were all elements delivered in a timely manner? Were some elements omitted? Was the balance across various elements appropriate?

Do the "Right" Students Attend our Academic and Student Support Services?

Many academic and student support services are designed to serve specific targeted student populations. It is important for such services to evaluate whether or not those targeted students participated. As an example, an academic tutoring program might have been intended to help "at risk" students raise their grades (i.e., from "F" to "D" or from "D" to "C"), but the students making use of the program may in fact be students with "C"s or "B"s trying to improve their grades. To effectively evaluate this process variable, program goals and definitions must be written that carefully delineate who should participate. It is then relatively easy to determine who actually participated and to compare the results with the intended target population. To do so requires that program participants are identified and appropriate indicators collected either at the time of participation or by tying their program participation to a larger database for tracking and evaluation purposes. A participant profile with summary statistics summarizing these indicators provides a way to judge how successful a program was in attracting its targeted student population.

Were Students Satisfied with the Program?

Student satisfaction is an important measure of how well a program was delivered. The measurement of student satisfaction should be a two-step process. First, what was the general level of satisfaction with the overall program as well as with individual components? Objective rating scales ranging from very dissatisfied to very satisfied can be used in this assessment. Another approach is to ask open-ended questions about the degree to which the participants were satisfied. A second question about what went wrong should be asked about those elements that received low satisfaction ratings. Was it poor organization? Did the program spend too much time on unimportant issues for the students? Were the students not engaged sufficiently to benefit from the program? Was it too boring? Both steps in the evaluation are important. The general assessment of satisfaction provides a way to pinpoint the elements of the program that worked well as well as those which did not. The second step provides important information for what, if anything went wrong.

What can be done to improve the program?

Evaluating the effectiveness of academic and student support programs would have limited value if institutional researchers could not provide information about how to improve those elements of the program that did not work as intended. There must be a "feedback" loop in the program for improvement to occur. For this reason, program participants must be asked their opinions about how to "fix" the program. Not only are program participants likely to identify what was wrong, but they may have excellent ideas of what to change about the timing, organization, delivery, and personnel involved with the program. In addition to asking the program participants, other stakeholders in the program should be queried as well. Gathering knowledgeable outside observers of the process may be useful in identifying weak links in the delivery. Total Quality Management and Continuous Quality Improvement techniques (Teeter and Lozier, 1993) are useful in gathering input about what went wrong and the necessary steps needed to fix the problem.

Does the Program Provide an Added Benefit?

One of the most difficult program evaluation issues is determining whether a particular effort produces learning outcomes over and beyond those expected after careful examination of the student's level of academic preparation, motivation, and readiness for college. Providing academic instruction in the form of tutoring or supplemental instruction or providing residential housing for well-prepared students may not yield higher levels of learning. These students may have learned the material well without additional assistance. One evaluation strategy for dealing with this issue is to use hierarchical linear regression models to statistically account for the contribution of student preparation (admission test scores, high school grades/class rank, curriculum patterns), motivation (academic and/or personal), and readiness for college (expectations, perceptions and knowledge about college) and then examine whether the program had an effect over and above these initial student characteristics. The important evaluation strategy for this issue is to collect appropriate measures of preparation, motivation and readiness for college in order to include them in the statistical modeling.

Does Student Participation Yield Better Outcomes Than Non-Participation?

If a support program works, students who participate should earn higher grades, return for another year of college more frequently, and graduate at higher rates than students who do not participate. Students who participate in these support programs, however, typically differ in important ways from those who do not. For example, students who elect to participate in a given program may be more highly motivated, be employed fewer hours, or have greater financial resources to purchase the services. These student differences must be considered when evaluating the effectiveness of the program. The chart below (Chart 1.3) shows the average grade point average, by SAT total score, of students who lived in residential housing their first year compared to those who did not.

The evidence is clear that well prepared students [i.e. high SAT scores] living in the residence hall did not do much better than students who lived elsewhere. However, students living in residential housing with lower SAT scores obtained higher grades than students with similar SAT scores who lived in non-residential housing. Without taking into consideration the academic preparation level, very different conclusions regarding the effects of residential housing may have been reached. This simple descriptive graphical analysis, however, does not take into consideration the effects of student motivation or other personal characteristics. More sophisticated research designs and statistical analyses are often necessary to provide an accurate portrayal of the situation. Another common strategy is to identify the background characteristics that may influence

Chart 1.3
A Comparison of the Mean Grade Point Average by SAT Total Category for Residential and Non-Residential Housing

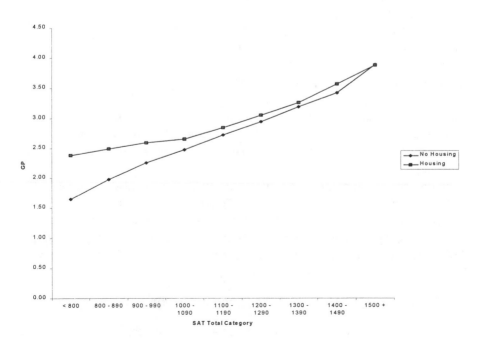

the outcome and provide matched samples of participants and non-participants on these characteristics. Another strategy is to use hierarchical linear models to examine the contribution of participation over and beyond the contributions of student characteristics or student behaviors outside the program. For example, one model might examine the relation of demographic characteristics such as gender, age, or race to academic outcome variables such as grade point average or first year retention. The next model might add academic preparation indicators such as SAT test score and high school GPA or class rank to the variables in the first model [e.g., demographics] to see if the combination of both adds to the model with demographics alone. Yet a third model may add a program participation variable and examine the relationship of all three categories of variables to the outcome measures. If adding the program participation variable in the third model increases the size of the relationship over the previous model, it may be concluded that participation in the program has a beneficial effect.

How Do We Isolate the Effect of a Single Program?

Isolating the effects of a given academic or student support program is one of the thorniest evaluation issues. The problem is that students live complicated lives, and they participate in many activities that may potentially influence their learning, retention, and graduation. For example, when students struggle to learn the material in a given course, they may seek assistance from a roommate, the course professor, a professional tutor, or they may enroll in a supplemental instruction discussion section. Often students engage in multiple activities and programs simultaneously. Assumptions that students only participate in one program may result in the attribution of the effects of one program to another. The use of multiple program impact evaluation strategy (Hanson & Swann, 1993) can counter this problem. This strategy requires the availability of a sophisticated longitudinal tracking system. By tracking student participation in multiple programs during a given semester, not only is the effect of a single program relative to other program participation program effects possible, but the combined effect of multiple participation over and beyond the effects of any single program may be determined. For example, Hanson and Swann (1993) found that participation in both summer orientation and residential housing during the first year reduced student attrition to half that of students who participated in neither program, resulting in a substantial improvement in the retention rate over students who participated in either orientation or housing, but not both. Isolating the effects of either housing or orientation would have been very difficult without the tracking system because unknown percentages of students were involved in both programs. Multiple program participation is the student norm rather than the exception.

Did the Program Contribute to the Broader Mission of the Institution?

The effectiveness of program participation in the achievement of student

34

learning outcomes has historically been evaluated on the basis of whether there was a program effect over and beyond the student's level of preparation, whether students who participated were more likely to achieve than students who did not, and more rarely whether there was a single or multiple program impact on the student's achievement. Interestingly, program contributions are almost never linked to the larger mission of the institution. For example, it may be shown that students who participate in a particular student retention program have higher graduation rates than those who do not. Yet, if the graduation rates for the institution remain low and unchanged for a decade, the embarrassing question of whether the support service programs made a difference on this important institutional goal may have to be asked.

There are many reasons why individual support services may be shown to work remarkably well, but the levels of achievement regarding important educational goals may not change. For example, a successful support program may have substantial evidence that students who participate have a much higher graduation rate than those who do not. However, if only small numbers of students participate because of cost or program design, the program may not have any impact on the overall institutional graduation rate or achievement of learning outcomes. Another reason may be that other factors (e.g., institutional policy) negate the effects of the program. If an academic department grades on the curve and always gives the same percentages of "A's" and "B's" relative to "D's" and "F's" then a retention program that helps a fourth of the students earn higher grades will be negated by the fact that other students in the class will move down in the grading distribution. Hence, the retention program changes the faces of those who succeed but has no impact on the institutional retention or graduation rate. The ability to link the impact of a given program to the mission of the institution is extremely important, but rarely is the effectiveness of programs evaluated relative to this criterion.

Helping Colleagues

Institutional researchers have an important role in helping their colleagues determine whether or not academic and student support services accomplish important and necessary institutional and program goals. Gathering and collecting information helps program developers examine the process and the outcome of their efforts. Collecting data for both purposes may avoid the pitfalls of conducting program evaluations that identify problems but offer no viable solutions for improvement. By summarizing data about the success of the program and how to improve it for the next time it is delivered, institutional researchers will have provided a valuable service.

Graduation and Retention Rates

Surveys show that graduation and retention rates are the most frequently used indicators in state level accountability and performance measure initiatives. The federal government has also begun to require reporting of graduation rate data. These rates have become standard indicators at the campus, state, and national level over the past 15 years. As a result, virtually all institutions are now able to produce graduation rate data. Turning this accountability data into information useful for managing enrollments, however, requires some thoughtfulness on the part of the institutional researcher. Beginning from an understanding of retention issues, this process can be thought of as first establishing a flexible system for answering simple questions with descriptive data, then moving to more multivariate or qualitative approaches, and, finally, placing the data and research into a meaningful context for managing student retention. In his chapter, "Using Retention Research in Enrollment Management," John Bean (in Hossler, Bean and Associates, 1990) describes and compares different methods for researching retention, making recommendations about using the various methods and about implementing research findings. A few of the important current issues facing colleges and universities are:

- Increasing retention and graduation rates
- Increasing transfer rates and baccalaureate degree completion of community college students
- Reducing time-to-graduation
- Closing the gap between underrepresented groups and other students
- Increasing academic preparation—the link between recruitment and retention
- Implementing and evaluating efficient and effective retention programs

Descriptive Data

Efficiency and flexibility are two fundamental requirements for a useful retention rate analysis system. The researcher will be asked to parse the data in many ways—and to do so quickly. Using statistical and other software with a longitudinal student cohort tracking system is one way to meet such requests. Ewell (1995) describes student tracking systems in detail in a *New Directions in Institutional Research* volume. Such a system allows the researcher to track cohorts of students over time as they progress through the institution.

Designing a format for summarizing some of the simple descriptive data can be useful. Table 1.3 provides an example that has proved valuable for enrollment management discussions at a large public university. Some of the issues that can be easily addressed include:

- Retention and graduation trends over time
- Differences in rates among ethnic groups
- Differences between state residents and non-residents
- Comparisons between academically well-prepared and less-prepared students

Table 1.3
Persistence and Graduation Summary: First-Time, Full-Time Freshmen

Cohort	Original Number	HS GPA	Mean SATC	1st YR CGPA	Number of Years After Entry						
					1	2	3	4	5	6	7
1987 Freshmen	4477	-	1060	2.511	-	-	-	-	-	-	-
Enrolled	-	-	-	-	76%	66%	61%	41%	13%	5%	3%
Graduated	-	-	-	-	0%	0%	0%	17%	42%	49%	52%
1988 Freshmen	5015	3.131	1076	2.578	-	-	-	-	-	-	-
Enrolled	-	-	-	-	78%	66%	61%	40%	12%	6%	3%
Graduated	-	-	-	-	0%	0%	0%	19%	45%	51%	54%
1989 Freshmen	5216	3.148	1079	2.564	-	-	-	-	-	-	-
Enrolled	-	-	-	-	75%	64%	59%	39%	12%	6%	3%
Graduated	-	-	-	-	0%	0%	0%	19%	43%	50%	52%
1990 Freshmen	4106	3.206	1082	2.654	-	-	-	-	-	-	-
Enrolled	-	-	-	-	76%	66%	62%	41%	13%	6%	3%
Graduated	-	-	-	-	0%	0%	1%	18%	44%	51%	55%
1991 Freshmen	3970	3.179	1073	2.622	-	-	-	-	-	-	-
Enrolled	-	-	-	-	76%	67%	63%	40%	14%	6%	3%
Graduated	-	-	-	-	0%	0%	1%	20%	44%	52%	55%
1992 Freshmen	3850	3.187	1069	2.645	-	-	-	-	-	-	-
Enrolled	-	-	-	-	78%	67%	62%	39%	12%	5%	3%
Graduated	-	-	-	-	0%	0%	1%	21%	46%	53%	56%
1993 Freshmen	4287	3.2	1073	2.619	-	-	-	-	-	-	-
Enrolled	-	-	-	-	75%	63%	59%	36%	11%	4%	-
Graduated	-	-	-	-	0%	0%	1%	23%	45%	52%	-
1994 Freshmen	4298	3.242	1079	2.669	-	-	-	-	-	-	-
Enrolled	-	-	-	-	77%	66%	61%	34%	10%	-	-
Graduated	-	-	-	-	0%	0%	1%	27%	48%	-	-
1995 Freshmen	4370	3.263	1080	2.632	-	-	-	-	-	-	-
Enrolled	-	-	-	-	75%	66%	62%	34%	-	-	-
Graduated	-	-	-	-	0%	0%	1%	26%	-	-	-
1996 Freshmen	4006	3.292	1085	2.646	-	-	-	-	-	-	-
Enrolled	-	-	-	-	77%	66%	62%	-	-	-	-
Graduated	-	-	-	-	0%	0%	1%	-	-	-	-
1997 Freshmen	4431	3.305	1085	2.623	-	-	-	-	-	-	-
Enrolled	-	-	-	-	77%	66%	-	-	-	-	-
Graduated	-	-	-	-	0%	0%	-	-	-	-	-
1998 Freshmen	5088	3.316	1095	2.629	-	-	-	-	-	-	-
Enrolled	-	-	-	-	77%	-	-	-	-	-	-
Graduated	-	-	-	-	0%	-	-	-	-	-	-
SUMMARY											
TOTAL					53114	48026	43595	39589	35219	30921	26634
ENROLLED					76%	66%	61%	38%	12%	5%	3%
GRADUATED					0%	0%	1%	21%	45%	51%	54%

- Transfer student rates, including comparisons of two-year and four-year transfers, as well as transfers admitted at different class levels
- Comparisons of full-time and part-time students; continuous and interrupted attendance students

Survey data can be a valuable adjunct to institutional data about attrition. Students who have recently withdrawn from an institution can provide useful feedback about their current situation, reasons for leaving, attitudes, and plans. It is very important for comparative purposes to also survey students who have returned. This permits the researcher to profile the similarities and differences between persisters and exiters.

Basic descriptive data provide a foundation upon which enrollment management decisions can be built. They are also useful for educating the wider campus community about retention issues and often become part of the set of accountability and performance measures at the state or governing board level. Descriptive data, along with the supporting infrastructure, become the springboard for more sophisticated questions and analyses.

Multivariate Analyses

Descriptive data alone will not be sufficient for a full understanding of retention and graduation rates. Retention is a subtle and complex issue with many different determinants. Multivariate analysis can help unravel some of this complexity. Perhaps the best known example of this approach is Astin's (1993) work, which examines the predictability of graduation rates from entry characteristics of students in light of his tri-partite model: input, environment, and outcome. Astin advocates computing a predicted graduation rate, which could then be compared with an institution's actual rate as an assessment of performance. Mortenson (1997) modifies this approach using a different set of predictors not within the control of institutions and then using the results to rank states as well as individual institutions based on differences between predicted and actual graduation rates. *U.S. News and World Reports* also uses a similar approach in their annual rankings. Although more sophisticated than simple descriptive statistics, this approach is not without controversy. Results can vary widely depending on the choice of independent variables and on any measurement error in the variables that are chosen. Kroc, Howard, Hull and Woodard (1997) point out how the choice of institutions (public vs. private, for example) can influence the results, and how logistic regression is superior to OLS regression when the dependent variable is a dichotomy.

Causal modeling, also known as path analysis or structural equation modeling, has been useful to some researchers as a method that helps to identify more accurately causal relationships among complex, interrelated data. In recent years, most volumes of *Research in Higher Education* contain examples of this method. Hazard or survival analysis, a relatively new method imported into higher education from medicine, promises to further refine and improve our analysis of graduation rates. DesJardins, Ahlberg and McCall (1999), for example, have used this method to better understand the temporal dimensions of first stopout or dropout.

Qualitative Methods

Although most retention studies use quantitative methods, qualitative approaches can be valuable in some situations, revealing issues and providing insights that will be otherwise missed. In situations where little is known, perhaps with small populations of students, these methods (interviews, case studies, ethnographies or participant observation, for example) can be particularly useful. The retention issues confronting students confined to wheelchairs, for example, may be best understood using qualitative methods. These situations should be carefully selected, because these approaches are labor intensive, and some administrators have serious misgivings about crafting policy from the small number of cases studied in most qualitative research.

Program Evaluation

A plethora of retention programs have sprung to life on many campuses. Administrators are increasingly concerned about the benefits produced by these programs, particularly during years of budget shortfall. Some programs may have on-going systematic evaluation efforts in place; others may not. Serving as an external evaluator for retention programs can be awkward both because of the time and effort required and because of the possible suspicion and wariness of the program coordinators. Another strategy might be to act as a consultant to program coordinators, providing design assistance and, perhaps, basic retention data for the program participants. The coordinators would then be responsible for the evaluation, which should be both formative and summative in nature. As supported by the "best practices" literature, program evaluation should be embedded into a program, rather than be episodic, and should be designed primarily for program improvement. The "Academic and Student Support" section of this chapter describes program evaluation in more detail.

The Context

Retention research can be made more difficult because the locus of control is not as well defined as with recruitment, where a single office often has primary responsibility. Retention is everyone's job, which can mean no one takes responsibility. A university or college needs to create a structure that supports enrollment management to be effective in this area. An enrollment management committee, for example, can identify critical issues, help shape the analysis, and facilitate recommended changes. Whatever the institution's structure may be, the institutional researcher needs to be aware of the local context both to understand important issues when designing studies and for implementing the results. It is often important to present to a number of audiences with differing perspectives, requiring both flexibility and the ability to simplify complex findings for non-statisticians. The researcher needs to be sensitive to the fact that there may often be competing perspectives about potential campus changes. It can be especially helpful, if not essential, to inform and engage high level administrators in the retention conversation.

In addition to understanding local concerns, the researcher needs to be informed about the national context. A number of sources for national graduation rate data now exist. One of the best is the Consortium for Student Retention Data Exchange (Smith, 1999), which provided data for 269 U.S. colleges and universities in 1999. Many groups of institutions now have data exchanges (the AAU Data Exchange is an example) to facilitate the sharing of more detailed information. In the age of attachments and electronic files, informal collaborations among institutions facing similar issues can be fruitful and engaging. E-mail or the *Electronic AIR* can help begin a conversation with colleagues.

Beyond Graduation

Consistent with our student flow perspective, enrollment management should not end when students graduate. Valuable insights can be gained from alumni as well as from employers of former students. These insights may help us to recruit and retain students and to enrich students' college experience. There is strong convergence here between student assessment and enrollment management. Student outcomes assessment has encouraged us to gather information after graduation that can also be useful for managing enrollments. We can complete the cycle that begins with student prospects by understanding the outcomes and by using this knowledge to improve our ability to attract new students, thus completing the feedback loop.

Alumni

Comprehensive surveys of alumni have become widespread among colleges and universities, partly as a result of assessment and accountability pressures. Much can be learned from these surveys.

- Where are our graduates? How many of them have stayed in the region or state? Are we educating our neighbors' workforce?
- Are they employed? For how long? Are they in an area for which they were trained? Did they receive adequate career preparation? What is their salary? Have they changed jobs?
- Have they continued their education? Where? What are their educational objectives?
- How do they view their academic experiences at your institution? Was the curriculum satisfactory? Their instructors?
- How do they view their extra-curricular experiences? Was the campus climate positive? Was the level of student services satisfactory?

- Would they recommend your college to others? Why or why not?

Non-resident enrollment is an example of a policy area where data from an alumni survey might be useful. Decisions about the appropriate mix of in-state and out-of-state students might be better informed if policy makers know how many non-residents remain in the state after graduation.

At community colleges, where students' educational objectives are more diverse, the situation is more complex than at four-year institutions. The relatively small population of alumni can be supplemented with students who have transferred to a four-year institution or for students who have vocational or other objectives. The college may wish to learn more about the transfer process and other outcomes in order to assess its educational programs and outcomes.

Employers

Employers are another group that can provide valuable feedback. Periodic surveys can be used to gather data for student assessment, accountability, and enrollment management needs. Such information might include:

- The overall quality and training of an institution's graduates/students
- The preparation of graduates in specific areas, such as writing skills, technical skills, quantitative reasoning, oral communication, leadership, and teamwork
- The accessibility of the campus and its students to the employer for interviewing
- Trends in past hiring and expectations for the future.

SUPPORTING ENROLLMENT MANAGEMENT

Organizing for Enrollment Management

The most elegant analyses will lie fallow unless an effective institutional structure exists for managing enrollments. Several components need to be interwoven to create an environment where good ideas can be implemented and necessary changes are fostered. These components include planning, the functional units responsible for implementing changes, institutional research, and administrative support.

Planning and Administrative Support

Enrollment management and enrollment planning are virtually synonymous. Enrollment management can fail if it becomes separated from other campus planning activities, particularly if these activities involve budgeting and facilities. A certain amount of education and, perhaps, change management may be needed to persuade key campus constituencies that enrollment issues are pervasive in their impact on the entire campus. Examples of this impact include:

- The total college budget is clearly affected by enrollment increases and declines
- Classroom and residence hall needs ebb and flow with enrollment
- Curricular and faculty needs shift not only according to student numbers, but also as demand for academic programs fluctuates and as the mix of lower division, upper division, and graduate students changes—in community colleges the mix between vocational and transfer track programs is important
- Student union, bookstore, library, student health, parking, and other disparate auxiliary needs can also be critically affected by changes in student enrollment

If the campus view of enrollment management is limited to student recruitment (to use a common example), then the researcher needs to facilitate a conversation designed to broaden the perspective. It may be best to begin by selecting a handful of campus enrollment issues that need to be addressed. The key stakeholders, both individuals and campus committees, should then be identified. This group might include curriculum, advising, and student assessment committees; admission, financial aid, and residence life directors; vice presidents for student or academic affairs; and perhaps even the president. Meetings with these stakeholders should be designed not only to discuss the specific issues, but also to instill a broad perspective of enrollment as an essential campus planning activity. Drawing on the professional literature in enrollment management can be helpful in infusing this broader perspective into campus discussions. *The Strategic Management of College Enrollments* (Hossler, Bean and Associates, 1990) is a comprehensive source of information about the various aspects of enrollment management, and includes chapters on strategic planning, organizational approaches, and case studies of institutions that have successful approaches to managing college enrollments. More recently, *A Practical Guide to Enrollment and Retention Management in Higher Education* (Dennis, 1998) discusses an array of useful ideas for the enrollment manager, including very specific suggestions about useful data and reports as well as some thoughtful ideas about future directions for enrollment management. These sources are useful for the institutional researcher, and they can also be very persuasive when placed into the right hands at the appropriate time. The national perspective reflected in these books, as well as in other publications and research studies, can be a critical element for educating the campus community and securing the administrative support needed to successfully integrate the enrollment management enterprise with the overall college planning processes.

Organizational Structures

Successful enrollment management structures come in all shapes and sizes. Some are centralized, some decentralized. Some depend on a hierarchical management structure; others invoke a flat structure. Some emanate

42

from student affairs and others from academic affairs. The person or agency responsible for coordinating the enterprise might be the admissions director, a faculty member, the vice president for undergraduate education, the provost, or a committee. New and radically different structures cannot easily be imposed in most cases. Changes need to be reasonably consistent with the existing organization or they are likely to fail. Enrollment management is usually an evolutionary process rather than one marked by sharp, sudden managerial change. As Hossler (1990, p. 44) puts it:

> Like planning, enrollment management must be adapted to the needs, organizational climate, and administrative skills available on each campus. Enrollment management activities, like any organizational task, need to be compatible with local campus issues, management styles, and traditions and cultures.

Some useful ways to conceptualize and describe alternative approaches and organizational structures do exist. This section describes a framework that can help guide a college or university toward more effective strategies. Originally developed by Kemerer, Baldridge, and Green (1982) in their book *Strategies for Effective Enrollment Management*, this framework continues to be instructive for understanding alternative structures for managing college enrollments. They describe four models: the enrollment management committee, the enrollment management coordinator, the enrollment management matrix, and the enrollment management division.

The simplest approach to enrollment issues or problems is to form a committee. Such committees are often initially charged with examining the institution's recruitment and retention efforts. The admissions director, a faculty member, or a student affairs administrator may chair the committee. This approach is quick, requires minimal investment of time and money, requires no organizational restructuring, and makes use of a problem-solving practice common to other campus issues. A committee can provide a useful forum for addressing enrollment management issues and for educating the wider campus community if problems are not severe or in need of immediate action. It can engage a diverse array of faculty and staff in an important campus conversation. This approach does have some serious, sometimes fatal, drawbacks. Because committees usually have no authority over institutional policy or practice, a committee structure is usually inadequate to accomplish significant change. Moreover, committee members generally are unable to devote the time needed to accomplish complex objectives—and the membership may change frequently. The committee structure can be a useful initial phase in the enrollment management enterprise, but a more complex structure will probably be needed before long.

Many colleges designate an enrollment management coordinator, a second common organizational strategy. This person is usually a middle level administrator, often the admissions director, who has some working knowledge of enrollment management issues and generally retains most of their original responsibilities. This model can more successfully produce change because some portion of the functional units responsible for implementing enrollment strategies often report to this person. In addition, having a specific person rather than a committee in charge focuses accountability, which is more likely to catalyze action. Conversely, having a specific person as coordinator can easily make effective enrollment management overly dependent on the abilities, personality, and influence of that particular person. If the coordinator receives little release time from other duties, then she may have insufficient time to devote to sometimes burdensome enrollment needs. Finally, although the coordinator role can provide more visibility within the administrative hierarchy, it still may not create sufficient linkage with senior level administrators to accomplish needed objectives.

Assigning a senior level administrator matrix management responsibilities for managing enrollments is a third, more centralized, organizational approach. In this model, the relevant units continue to maintain their formal reporting relationships but also report to the designated senior administrator for enrollment management activities. The director of residence life, for example, would continue to report formally to the dean of students but would also report to the vice president for undergraduate education with regard to those activities and initiatives that directly impact enrollments. This model creates an important direct connection to the resources and influence of the senior level administration. It can also, however, create considerable confusion because many units may now report to two people. Difficulties can easily arise unless good communication and cooperation exists, particularly if the senior level administrator has too little time and inadequate understanding of enrollment management issues.

Finally, a campus can organize an enrollment management division with units reporting directly to a senior level administrator, usually a vice president, who is specifically responsible for enrollment management. In this most centralized model, the functional units responsible for implementing enrollment policies report directly to the vice president for enrollment management. These units may include admissions, financial aid, registrar, bursar, academic advising, residence life, student activities, career services, academic support services, institutional research, and faculty development. A separate institutional research function may be established to support this division in some cases. This model can and should result in a highly effective enrollment management program, one that is closely bound to other campus processes. It can also be the most difficult, costly, and disruptive model to implement. Units must be organizationally, and sometimes, physically moved. The political and economic costs may be significant— people may become angry and processes may be disrupted. For these reasons, it may take an enrollment crisis to propel an institution toward this model.

The Role of Student Affairs

The vice president for student affairs is the chief enrollment management officer in some colleges and universities. This model can work well, particularly if many of the functional enrollment units report to student affairs. Student affairs professionals focus sharply on student and enrollment issues in their education as well as in their work. They may also be less distracted by the research and teaching responsibilities that can divide faculty attention. Increasingly, however, changes in postsecondary education complicate the picture. The growth of student assessment and accountability has focused increasing attention on undergraduate education and on the role of faculty. The view that faculty need to take greater responsibility for undergraduate teaching and learning has sometimes resulted in an increased role for academic affairs in enrollment management, particularly at research universities. Enrollment related functions and units, such as admissions and financial aid, in some cases have been reorganized from student affairs to academic affairs, bringing them together with more typical academic affairs units such as academic advising and faculty development. This creates a larger enrollment management division, which can be used to leverage change at a time when improving undergraduate education is often the top priority for provosts and presidents. These issues may place a student affairs division in the difficult position of defending and justifying its efforts without appearing defiant or uncooperative.

Technical and Analytic Skills

In his reflective article about the nature of institutional research, Pat Terenzini (1993) conceptualizes three tiers of organizational intelligence that need to be present for effective research: technical/analytic, issues, and contextual intelligence. Most of this chapter has been devoted to an overview of the second tier, the many issues involved in enrollment management. Some discussion of the third tier, which "involves understanding the culture both of higher education in general and of the particular campus where the institutional researcher works" (Terenzini, 1993, p.3), has also been included. This chapter would be incomplete, though, without some discussion of the first tier of organizational intelligence, the technical and analytical skills needed to undertake enrollment management research. Although this tier is insufficient by itself, it is "fundamental and foundational" (Terenzini, 1993, p.2) to the two higher level tiers and to an effective enrollment management program.

Factual Knowledge

Terenzini (1993) distinguishes factual knowledge, which is usually acquired on-the-job, from methodological skills, which are initially learned more formally from coursework. Characteristics of factual knowledge include familiarity with standard categories and definitions; counting rules and formulae; and data administration and structure issues. For the enrollment management analyst, standard categories and definitions include such things as prospective student, applicant, admitted student, matriculated student, alumnus, high school background characteristics (SAT/ACT scores, class rank, high school GPA, etc.), first-time freshman, transfer student, degree-seeking, headcount, part- or full-time, race/ethnicity, domicile, class level, career (graduate, undergraduate, or other), financial aid type (grant, scholarship, waiver, loan, employment, etc.), academic program, grade type, course level, course site, course delivery mode, degree type, credit hours, contact hours, tuition, and fees. Counting rules and formulae include calculating the number of FTE students, the price of education, students' grade point averages, costs per credit hour, student financial need, student/faculty ratios, and others. Data administration and structure issues will be considered in more detail in the next section of the chapter. Although this type of knowledge can be learned from an institutional research and planning course or from directed readings, most analysts acquire this content as dictated by their work responsibilities.

Methodological Skills

Knowledge of methodological skills is generally best acquired through formal coursework at the graduate level, most often in education or the social sciences. Departments of educational psychology, psychology, statistics, sociology, anthropology, or public administration may also offer such courses. The methodological skills needed include research design, statistics, survey design and sampling, qualitative methods, psychometrics, and evaluation.

A solid understanding of research design is the essential methodological foundation for the enrollment management analyst. When an enrollment question is posed, the analyst needs to have a working understanding of an array of research design strategies from which to choose. In many cases, more than one alternative may be possible, so an informed choice can make the difference between a successful and unsuccessful outcome. Deciding between a survey or focus group approach, or using a matched pairs design instead of regression, for example, may be important. Because most higher education interventions create situations that are quasi-experimental in nature, the researcher needs to have a solid grasp of these techniques. Rarely is random assignment used to place students into retention programs, so comparing the "control" and "experimental" groups can be difficult. Fortunately, much has been written in this area. A good place to start is the classic text, *Quasi-Experimentation* (Cook and Campbell, 1979). While coursework and readings are the essential starting point for a mastery of research design, only the trial and error process of engaging in actual studies can complete the analyst's training.

The statistician has been scorned as a person who drowns in a river with an average depth of three feet. Nonetheless, a working understanding of statistics is also an important part of the analyst's arsenal. This understanding should begin with basic descriptive statistics and exploratory data analysis (Tukey, 1977). It should also include basic probability, inferential statistics, measurement error, hypothesis testing, and bivariate and multivariate techniques. Regression and structural equation modeling have become increasingly popular and valuable for analyzing retention outcomes. Although the analyst will want

46

to bring the best statistical techniques to bear on an issue, too much statistical detail in a report or presentation can be distracting.

Survey design and sampling have also become increasingly important skills for the enrollment management analyst in recent years. Surveys are used to assess the reasons why students do not matriculate, why they withdraw, how they view instructors and the curriculum, and what their lives are like after graduation. Student outcomes assessment programs make particular use of surveys that may also be helpful for the enrollment analyst. Two useful sources for practical survey design information are *Mail and Internet Surveys: The Tailored Design Method* (Dillman, 2000) and the Association for Institutional Research handbook, *Questionnaire Survey Research: What Works* (Suskie, 1992).

Qualitative methods can be employed usefully by the enrollment manager, particularly in situations where little is known or where detailed and richly descriptive analysis is needed. This is more than a choice of methods—it is also an epistemological decision. Because of these philosophical differences, a debate continues about appropriate uses of these methods and about the wisdom of blending qualitative and quantitative methods in program evaluation or research studies. Hathaway (1995) has published an article for institutional researchers comparing and contrasting the two approaches. The disciplines of anthropology and sociology, which have pioneered these methods, usually offer course work. Another source of information is *Using Qualitative Methods in Institutional Research* (Fetterman, ed., 1991). Since some issues lend themselves to these methods, and some stakeholders are very responsive to case studies and "thick description," enrollment analysts should consider using qualitative techniques more often.

A cursory understanding of measurement issues can also assist the enrollment analyst. Although enrollment studies are more likely to require the construction of affective scales, it can be useful even in the cognitive domain to understand reliability and validity issues, item analysis techniques, scaling, and other related concepts. Departments of educational psychology typically offer course work in psychometrics.

Interest in program evaluation has increased in recent years as the number of retention programs has grown. Institutional researchers and enrollment analysts sometimes find themselves asked to be program evaluators. What might seem to be a simple assignment can turn out to be a complex and time-consuming task. *Evaluating with Validity* (House, 1980) provides a sense for many of the issues and an excellent overview of evaluation. Evaluation can require knowledge of all of the domains that have been described—research design, statistics, qualitative methods, and psychometrics. Understanding the politics and economics of the situation, including the interests of the various stakeholders, is often also essential.

Third Party Vendors

Sometimes it makes more sense to have someone else do the research.

Educational Testing Service (ETS) and the American College Testing program (ACT) offer an array of services related to enrollment management and assessment. The Admitted Student Questionnaire (from ETS), for example, can help reveal why students chose to attend another college. Differences by market segment can be especially helpful. Because the testing companies have access to data that individual institutions do not have, such as where students have sent applications, their services may be particularly valuable. Other firms offer their services in the area of financial aid leveraging.

Using outside sources should be seen as an adjunct to, rather than a substitute for, an in-house enrollment management program. Although these companies can provide valuable services, they are most useful in the context of an active enrollment management program that is staffed by analysts with strong research and methodological skills.

Data Sources

The analysis of enrollment management issues requires a wide array of data, both internal and external to the institution. Obtaining the data needed for an analysis can be a major obstacle. Simple, critical analyses are sometimes not possible because data are either unavailable or inadequate. Understanding where to find data, how it is collected, who the steward is, and how it may be accessed are essential aspects of the enrollment management enterprise.

Institutional Data

Most institutional data is collected for purposes that may not be directly related to the needs of the enrollment management researcher. Admissions offices need to attract and admit students, financial aid offices need to disburse aid, the Bursar needs to collect tuition and fees, etc. Understanding how and why such offices do their business can be essential to understanding the data needed by the researcher but collected and controlled by other offices. Student ethnicity, for example, is often initially collected by the admissions office. Typically students self-report this data on their admissions application, but the format and labels can vary considerably. If applicants can check "other," for example, there may be large numbers of students whose ethnicity is unknown, thereby affecting analyses. Analyses may also be impacted if labels for ethnic groups are unclear or misleading. Years ago, the University of Arizona began using "American Indian or Alaskan Native" rather than "Native American" on the admission application, which apparently resulted in an unexpected drop in the enrollment of these students. Investigation revealed that a number of non-Native American applicants born in the United States had been reporting themselves as "Native American." The lesson is clear: good enrollment management research requires a thorough understanding of how, why, and by whom data are collected. Institutional researchers need to be on good terms with the offices on which they depend.

Many institutions are faced with the uncertainty and expense of replacing outdated, inflexible administrative data systems—systems that have often been poorly designed to meet institutional research needs. Fortunately, vendors are now more aware that their systems need to meet both business transaction needs (admission, registration, aid, fee payment, etc.) and decision support needs, including enrollment management analysis. Particularly when student information systems are replaced, it is essential that enrollment management researchers be engaged with the project teams that craft the RFP, select the vendor, and implement the new product. Even if it is the process used to collect data rather than the data structure that creates difficulties, replacing an administrative system often provides the opportunity to change business processes as well as data systems. The researcher who does not become involved in system replacement loses an ideal opportunity to improve the quality and accessibility of data needed to meet enrollment management needs.

Peer Data and Performance Indicators

Peer data can provide valuable comparisons that help establish a context for strategic enrollment planning. The World Wide Web and other advances in technology have helped make access to such data much easier. The rich array of NCES Integrated Postsecondary Education Data System (IPEDS) data and reports is now available through their Web site. The accelerating need for information has also spawned a number of data exchanges and peer databases. The Association of American Universities Data Exchange, for example, provides data in a variety of areas to its member institutions. This group is currently working to refine definitions and data collection; expand the data to include institutions that are not AAU members; and to make data collection and dissemination "paperless" (including development of a Web front end). Some individual institutions have obtained funding to compile peer data, making their databases available to others through paper reports, Web sites, spreadsheets, CD-ROM, or some other means. The Consortium for Student Retention and Data Exchange (Smith, 1999), for example, annually publishes student retention and graduation rates for its 330 members. As another example, the University of Delaware has compiled, analyzed, and widely distributed data about faculty workload and academic program costs. This project was developed as a response to the need for overall workload and cost data and the need for data both at the institution and program levels. Researchers increasingly need such multi-level data. Finally, the data found in publications like *U.S. News and World Report* and *Peterson's Guide* have become increasingly useful as sources for peer data. The Common Data Set, which many institutions update annually for use in these publications, has helped considerably to standardize and facilitate this process. In summary, peer data useful to meet enrollment management needs has become more available and more useful.

Performance indicators are becoming increasingly common in higher education. Graduation rates, for example, may be the most common indicator required for state-level accountability. Colleges and universities may need to establish sets of peer institutions and gather comparable peer data to interpret and analyze these indicators. Such data can be influential in statewide conversations about managing enrollments, particularly since governing boards and legislative staffs may be familiar with these indicators and more likely to use them (wisely or not) when crafting policy.

Other Data

Collecting and maintaining additional data has become a more important aspect of enrollment management in light of growing assessment and accountability needs. Although surveys have been used for many years in marketing research needed to manage student recruitment, student surveys are now often administered at many other points in time to obtain data about student background, activities, attitudes or satisfaction. Many colleges and universities are also collecting new data to assess the "value added" by students' academic experiences. Particularly when linked to existing institutional data, such data may be useful for enrollment management studies. On campuses where assessment is organizationally separated from institutional research, it may be important to become familiar with assessment activities and data and to develop efficient ways to integrate assessment and administrative databases.

Organizing Data

When recent technical advancements are coupled with the need to integrate diverse, disparate databases, the result is sometimes the creation of data warehouses and data marts. These repositories can provide an analytic environment allowing more efficient access to data needed for enrollment management purposes and, more widely, for what some are calling enterprise reporting needs. A wide array of current data and a more parsimonious array of historical data may often be available from such systems. Warehouses facilitate retrieval and analysis of data across different administrative systems and can provide linkages with ancillary databases. They also permit the construction of standard queries, which can be run at any time by anyone with the proper access. With minimal time and effort, for example, a vice president or provost could run a query to retrieve headcount enrollment and FTE counts at any point during the course registration cycle. The primary pitfalls are the effort required to develop comprehensive warehouses and the administrative overhead needed to maintain them. Third party vendors have begun developing products to meet this need (Cold Fusion, for example). Data warehouses and data marts can offer significant benefits to the policy analyst when adequately developed and maintained.

Communicating Results

Effective enrollment management demands that we share information with others about the recruitment, enrollment, retention, and graduation of students. Because students flow "through" our institutions, how and when we communicate information is as important as what we communicate. In this section, we want to share important principles for placing enrollment management information in the hands of the decision-makers who need it.

The first principle of effective communication is knowing who needs the data. The organization of the institution may determine key decision makers who must have the information, but political considerations may determine who receives the information first. Every organization has a network of individuals who use the same information in different ways or need very different kinds of information for their specific decisions. For example, college recruiters may not only need different information about who is considering their institution but may need it sooner than the financial aid advisors. Another factor in knowing who needs the data is understanding how key decision-makers process the enrollment management information given to them. Consequently, it is important to analyze each individual in the reporting hierarchy and to determine whether they prefer processing information using text, numbers, or graphical interpretations (Brigman and Hanson, 2000). Some decision-makers process information most effectively by reading text. Provide them with key findings summarized early in the report. Other decision-makers may prefer analyzing detailed numerical tables to arrive at their own conclusions. Simple one-page reports with a table or two are the best way to share information with these "number processing" decision-makers. The decision-maker may instead prefer processing information by quickly scanning a chart or graph that visually summarizes the key points of information. The best reporting formats combine some elements of all three reporting formats and satisfy the largest variety of enrollment management information users.

A second principle is knowing when the information is needed. If the right information is provided a day late, the decision will have been made without it. Being aware of when important decisions are being made on your campus is critical. Letting decision-makers know ahead of time how long a particular analysis or report may take will allow creation of a "time buffer" or "slippage factor" in getting the report finished before the decision is made. Creating a dissemination plan for the academic year that highlights when key reports are needed may help avoid the "avalanche" syndrome, that period of time when everyone wants everything yesterday.

A third principle is knowing the best information reporting format and mode. Not only must the information processing style of the decision-maker be considered, but the mode by which it is delivered is an important consideration in designing the format. Traditionally, a print or text mode has been used for communicating information. While all findings should be documented in a written report for purposes of archiving the information for historical reference, long and detailed reports are rarely read or used. Technology offers other options for sharing our enrollment management information. Colleges and universities increasingly use the Web for disseminating key information. The advantages of using the Web is that it is widely accessible, relatively inexpensive to produce, and available 24 hours a day. Yet another advantage of using the Web is that the production of reports can be automated or semi-automated by commercial statistical analysis software packages. Enrollment management information can be collected, analyzed, and reported on the Web in a few hours or days, compared with the weeks or months using more conventional methods. Sharing information using interactive data presentation methodology or On-line Analytic Processing (OLAP) techniques is another way to use technology to enhance the production and use of information. The report audience can analyze raw data from a database with interactive data analysis software program that provides "real-time" query. "What if" and "simulation" questions can be analyzed and reported within seconds. This technique provides a very powerful way of reporting relevant information because the decision-makers generate the questions that drive the analysis. Finally, providing oral reports using computer-assisted presentation techniques is an excellent way to share information. This presentation mode provides the decision-makers an opportunity to query the presenter and pursue special topics related to the decision at hand. Questions can be raised and discussions initiated that may have implications for action.

A fourth principle when communicating enrollment management information is the content of the report. The nature of the decision must be considered in light of the statistical sophistication of the user audience. The most appropriate statistics should be used to analyze the data, but it may be necessary to transform the findings to simpler, more meaningful information if the decision-makers are to understand it. Most decision-makers want to know what the reported data means and what implications it may have for the decision they are trying to make. Reporting a detailed description of data analytic techniques should be avoided because most decision-makers will trust that the appropriate statistics have been chosen. The focus should be on what the information means. That meaning should be communicated using simple numbers, percentages, and statistical averages (e.g., mean, median, or mode). Descriptions of complex multivariate analysis, discriminate function analysis, or logistic regression analysis used to understand data are more likely to confuse than illuminate the important issues in a report. Increasingly, exploratory data analytic techniques and data analytic visualization software are being used to share information.

A fifth principle to consider is the "formality" of a report. While one may be asked to produce a long formal written report with extensive data analysis and strong recommendations for practice, it is more likely that a brief report with a single table of data, one or two charts, and one or two recommendations for action will be requested. Other reporting forms bring with them their own implications (e.g., a 10-minute presentation in a meeting with a long agenda versus a five-minute phone report to a key decision-maker). It is important to clarify the level of formality of the information requested. Over time, a sense can be developed of how much detail, statistical analysis, and specificity of recommendation particular decision-makers on campus desire. In general, "less-is-more" is a good rule to follow. Too much data and not enough information merely frustrate decision-makers and interfere with the decision-making process.

A sixth principle is knowing how to deliver bad news to a decision-maker. If enrollment drops dramatically when an increase was expected, key decision-makers do not want to be told after the fact. If the information they request contains bad news, it may be helpful to release preliminary findings to key decision-makers in time for them to develop a plan of action for dealing with the negative news. Few decision-makers want to look at a final draft or a formal report and be surprised by the findings without having the opportunity to think of ways to consider the implications for dealing with it.

A final principle is to think of communicating information as a process rather than a product. Thinking of sharing information as a process will encourage searching for ways to provide systematic institutional structures for sharing information with the right people, in the right format, at the right time. Creating database or data warehouse information systems that provide a level of "on-demand" report generation can be helpful. McLaughlin et. al. (1998?) provide an overview of information system development that facilitates "query friendly" use. Another guideline is to engage the decision-makers in the design of an information reporting system. The end-user's needs for information and their critical time demands are ignored too often. Thinking of an information sharing process as providing "their" information rather than "your" information will make a huge improvement in getting decision-makers to use information.

In summary, effective communication of enrollment management information means getting the right information to the right people at the right time to do the right thing. An institution has done a good job of communicating information when the flow of students to its doorstep, through college, and into the world of work happens as planned. Making this communication of information an open, public, and continuous process will enlighten more people involved in educating students. Perhaps most importantly, efforts to share information will have been successful when the external public recognizes that educational institutions are effectively and efficiently managed.

The Future of Enrollment Management

Higher Education Trends

The future of enrollment management depends on the national higher education environment in which it will exist and to which it must respond. We would suggest that this environment might have the following characteristics:

- All national projections (WICHE, 1998; NCES, 1998; ETS, 2000) forecast sharp growth in higher education over the next 10-15 years as the baby boom echo (sometimes called "Generation Y") attends college.
- Demographic changes will cause the South and West regions of the

U.S. to have large enrollment increases while other areas experience smaller increases.

- Hispanic and Asian enrollment will increase faster than the enrollment of other groups.
- Funding for higher education will become increasingly competitive, complex, and in many cases scarce.
- Accountability demands will continue to accelerate.
- Technology-delivered education coupled with growing demands for wider access to academic programs will blur geographic and educational sector boundaries.

Implications for Enrollment Management

Within this wider higher education context, enrollment management analysts may expect to observe several trends:

- **Enrollment management will become increasingly central to college and university missions**. Managing enrollments will become increasingly important as institutions compete for students in an environment where funding is often insecure. This will extend a trend that began for some institutions in the 1980s or even earlier. Researchers can expect to be asked for increased depth and breadth in their policy analyses. This might include better institutional data, multi-level analyses, more refined peer data, consideration of more issues, quicker response time, and dissemination to a wider audience.

- **Better integration with strategic planning and budgeting processes will occur**. Enrollment growth will become a more critical avenue for maintaining the revenue stream and developing discretionary funds for many institutions. Tuition increases and, in public institutions, the marginal revenue derived from state appropriations will forge stronger linkages with the budgeting and planning processes. Enrollment researchers will also need to be fiscal analysts.

- **The partnership between enrollment management and student assessment will strengthen**. As described in this chapter, assessment programs and enrollment management have a variety of common interests. As the assessment "movement" matures, enrollment researchers will increasingly integrate assessment data into their work, particularly with regard to student flow. Assessment studies and data will help understand how students move through the curriculum—and may also help us to design better recruitment strategies as we get to know our students better.

- **Collaborations with other sectors and other institutions will increase**. Higher education boundaries are becoming less distinct. Technology-delivered education, dual enrollment of students in high school and community college courses, and baccalaureate degrees offered by community colleges are examples of initiatives that are changing the boundaries and increasing collaborative efforts across sectors and among institutions. The enrollment analyst will be working more with colleagues from other institutions as we address these complex issues.

References

Adelman, C. (1999). Answers in the toolbox: Academic intensity, attendance patterns and bachelor's degree attainment. Washington D.C.: U.S. Dept. of Education, Office of Educational Research and Improvement Admitted Student Questionnaire. Princeton, NJ: College Board

American College Testing Program. (2000a). College dropout rates improve, but graduation rate falls. News release: February 16, 2000. Available on the web at http://www.act.org/news/releases/2000/02-16-00.html. Downloaded on November 28, 2000.

American College Testing Program. (2000b). Prediction Service Report. Available on the web at http://www.act.org/research/services/predict/index.html. Downloaded on November 28, 2000.

Andrade, S. J. (1999). Assessing the impact of curricular reform: Measures of course efficiency and effectiveness. Paper presented at the Annual Forum of the Association for Institutional Research, Seattle, WA.

Astin, A. W. (1968). The college environment. Washington DC: American Council on Education.

Astin, A. W. (1993). What matters in college?: Four critical years revisited. San Francisco, CA: Jossey Bass.

Astin, A., Parrott, S. A., Korn, W. S., & Sax, L. J. (1997a). The American college student: Thirty year trends, 1966-1996. Higher Education Research Institute, Graduate School of Education and Information Studies, University of California, Los Angeles.

Astin A. W. (1997b). How good is your institution's retention rate? Research in Higher Education, 38 (6), 647-658.

Astin, A. W. (1998). The changing American college student: Thirty-year trends, 1966-96. Review of Higher Education, 21 (2), 115-35.

Bauer, K. (1998). (Vol. Ed.). New Directions for Institutional Research: No. 98. Campus climate: Understanding the critical components of today's colleges and universities. San Francisco, CA: Jossey-Bass.

Baum, S., Choy, S. P., Cofer, J., King, J. E., Saunders, D., Scherschel, P.M., & Somers, P. (1998). Student loan debt: Problems and prospects. Proceedings from a National Symposium (Washington, DC, December 10, 1997). Boston. MA: Education Resources Institute.

Bean, A.G. (1990). Using retention research in enrollment management. In D. Hossler (Ed.), The strategic management of college enrollments. San Francisco, CA: Jossey-Bass.

Bean, J. (1980). Dropouts and turnover: The synthesis and test of a causal model of student attrition. Research in Higher Education, 12 (2), 155-187.

Bean, J. P. & Metzner, B. S. (1985). A conceptual model of nontraditional undergraduate student attrition. Review of Educational Research. 55 (4), 485-540.

Boyer, E. L. (1990). Campus life. The Carnegie Foundation for the Advancement of Teaching. Lawrenceville, NJ: Princeton University Press.

Brigman, L. & Hanson, G. R. (2000). Making things happen in higher education: Dissemination of student affairs research results. In W. Pickering & G. R. Hanson (Vol. Eds.), New Directions for Institutional Research: No. 108. Collaboration between student affairs and institutional researchers to improve institutional effectiveness. San Francisco, CA: Jossey-Bass.

Brinkman, P. T. & McIntyre, C. (1997). Methods and techniques of enrollment forecasting. In D. T. Layzell (Vol. Ed.), New Directions for Institutional Research: No. 93. Forecasting and managing enrollment and revenue: An overview of current trends, issues and methods. (pp. 67-80). San Francisco, CA: Jossey-Bass.

Caldwell, R. (1999). Personal communication.

Clagett, C.A. & Kerr, H. S. (1992). An information infrastructure for enrollment management: Tracking and understanding your students. (ERIC Document Reproduction Service No. ED351075).

Cohen, A. M. (1998). The shaping of American higher education: Emergence and growth of the contemporary system. San Francisco, CA: Jossey-Bass Publishers, Inc.

Cook, T. D. & Campbell, D. T. (1979). Quasi-experimentation: Design and analysis issues for field settings. Boston, MA: Houghton Mifflin.

Davis, J. S. (1997). Student aid research: A manual for financial aid administrators. Washington D.C.: National Association of Student Financial Aid Administrators.

Dennis, M. J. (1998). A practical guide to enrollment and retention management in higher education. Westport, CT: Greenwood Publishing Group.

DesJardins, S. L., Ahlburg, D. A., & McCall, B. P. (1999). An event model of student departure. Economics of Education Review, 18 (3), 375-90.

DesJardins, S. L., Ahlburg, D. A., & McCall, B. P. (1999). Are factors that affect students' chances of graduating time-invariant? Paper presented at the Annual Forum of the Association for Institutional Research, Seattle, Washington.

Dillman, D. A., (2000). Mail and internet surveys: The tailored design method (2nd ed.). New York, NY: Wiley.

Durkheim, E. (1951). Suicide: A study in sociology. New York, NY: Free Press.

Durkheim, E. (1961). Moral education: A study in the theory and application of the sociology of education. New York, NY: Free Press.

Educational Testing Service (ETS). (2000). Crossing the great divide: Can we achieve equity when generation Y goes to college? Princeton, N.J.

Ewell, P. T. (1995). Working over time: The evolution of longitudinal student tracking data bases. In P. T. Ewell (Vol. Ed.), New Directions for Institutional Research: No. 87. Student tracking: New technologies, new demands. (pp. 7-19).

Ewell, P. T. (1997). Is there something wrong with academic advising at the research universities? Panel discussion at Association for Institutional Research Annual Forum, Orlando, Florida.

Fetterman. D. M. (Ed.). (1991). New Directions for Institutional Research: No. 72. Using qualitative methods in institutional research. San Francisco, CA: Jossey-Bass.

Griswold, C. P. & Marine, G. M. (1996). Political influences on state policy: Higher-tuition, higher-aid, and the real world. Review of Higher Education, 19 (4), 361-89.

Hanson, G. R., and Swann, D. M. (1993). Using multiple program impact analysis to document institutional effectiveness. Research in Higher Education, 34 (1), 71-94.

Hanson, G. R., Ouimet, J. & Williams, A. (1997). Quality of Freshmen Student Life. University of Texas at Austin Student Affairs Research Report available at http://www.utexas.edu/student/research/reports/Survey97/survey97.html. Downloaded on November 28, 2000.

Hanson, G. R., Norman, P., & Caillouet, C. (1998). Conquering calculus: Intra-departmental variability in the efficiency and effectiveness of moving students through the math curriculum. Paper presented at the 1998 AIR Forum. Seattle, WA.

Hanson, G. R., Norman, P., & Williams, A. (1998). The Decision to attend UT-Austin: What makes a difference? Student Affairs Electronic Research Report available at http://www.utexas.edu/student/research/reports/ccweb/CCweb.html. Downloaded on November 28, 2000.

Harvey, J., Williams, R. M.., Kirshstein, R. J., O'Malley, A. S., & Wellman, J. V. (1998). Straight talk about college costs and prices. Washington D.C.: National Commission on the Cost of Higher Education.

Hathaway, R. S. (1995). Assumptions underlying quantitative and qualitative research: implications for institutional research. Research in Higher Education, 36 (5).

Heller, D. E. (1997). Student price response in higher education: An update to Leslie and Brinkman. Journal of Higher Education, 68 (6), 624-59.

Hossler, D. & Bean, J. P. (1990). The strategic management of college enrollments. San Francisco, CA: Jossey-Bass.

Hossler, D., Schmitz, J., & Vespar, N. (1999). Going to college: How social, economic, and educational factors influence the decisions students make. Baltimore, MD: Johns Hopkins University Press.

House. (1980). Evaluating with validity. Beverly Hills, CA: Sage Publications.

Institute for Higher Education Policy. (1998). Student Loan debt: Problems and Prospects. Washington, D.C.

Kemerer, F. R., Baldridge, V. J., & Green, K. C., (1982). Strategies for effective enrollment management. Washington, D.C.: American Association of State Colleges and Universities.

Kroc, R., Howard, R., Hull, P., & Woodard, D. (1997). Graduation rates: Do students' academic program choices make a difference? Paper presented at the Annual Forum of the Association for Institutional Research, Orlando, FL.

Kroc, R., Howard, R., Hull, P., & Woodard, D. (1995). Predicting graduation rates: A study of land grant, research 1 and AAU universities. Paper presented at the Annual Forum of the Association for Institutional Research, Boston, MA.

Kuh, G. D., Schuh, J. H., Whitt, E. J., & Associates. (1991). Involving colleges. Successful approaches to fostering student learning and development outside the classroom. San Francisco, CA: Jossey-Bass.

Leslie, L. L., & Brinkman, P. T. (1987). Student price response in higher education: The student demand studies. Journal of Higher Education, 58, (2), 181-204.

Leslie, L. L. & Brinkman, P. T. (1993). The economic value of higher education. Phoenix, AZ: American Council on Education, Oryx Press.

McLaughlin, G. W., Howard, R. D., Balkan, L. A., & Blythe, E. W. (1998). People, Processes, and Managing Data. Tallahassee, FL: Association for Institutional Research.

Milem, J. F. & Berger, J. B. (1997) A modified model of college student persistence: Exploring the relationship between Astin's theory of involvement and Tinto's theory of student departure. Journal of College Student Development, 38 (4), 387-400.

Mortenson, T. (1997). Actual versus predicted institutional graduation rates for 1100 colleges and universities. Post-Secondary Opportunity, 58.

National Center for Education Statistics (NCES). (1998). Pocket projections: Projections of education statistics to 2008. Washington, DC: U.S. Department of Education.

Pascarella, E. E. (1985). Students' affective development within the college environment. Journal of Higher Education, 56 (6), 640-63.

Pascarella, E. T. & Terenzini, P. T. (1991). How college affects students. San Francisco, CA: Jossey-Bass.

Ross, S. M. & Morrison, G. R. (1992). Getting started as a researcher: Designing and conducting research studies in instructional technology. TechTrends, 37 (3), 19-22.

Ruddock, M. S., Hanson, G., & Moss, M. K. (1999). New directions in student retention research: Looking beyond interactional theories of student departure. Paper presented at the Annual Forum of the Association for Institutional Research, Seattle, WA.

Seymour, E. & Hewitt, N. M. (1997). Talking about leaving: Why undergraduates leave the sciences. Boulder, CO: Westview Press.

Smith, T. Y., (Ed.). (1999). 1998-99 CSRDE report. University of Oklahoma: Center for Institutional Data Exchange and Analysis.

Spady, W. G. (1970). Dropouts from higher education: An interdisciplinary review and synthesis. Interchange, 1 (1), 64-85.

Stampen, J. O. & Layzell, D. T. (1997) Tuition and student aid in public higher education: Searching for an organizing principle. In D. T. Layzell (Vol. Ed.), New Directions for Institutional Research: No. 93. Forecasting and Managing Enrollment and Revenue: An Overview of Current Trends, Issues and Methods. (pp. 25-42). San Francisco, CA: Jossey-Bass.

Suskie, L. A. (1992). Questionnaire survey research: What works (second edition). Tallahassee, FL: Association for Institutional Research.

Teeter, D. J. & Lozier, G. L. (Vol. Eds.). (1993). New Directions for Institutional Research: No. 78. Pursuit of quality in educational research: Case studies in total quality management. San Francisco, CA: Jossey-Bass.

Terenzini, P. T. (1980). An evaluation of three basic designs for studying attrition. Journal of College Student Personnel, 21 (3), 257-63.

Terenzini, P. (1982). Studying student attrition. In E. T. Pascarella, (Ed.), New Directions for Institutional Research: No. 36. Studying student attrition. San Francisco, CA: Jossey-Bass.

Terenzini, P. T. (1993). On the nature of institutional research and the knowledge and skills it requires. Research in Higher Education, 34 (1), 1-10.

Tinto, V. (1975). Dropout from higher education: A theoretical synthesis of recent research. Review of Educational Research, 45 (1), 89-125.

Tinto, V. (1987). Leaving college: Rethinking the causes and cures of student attrition. Chicago, IL: University of Chicago Press.

Tukey, John W. (1977). Exploratory data analysis. Reading, MA: Addison-Wesley Publishing Company.

Velleman, D. J. (1996). Vision 2010 website. Ann Arbor, MI: University of Michigan School of Information

Voorhees, R. A. (1997). An action agenda for researching student aid. In D. T. Layzell (Vol. Ed.), New Directions for Institutional Research: No. 93. Forecasting and managing enrollment and revenue: An overview of current trends, issues and methods. (pp. 99-107). San Francisco, CA: Jossey-Bass.

Western Interstate Commission for Higher Education (WICHE), (1998). Knocking at the college door—projections of high school graduates by state and ethnicity: 1996-2012. Boulder, CO.

CHAPTER 2: INSTITUTIONAL EFFECTIVENESS, STUDENT LEARNING, AND OUTCOMES ASSESSMENT

Author: John Muffo

This chapter focuses on the assessment of institutional effectiveness and student outcomes. Related topics include the assessment of general education; the academic major; affective student learning; retention; and other aspects of student life related to teaching and learning. Measurement issues and effective data collection techniques related to these topics are especially relevant.

Introduction

It has been over two decades now since the performance funding program was initiated and implemented at the University of Tennessee (Banta, 1986). For many of us the efforts in Tennessee mark the beginning of the outcomes assessment movement in the U.S. Since then a great deal has been happening over a wide range of topics related to assessment. This chapter will attempt to provide an overview of what we have learned in the past 20 years, and how the many activities related to assessment affect the day-to-day lives of those studying and working in U.S. higher education.

DEFINITION

The first question to be addressed regarding assessment has to do with its definition. What do we mean when we discuss assessment? Confusion on this point often leads to large amounts of negative energy being spent unnecessarily.

A basic definition of assessment would take into account the fundamental shift from an emphasis on inputs to one on outcomes. The traditional view of quality in American higher education is to study the amount of human and material resources involved, along with the relative status of the human resources in particular, and to declare something of high or low quality as a result. (The current emphasis on ranking reports at the undergraduate and graduate levels is a good example of that. They emphasize inputs such as average standardized test scores of students and proportion of terminally educated faculty without attempting to measure if anybody has learned anything as a result of these inputs.) The traditional assumption has been that when the best students and best faculty are mixed with the best resources, then it is only logical to conclude that excellent education must be taking place. This approach has been the foundation of regional and disciplinary accreditation until recently.

The assessment movement tends to be more interested in the quality of the end product and the value added to it than the status of the players involved. Assessment asks the question regarding what students know and how they came to know it. What is important is how much a student knows and is able to do upon graduation, as well as perhaps what values (professional and personal) the new graduate has. Resources, including faculty, might be of some secondary interest, but the primary focus is on student learning against a stated set of goals and objectives. Terenzini describes this as a "redirection of institutional attention from resources to education" (Terenzini, 1989, p. 645).

A good way to conceptualize the term "assessment" is to ask, as suggested by Terenzini (1989, p. 646-647), three questions. These will determine the specifics of what is meant by assessment, direct the methods use, and guide the utilization of the results. The three questions are:

- What is the purpose of the assessment? Why is it taking place?
  - ➤ Enhancement of teaching and learning or **formative** assessment?
  - ➤ Accountability to external organizations or **summative** assessment?

- What is the level of assessment? Who is to be assessed?
  - ➤ Individual students?
  - ➤ Groups – aggregation by course, department, college, gender, race, etc.?

- What outcomes are to be assessed? For example,
  - ➤ Knowledge?
  - ➤ Skills?
  - ➤ Attitudes?
  - ➤ Behaviors?

In some respects there are inherent contradictions in the way that assessment is implemented today. Most assessment programs appear to be driven by external mandates from accrediting organizations and, in the case of public institutions, state requirements. At the same time, institutions try to use the results of assessment efforts for internal improvement purposes. Thus formative purposes are integrated into summative programs with the hope of making them internally acceptable and useful. The end result may not satisfy either purpose if not implemented with great care. In addition, the work and opinions of individual students are measured, then generalizations are made about groups. One must be especially careful in specifying the level of precision of such measures.

Despite the challenges present beginning with the very definition of assessment itself, interest remains high in a number of quarters.

NASULGC STATEMENT OF PRINCIPLES

Relatively early on it became apparent that the assessment movement, especially since it has been driven by powerful external forces such as the federal and state governments, has had the potential for administrative abuse if done improperly. Consequently, as the movement has picked up steam, a general sense has arisen in the higher education community that statements of principles are needed to guide action. Such statements of principles might be considered similar to codes of ethics for professional groups. The intent has been to develop guidelines for proper behavior in the use of outcomes assessment data, particularly at the institutional level. That it has taken American higher education over 350 years to be concerned enough about the results of its labors to develop the first such principles says a lot about traditional institutional autonomy, among other things.

One of the early public statements about assessing learning in higher education at the institutional level came from the National Association of State Universities and Land Grant Colleges (NASULGC) Council on Academic Affairs in 1988. The Statement of Principles on Student Outcomes Assessment was produced by a group of experts selected by NASULGC. Among their major conclusions are the following. (The statements following the bullets below are from NASULGC; the text is my own.)

- "Institutional, program, and student outcomes assessment should focus, primarily, on the effectiveness of academic programs and on the improvement of student learning and performance."

It is no mistake that this is the first principle, in that it is one of the most basic tenets of assessment: to work, it must be aimed at improving teaching and learning. If its purpose is accountability, i.e., deciding whether the institution (or department or faculty member) is doing the "right thing" or not; however, the "right thing" is determined, then assessment is dead in the water. That's because everybody will be defensive, looking over their shoulders and worrying about their jobs. All reports from self-studies will be glowing, with nobody being honest, often even with themselves. Accountability can and should occur, but that is separate from assessment. It only muddies the waters and sabotages assessment when the two are mixed.

- "States and institutions should rely primarily on incentives rather than regulations or penalties to effect student outcomes assessment and foster improvement."

This follows on the first principle. People in higher education generally respond much better to positive incentives rather than to negative penalties. The incentives can be financial, as might be the case for a public institution dealing with the state, or some other type, such as program approval by a state board or accrediting body. Unfortunately, because higher education funding tends to be a zero sum proposition, the state level financial incentives tend to work something like the following: the state takes the money that it intends to give higher education, sets aside a small amount such as five percent, and has the institutions jump through various hoops to get the full five percent that they should have gotten in the first place. Failure to satisfy the assessment requirements means that each institution gets less than it might have received otherwise, with the state pocketing the difference.

- "Institutional programs for evaluation and assessment should be developed in collaboration with the faculty."

It is unfortunate that this principle uses the terms evaluation and assessment interchangeably, because this tends to cause confusion. While there is no standard to which all experts agree, the most common distinction is that assessment is for improvement and evaluation is for accountability. (An example of the latter would be faculty evaluation of teaching. Never, ever use assessment data for that purpose, because the faculty will not cooperate with assessment again if this is done.)

The basic assumption of this principle is one that makes a lot of sense on the surface but is sometimes forgotten, especially in political circles. Who does the teaching that leads to the measured learning? Clearly the faculty do. If one wants to impact the learning in a positive way, only the faculty can accomplish that, since they are the ones in the classrooms and laboratories on a daily basis. Without the faculty there is no assessment.

- "Assessment requirements should permit colleges and universities to develop institutional programs and define indicators of quality appropriate to their missions and goals and consistent with state-wide objectives and standards."

This is another principle that seems like common sense but which is ignored sometimes in the political arena, though thankfully not often among institutional and disciplinary accreditors. One of the greatest strengths of the postsecondary education system in the United States is its tremendous diversity. There is literally a college or university for everybody, from the most selective to open admissions, and ones supporting a wide variety of religious and philosophical traditions as well. In doing assessment, then, one size cannot fit all. Clarify and explain the institutional mission first, then assess the institution and its units. The assessment should look different based on different missions. Blindly copying somebody else's assessment tools when they have different missions is just plain wrong and might do serious damage in the end.

- "Colleges and universities should be encouraged to use multiple methods of assessment for improving teaching and learning and demonstrating achievement."

Sometimes even good measurement techniques provide results that tell only part of the story. Occasionally a sound technique will provide data that are misleading for any number of reasons. Using multiple measures, however, is much more likely to provide the kind of overview necessary for improvement. (The use of multiple measures sometimes is called triangulation.) When multiple measures are used, and the data are not consistent with each other, then that tells a story in itself. It says that the results are inconclusive and that further research is needed before any conclusions can be drawn with confidence.

- "Requirements for assessment should be fiscally conservative and avoid imposing costly evaluation programs on institutions or state agencies."

"Do it on the cheap" seems to be the battle cry of higher education, but in this case it appears to make sense. Funding is tight everywhere and at every level, including the state and federal levels. Money spent on assessment is not being spent on direct instruction or for other important purposes. There are relatively efficient, inexpensive ways to gather data that yield good information, and those should be tried first. Spending a lot of money on assessment is analogous to wrecking many expensive automobiles to ensure that they are of good quality and are safe. It is not free, especially when one considers the most expensive cost of all, faculty and administrative time. This is another area where good sense can go a long way.

- "Within an institution, assessment programs should be linked to strategic planning or program review, or to some comprehensive strategy intended to encourage change and improvement."

While well intended, this principle too seems to confuse improvement or formative assessment with evaluation or summative assessment. Creating a direct, required link between assessment and program review for resource allocation purposes primarily will yield glowing self-studies extolling the virtues of the units and institutions involved. A lack of such linkage, however, can lead to a perfunctory process that nobody takes seriously, much like many planning processes which have no link to the budget.

A middle ground approach would be to ask what things have changed in the, e.g., past five years based on assessment. In addition, units and institutions can be allowed and even encouraged to use data gathered in a self-study assessment process for planning and budgeting purposes, as long as control stays with those collecting and analyzing the data. For instance, a department may determine through assessment that its students are weak in a certain specialization necessary for success in the field after graduation. Assuming that there are no faculty in that specialization within the department, such information can be used to request a faculty position or some retraining of a current faculty member. Likewise alumni or employer data might be used to show that laboratories are not up-to-date or that there is some other program weakness that might have budgetary repercussions. For assessment to be successful, however, such connections should be from the bottom up and not the top down.

AAHE PRINCIPLES OF GOOD PRACTICE

The NASULGC principles have been highly regarded since their release but still represent the thinking of a body of state-supported universities, and not even most of them. As a consequence, another group representing a much wider sector of higher education felt it necessary to develop its own set of principles, one with less emphasis on state funding, even though there is substantial overlap between the two. Hence the American Association for Higher Education (AAHE) Principles of Good Practice for Assessing Student Learning was born in 1992. The basic principles are as follows, again with personal comments below each of them.

- "The assessment of student learning begins with educational values."

"Assessment is not an end in itself but a vehicle for educational improvement." The purpose of assessment as well as the means of assessment should be driven by what the organization is trying to achieve. Sometimes the most difficult part of assessment is getting people to reach agreement upon and explain, even to themselves, what they expect a student to know and be able to do, what values they expect the student to have upon graduation. The reality is that most of us have a vague idea of educational goals but struggle in defining them precisely. Measurement is impossible if we don't know what it is we are trying to measure.

- "Assessment is most effective when it reflects an understanding of learning as multidimensional, integrated, and revealed in performance over time."

"Learning is a complex process." As such it requires a range of ways to measure it. Here again the concept of triangulation is repeated, with even more emphasis on the complexity of the learning process and consequently diversity of measures necessary to begin to comprehend it.

- "Assessment works best when the programs it seeks to improve have clear, explicitly stated purposes."

"Assessment is a goal-oriented process." Essentially this further explicates the concepts introduced in the first principle above.

- "Assessment requires attention to outcomes but also and equally to the experiences that lead to those outcomes."

"To improve outcomes, we need to know about student experiences along the way." Obviously the focus on outcomes assessment is on the end result, but this is done only as a guide or indicator of where to look closer at processes. Why do our students achieve better in mathematics but worse in written communication than similar students at another college or university? What experiences are leading to those results? How might the experiences be adjusted to yield results more in line with our stated goals and objectives? If the end result is at a desired level, there is no need to look further at results. If it is not, then the need is to find out why and attempt to correct that.

- "Assessment works best when it is ongoing, not episodic."

"Assessment is a process whose power is cumulative." Basically this builds on the notion of triangulation but introduces the time factor, which can work several different ways. For example, different student classes bring with them differing abilities and skills, so what worked for freshmen of 10 or 20 years ago may not work for freshmen or today or a decade or two down the road. In addition, once enrolled, student growth over time might be a major goal, so only tracking over time will tell whether the goal is being achieved and in what areas. (Some communication goals, for instance, might even decline if a curriculum does not require writing and/or speaking on a regular basis.) Testing and re-testing within a few days or weeks helps establish the validity of baseline data. In summary, time is one of the important factors to be considered in identifying which experiences lead to which outcomes.

In the end this is the principle that is most likely to make chins drop around any meeting of faculty and administrators, though it is considered basic by most accrediting groups and others responsible for assessment. No longer does the college or university gear up for a site visit a year or two in advance, then go back to business as usual the day after the visiting team leaves. True assessment requires data over time that cannot be gathered in short, spasmodic periods. The increased number of probationary regional and disciplinary accreditation decisions, even among some very well known institutions, is beginning to produce more believers of this principle, but the cultural change has been slow for many.

- "Assessment fosters wider improvement when representatives from across the educational community are involved."

"Student learning is a campus-wide responsibility." Faculty are key parties, as is mentioned in the NASULGC principles, but certainly administrators, support staff, and others in the academic community have roles to play also. One need only to read alumni survey results, where alumni discuss how they learned more out of class than in traditional classes while at an institution, to be convinced that all have a role to play.

- "Assessment makes a difference when it begins with issues of use and illuminates questions that people really care about."

"To be useful, information must be connected to issues or questions that people really care about." How will the data gathered be used, and by whom? Involving the key decision-makers in the gathering and interpretation of the data is absolutely fundamental to the process. As a side benefit, the process of getting clarification regarding the issues assists those making the decisions to clarify in their own minds what their goals and objectives are for the institution and their areas of responsibility. Be careful to avoid the tendency to gather data due to vague curiosity. "Wouldn't it be nice to know" are words that should send a shiver of revulsion among all present and that should be quashed immediately.

- "Assessment is most likely to lead to improvement when it is part of a larger set of conditions that promote change."

"Assessment alone changes little." This is similar to the last NASULGC principle; assessment has to be integral to the decision-making processes of the institution in order to be successful. If it is optional and ignored by students, faculty, administrators, and the public alike, then the resources should not be wasted going through the motions. What seems to be more common is wide variation of adoption of assessment principles within a single institution. Some academic and administrative departments can be doing excellent work while other colleagues remain convinced that the way that they were taught is the only way to do things. Though some disciplines seem to be more assessment-friendly than others, especially at the national level, it's not easy to predict which ones will be that way within a college or university. Personalities and local politics appear to have a stronger impact than national disciplinary leadership.

- "Through assessment, educators meet responsibilities to students and to the public."

"Those to whom educators are accountable have an obligation to support attempts at improvement." This principle is a means by which AAHE recognizes the accountability mandates outside of postsecondary education while also resisting a one-size-fits-all approach. The act of doing a good job of assessment in itself meets the accountability obligation, or so goes the argument. Such an approach has been the driving force behind many state assessment movements, for example, where the institutions have been obligated to implement a defensible assessment process without gathering measures that would allow for institutional comparability between colleges and universities with unlike missions. Unfortunately in some states this approach is no longer sufficient to satisfy the political forces which are seeking comparability, or so they think. More on this later.

SOME PRACTICAL PRINCIPLES

The NASULGC and AAHE principles reflect somewhat philosophical points of view, often from high levels of institutions, though they are quite sensible in driving actions at the unit level. The section below takes a different approach and is based on well over a decade of practical experience involved in assessment with a wide variety of academic, student affairs, and other administrative units at a number of colleges and universities. The purpose of these principles is to share with institutional research and assessment practitioners some ideas that work and don't work at the operational level so that others need not learn from experience what those of us who have gone before have learned the hard way. Be forewarned, however, that not all of those employed in the field would necessarily agree with all of the principles outlined below.

The following principles are adopted from "Lessons Learned from a Decade of Assessment" (Muffo, 1996b) as well as the original AIR Forum paper from which the *Assessment Update* piece was adapted (Muffo, 1996a). For ease of reading, the issues are split into the following categories: faculty/academic issues; administrative issues; state/regional/ national issues; and future trends.

Faculty/Academic Issues

- Faculty are going to resist assessment and identify it with accountability.

It is uncomfortable to be assessed, even when one is in charge of the assessment process. In addition, in the eyes of faculty, assessment frequently is associated with student evaluations of teaching and other accountability processes. The assessment officer or institutional researcher is viewed as the stooge of the administration who is out to "get" the faculty. The potential loss of control and time consuming nature of the process does not endear it to faculty either. Frequently in the end, however, the faculty are pleasantly surprised by what they discover. An example of this is where a liberal arts department discovers that most of its graduates are gainfully employed and then uses that information as a recruiting tool to share with potential students and their families.

- Faculty do not know how to do assessment properly.

Even when they are willing to cooperate, most faculty do not know how to go about assessing their own programs or even courses without some outside assistance, as from an assessment professional. The fact is that most of us are not trained to assess programs. Faculty learn disciplinary content and then go out to teach it, often with little or no training in pedagogy. Most assume that the way to teach is the way that they were taught, and that student learning is reflected in student grades. The fact that grades vary substantially from teacher to teacher, even where the subject matter supposedly is the same, is a topic that most prefer to avoid. Student learning, as opposed to faculty teaching, is another topic to be avoided. A common response is, "I teach the material; it's up to them to learn it."

- Faculty (and others) will only accept the results of studies if they gather the data themselves, especially if the data are about their department or unit.

Faculty "ownership" of data comes when they gather the data, not when an outsider does, because it's much easier to dismiss the results in the latter case. It's far better to have less-than-perfect data gathering by departmental faculty than perfect data from somewhere else. Only when they trust the veracity of the data are they likely to act upon the findings. A compromise case would be where faculty sign off on the data gathering process, such as might take place in a small college alumni survey, but one must still be vigilant about the possibility of data rejection due to lack of trust in those gathering the data.

- Improvement of individual teaching inevitably enters the assessment discussion no matter how much assessment and accountability are kept separate.

Faculty evaluation, development, and assessment cannot be kept artificially separated indefinitely even when the purpose is assessment of programs and not individuals. This is particularly true in smaller institutions or regarding courses taught by a single individual. If assessment data show that graduates of a program are weak in statistics, for instance, and only one person teaches that subject, then inevitably the discussion gets back to that one person, thereby confirming the worst fears of the faculty. A true assessment process will use such information for program improvement purposes only, however, and not for faculty salary, promotion, and tenure decision-making.

- Continuity is easily lost year-to-year.

Departmental and other unit leadership changes over time, and often the turnover of records is not a smooth one. The new head may not be familiar with assessment. This is especially true if the head was hired from outside the institution and came from somewhere where assessment was weak or done differently. Committee leadership among the faculty turns over even more frequently on average as well. It is therefore important to emphasize continuity over time in planning and reporting, as well as to keep good records centrally. If one has a Web site where assessment reports are available, for instance, then most know where the prior report is and how to access it.

Assessment and institutional research professionals are known to change jobs occasionally also, so planning for continuity at the institutional level likewise is necessary.

- Assessment and the resulting curricular adjustments go on constantly in good academic units.

As noted above, assessment cannot be effective if it is episodic. Nowadays many disciplinary as well as regional accreditation standards require assessment. Whenever possible, however, tie institutional and other assessment efforts together to minimize the impact on faculty and others, even if some data gathering will have to continue on a regular basis. Assessment exhaustion can and does set in. Faculty need to have periods when their programs are not being assessed intensively.

- There is little or no need to force people to take action on assessment results.

Most people working in higher education want to do a good job, the right thing. As a result, the most common occurrence is for them to use the results of assessment to make adjustments in the programs. No inducements or penalties are required. A few will be unmoved by the data, but they are a distinct minority.

Administrative Issues

- Data must be disseminated in an easy-to-understand manner in order to be effective.

One of the common problems facing assessment efforts is the failure to share data with the larger academic community. A relatively easy and effective way to do this is through a monthly or bimonthly one-page (front and back) newsletter. This might use graphics, summary statements in bullet format, self-quizzes, and even cartoons to get the attention of the faculty and staff readers. However done, it should be short and to the point; anything longer is less likely to be read. More detailed back-up reports may be necessary for the small number of people desiring more information.

Student media, student government, and the college/university library should be on the mailing list as well. Coverage of information in student publications is aimed at, among other things, showing students that the results of their participation in assessment activities are utilized for decision-making purposes. The library's interest normally is in capturing some of the history of the institution. Data gathered in assessment, and their reporting, become part of the institutional history.

- A little bit of financial support goes a long way towards changing attitudes.

It's less the amount of money than the principle that counts, but people in academic and administrative units being asked to perform assessment activities tend to respond more positively when offered financial assistance to aid them in their efforts. When asking people to spend a substantial amount of time doing something that they are not very enthusiastic about doing in the first place, it helps to be able to offer a few dollars to assist them in defraying out-of-pocket expenses such as costs associated with surveys and student testing. Normally the greatest cost involved, that of personnel time, cannot be reimbursed.

As one chair of a large department noted, he frequently gets asked to do things not normally part of his job description, but seldom does anybody offer to help out financially even in a small way. That chairman's attitude changed perceptively when told that a small amount was available to offset assessment costs, some of which he might have absorbed without a required assessment process (e.g., for an alumni survey). In some cases the money is not even requested; it's the thought that counts.

In order to be able to do this, the budget for assessment has to allow for substantial flexibility, including money that can be passed through to other units undergoing assessment. As with many academic and other departments, such flexibility is greatly limited if the budget becomes tied up to a great extent in personnel costs only.

- Changes in the curriculum that are the result of assessment efforts often lead to improved student satisfaction, but not always.

This is the case where the "customer" is not always right if the student is considered to be a customer. Sometimes students do not appreciate immediately curricular changes which result in teaching and learning occurring in a manner different from what they are used to experiencing. This can be the case even when they are learning more in the process.

As an example, a highly regarded professor found that his students learned better than a comparative group when he employed interactive software in his class. Despite the improved learning, he received the lowest student evaluations of his teaching career. It appears that the students preferred the role that they played normally in classes, i.e., being passive recipients of lecture material rather than active problem solvers as required by the software. Blind adherence to the student evaluation numbers in salary, promotion, and tenure considerations would have discouraged this faculty member from going forward pedagogically despite the improvements in student learning.

- Not all changes resulting from assessment will yield positive results.

One of the reasons that assessment needs to be ongoing is that even the best intended changes made because of assessment results sometimes lead to decreased rather than increased student learning. This is to be expected to a certain extent; to be right two-thirds of the time is quite good. The only way to determine how well things are going afterwards is to continue assessing. Healthy

71

skepticism and flexibility are desirable personal characteristics in working with assessment and resulting curricular change.

- There is strong evidence that student involvement in learning leads to improved retention of material over both short and long periods.

Hands-on experience with class material has for many years been known to improve student learning. Technology is making it easier and less costly to involve students in their own learning and to assess that learning. One must keep in mind, however, that it is the hands-on activity, and not the technology as such, which makes the difference. Technology is simply a tool that will work only as well as the teaching behind it. A poorly constructed laboratory exercise, for example, will not lead to better learning because it is done on a computer rather than in a laboratory.

- When testing for placement in particular, locally developed tests are usually better than standardized ones.

Locally developed tests, e.g., to place students in English I or English II, normally are developed by the faculty who teach the classes involved. Consequently they are better predictors of student performance than a test developed by a body of experts drawn from a wide range of institutions. One need not be a statistics expert to see this. Place the results of the English or mathematics portions of the SATs, for example, next to grades in the first class of the English or math sequence and look at the correlation, which tends to be zero or near zero. Place the local placement results along side the same grades; more of a correspondence is evident.

Simply stated, the local faculty know what their program is trying to achieve and what entering knowledge and skills are likely to result in that achievement. Similarly, in determining if a program has been successful in producing the kinds of graduates that it desires, a local examination is far better than a standardized one. The latter is simply a compromise among experts and seldom matches exactly what any particular program is trying to accomplish. In addition, standardized tests sometimes do not report sub-scores to allow feedback on areas of strength and weakness, or they report scores to individual students only as opposed to the academic program attempting to measure student learning.

Ability to compare the performance on a program's graduates versus those of other programs does have its attractions nonetheless; a locally developed test does not tell how well one's students are stacking up against the competition. As with other areas of assessment, these can be used productively as long as they don't end up driving the curriculum as a result. One case of this is a professional program with a licensing requirement that reported a sure way to increase its first-time pass rates on the licensure examination – drop all computing from the curriculum. That's because those creating the examination had not yet determined an acceptable way to test knowledge of computing. The program's graduates would be virtually unemployable as a result, but they would have terrific pass rates! Appropriate interpretation of data matched with common sense are needed when evaluating the results of such standardized tests in order to ensure that counterproductive curricular changes are not an outcome.

- In beginning subjects such as mathematics, chemistry, biology, English, etc., the true measure of student academic success is student performance in higher level courses in those or related subject areas.

Tracking students over time provides perhaps the best and most valid measures of success in earlier courses, such as those contained in many general education or core curriculum programs. This can be especially useful if the beginning courses are taught in multiple sections using different modes of instruction. It can also help settle faculty disagreements about which mode of instruction is more effective. Some would argue that, in the end, the true measure of educational effectiveness is student performance in the career and in life in general.

- Assessment personnel often are from non-technical backgrounds and are selected because of perceived personal integrity and respect by other faculty.

Such characteristics often become insufficient for success in more mature programs where technical skills are necessary in order for progress to be made. A compromise position would be to have an assessment program led by such a faculty member with help from a technically qualified assistant. That still places limits on what the assessment head can accomplish in evaluation and interpretation of data in various situations, however, so another compromise is to have the respected faculty member help get the program started, then bring in a more technically proficient director once it is established.

This leads to the issue of where to place assessment in the administrative structure. Obviously it must report to the academic dean or vice president somewhere up the line, but should it be part of institutional research or institutional effectiveness? I would argue that it should not be connected with institutional research and/or planning at the beginning because of inevitable faculty resistance to the concept. If it is put under institutional research, for instance, it will tend to be considered an administrative function for somebody other than the faculty to do, similar to external reporting of enrollment data. The faculty have to understand from the beginning that only they can do academic assessment; the same is true for student affairs and other administrative staff. Once running smoothly with understandings in place, it may be possible and even desirable to move assessment and institutional research closer to each other in the administrative structure as long as IR is part of the academic reporting line.

- There is a need for strong cooperation between assessment, institutional research, planning, and faculty/staff development in order for all of the programs to be successful.

Despite faculty distrust of administrators, it is critically important that assessment work well with these other support units and vice versa. It is common, for example, for assessment staff to require access to institutional research data. The reverse also occurs. In addition, there is some potential overlap that can be avoided through good communication. The institution is poorly served if those responsible are more interested in turf protection than service. This has led to combining the three areas of assessment, institutional research, and planning in particular under the same supervisor in order to improve the cooperative environment. (For a summary of related issues, see McLaughlin, Muffo, and Calhoun, 1995.)

- Feedback is absolutely necessary.

A common criticism on campuses, not just regarding assessment, is that many studies and reports are done with little or no feedback afterwards. All that work without feedback tends to dampen the enthusiasm of faculty and others to take on new endeavors such as assessment. People want to have reactions to their work, positive as well as negative, and really deserve it as a common courtesy. The extra labor of reacting can also lead to further dialogue about curricular and co-curricular issues.

- Assessment offices and personnel must be assessed themselves.

This is where the old adage about practicing what one preaches applies. The assessment officer cannot expect others to assess themselves while avoiding it for his or her own office. Not only does it undermine credibility, but it also defies regional assessment criteria in some regions. Perhaps most important of all, it limits program improvement and feelings of affinity for those being assessed.

In my own case, a number of activities that I do now, such as a bimonthly newsletter and writing responses to all assessment plans and reports, are the direct result of having professional quality assessments done of my own office. I also have a much better appreciation for the feelings of those whose programs are being assessed; I don't enjoy it any more than they do.

CLASSROOM/ACADEMIC UNIT ASSESSMENT

Essentially assessment begins and ends at the department or unit level. Focusing on academic departments or units for the moment [co-curricular and non-academic units are addressed later in the chapter], the very reason that assessment is done is for program improvement; for improved student learning. In fact, one of the difficult adjustments for many faculty in addressing assessment is the inherent assumption that it is what the student learns, not what the faculty member teaches, that is most important. The threat inherent in that is one can do the most wonderful teaching job in the world and still yield poor results in the presence of lazy, disinterested, and ill-prepared students. While acknowledging that to be true, assessment takes the view that wonderful teaching with poor learning on the other end is problematic and requires further attention. That is not the same as "blaming" the faculty member for poor student learning, however.

Bloom's Taxonomy

One of the most useful tools in working with faculty regarding assessment is the use of what has become known as Bloom's Taxonomy (or) Classification of Cognitive Skills (1956). Bloom divided knowledge into categories, each with its own definitions and key words. The categories include: knowledge, comprehension, application, analysis, synthesis, and evaluation. The reason that this taxonomy is useful is that it can be used to be shown that, while we in higher education supposedly teach students higher order learning skills, the evaluation of those learning skills tends to remain at the lowest levels of the taxonomy, often at the knowledge or memorization level. Discussions with faculty about what is taught and tested often lead to richer reflection regarding teaching and testing methods and, in the end, student learning, and frequently even lead to changes in both faculty teaching and testing behaviors.

A good example of this phenomenon is when discussions occur about pre-test/post-test methods of assessment. For instance, if one wants to determine whether or not a general education/core curriculum course is meeting the goals of that section of the core curriculum as stated in the institutional catalogue and/or core curriculum guide, a pre-test at the beginning of the course, followed by a post-test at the end, might be the logical approach. The test items might reflect the goals in some way and thereby determine to what degree the course is meeting those goals. The most common approach taken by faculty to such a chore is to ask the kinds of memorization questions that are covered in the course, e.g., "Name the five different schools of thought of xxx." Bloom's taxonomy can be used to get them to consider more thoughtful questions which ask students to apply, demonstrate, analyze, compare, contrast, interpret, predict, etc. Such an approach determines if students really are improving their higher order thinking skills or simply memorizing material which often is forgotten soon after the class is over. This type of process also can unleash the creative juices of the faculty and lead to substantial personal growth and development on their part while meeting assessment requirements for objective data.

Experimental versus Control Groups

In addition to pre-test/post-test methods of assessment, another way of determining the extent of growth of student learning is using control groups, though scientific measurement by using this method tends to be difficult. A control group is basically one that is similar to the treatment group in all other ways but the treatment. For instance, two different sections of Mathematics 01 are taught what is essentially the same material by two different methods, the traditional one and the new, experimental one. Ideally the two sections would have similar students in terms of ability and any other characteristics that might affect academic performance. It would be better still if the same faculty member taught each, because that would take away the possibility of one professor being a better instructor than the other. Better still they would be taught at the same time of day and in very similar classrooms. Obviously the goal here is to eliminate as many biasing factors as possible.

The problem with this scenario is that we seldom have the luxury here in the real world of working with such treatment and control groups. The students, faculty, locations, times, etc. often are not the same. When the faculty member *is* the same, the level of enthusiasm for the two types of teaching may not be. In short, the best that we can do often is to seek to minimize to the extent possible those factors which might bias the results of such experiments while recognizing that not all sources of bias can be eliminated completely. Faculty who do not want to recognize one method as being superior based on the results of such experiments will go to great lengths to pick apart the methods employed. In the end it is the task of the assessor(s) to do the best job possible under the circumstances and to tentatively accept the results while seeking more information. Absolute certainty is not normally available, and this is something which disturbs scientists and other faculty accustomed to operating in a much more certain environment.

In addition to the use of control groups in the same time frame, one can also compare results of student learning using past performance of similar groups as the control. Are students who study the material in the new way learning as well as students who studied it in the old way? Sometimes similar examinations are available to test student knowledge, but sometimes the new way of teaching demands new ways of testing as well. Sometimes too there are little or no baseline data available from prior years; nobody thought to collect it before the experiment began. Here again we have to take what we can get and move on as best as we can.

Assessing General Education and Majors

Normally assessment at the department or unit level begins with assessment of the academic major, because that is the purview of the unit. Departmental faculty can examine the goals and objectives for its majors and whether or not those are being met by examining student, alumni, and employer opinion as well as various measures of student learning. The latter need not be a test, especially a standardized test that does not match the program well.

Course-based assessment, where student achievement is measured on the basis of performance in an assignment for which they are graded (and hence are motivated to achieve well), often is the best approach. While there are many ways to do this, senior capstone experiences resulting in culminating projects lend themselves quite well to assessment by multiple evaluators. Such experiences might be simulations, such as student teaching or an internship, or a senior performance in art or music or theatre, or a senior project such as solving an engineering or business problem and reporting on it in written and oral presentations. Any experience that requires the pulling together of what students learn into a single entity seems to work well.

There is no question that agreeing upon goals and objectives and then measuring achievement of those is no small task for a department, yet the challenges of doing that often pale when compared to assessing general education, also known as liberal education or the core curriculum. First of all, it must be determined who "owns" it, because it is spread over a number of academic units. When "ownership" is determined to reside with a committee, which it often does, institutional memory becomes a major problem. The tendency is to write general goals that cover a wide range of territory, resulting objectives which are difficult if not impossible to measure against. Standardized tests such as the ACT Comp have been used to test general education, leaving the faculty off the hook so to speak, but their results are difficult to interpret for purposes of improvement, which is the primary goal of assessment. Standardized tests also have tended to be expensive, time consuming, and challenging in terms of student motivation. In short, they have not been found to be the magic bullet sought by many.

One of the best methods available for assessment of general education is one that involves the faculty in the process centrally and which focuses on faculty and student growth rather than psychometrics. It can be used with or without student opinion surveys. Basically this approach takes the stated goals for various areas of the general education curriculum and asks the faculty to show how their particular course or courses meet those goals. Workshops and continued dialogue, often via electronic mail, are needed to assist the faculty in addressing the issues involved and in developing good ways of measuring against the goals. The end result is greater attention to the goals in teaching among faculty who sometimes don't know what the general education goals are for the courses that they are teaching, as well as increased attention to pedagogical issues.

Student opinion surveys can be used to complement the testing to determine to what extent the courses are meeting the goals in their eyes. [The goals usually have to be translated into plain English in order for the students to understand them.] The motivation on the part of the faculty for participating in such an effort is the ability for their courses to remain in the pool of general education courses. The assessment should be done by other faculty, with the assistance of assessment professionals, and should be on a five-year or other cycle. Feedback to faculty is critical, and it may be necessary to move courses out that do not meet the standards. The end result of the process, however, can go far beyond the usual animosity that normally results from required reports of any kind, resulting in a pedagogical dialogue as opposed to the more typical complaining about bureaucracy.

Disciplinary Accreditation

Disciplinary accreditation, which is more common in applied disciplines (with the possible exception of chemistry, which some might argue also is an applied discipline), traditionally has relied heavily on input measures such a sufficiency of human, financial, and space resources. Disciplines have aimed at ensuring the quality of the graduating student product and, in the case of professions such as law, dentistry, medicine, nursing, veterinary medicine, etc., have attempted to ensure the quality of professionals serving the public. As with regional accreditation, the traditional disciplinary accreditation process has focused on input variables under the assumption that the output would be of high quality if all of the input variables were also of high quality. A side issue of the traditional disciplinary accreditation has been the tendency to threaten probation or total loss of accreditation if more resources are not directed to the discipline, a type of academic blackmail not particularly welcomed by chief academic officers and presidents.

As with regional accreditation, the approach to disciplinary accreditation has shifted substantially, perhaps dramatically, in recent years to much more of an outcomes focus. Fields such as architecture, education, engineering, nursing, and veterinary medicine all have developed new standards for accreditation that require extensive analysis of the program outcomes, though inputs normally are not totally ignored either. (See the Web page addresses at the end of this chapter for more information on accreditation standards in these fields.) Interestingly, the shift of emphasis among the disciplinary accrediting organizations has had a greater effect on many faculty, particularly at large colleges and universities, than the changes at the regional accreditation agencies. The fact is that most faculty know and care little about regional accreditation but are much more sensitive to disciplinary accreditation, because the latter affects them most immediately. The relationship can be symbiotic, however; good disciplinary accreditation efforts can support regional accreditation requirements and vice versa.

A prime example of what has been happening in this arena in recent years is the new criteria for accreditation of engineers, labeled ABET 2000 for the year in which all programs had to be accredited under the new criteria. (ABET stands for the Accreditation Board for Engineering and Technology.) Historically ABET accreditation was about rules and regulations of nearly everything, and slavish obedience to those rules and regulations with the constant threat of loss of accreditation hanging over the process. To those who have witnessed it as outsiders, engineering accreditation appeared to focus heavily on obscure detail or "bean counting." Any attempt to change anything in the curriculum, even in general education, was met with the statement that ABET required things to be done in a certain way. The process certainly seemed rigid from afar.

The new ABET criteria are quite different and involve a radical shift from the old. Now engineering departments and colleges have to show how their mission statements fit with institutional mission statements as a first step. Next they must explain what their goals and objectives are regarding the following 11 criteria, along with describing how the unit measures achievement of those goals and objectives. No longer are the rules spelled out for the engineers; they must spell them out themselves to the reviewers and demonstrate outcomes. The old process has been turned on its head. The new criteria are as follows:

- an ability to apply knowledge of mathematics, science, and engineering
- an ability to design and conduct experiments, as well as to analyze and interpret data
- an ability to design a system, component, or process to meet desired needs
- an ability to function on multi-disciplinary teams
- an ability to identify, formulate, and solve engineering problems
- an understanding of professional and ethical responsibility
- an ability to communicate effectively
- the broad education necessary to understand the impact of engineering solutions in a global/societal context
- a recognition of the need for and ability to engage in lifelong learning
- a knowledge of contemporary issues
- an ability to use the techniques, skills, and modern engineering tools necessary for engineering practice

What has been so remarkable about all of this, aside from the emphasis on outputs over inputs, has been the strong emphasis on topics not traditionally considered by many to be engineering matters, such as teamwork, ethics, communication, and lifelong learning. This has left many engineering faculty confused and uneasy. They understood the old input criteria but are not used to writing goal and objective statements, especially on non-technical topics, and then developing ways of measuring achievement of the goals and objectives. It has been a real culture shift and one that is still in process. Why has the discipline moved in this direction? Probably the best explanation has to do with the make-up of ABET itself and the visiting teams. Private industry has provided a lot of input in developing the new criteria, and up to half of the visiting teams are industry representatives and not faculty. Assessment techniques, perhaps labeled differently, are common in the private sector. Industry representatives don't see what the fuss is about regarding the new criteria; these things are done in the "real world" all of the time. Although most other disciplines do not have as much influence from outside of academe as the engineers do, most have felt the external pressure from the professions.

Disciplinary accreditation itself seems to have resulted from the meeting of academe and the society outside of the ivy covered walls, hence the heavy emphasis on professional fields among the disciplinary accreditation groups and the general absence of traditional arts and sciences areas. Likewise the current emphasis on assessment appears to be an outgrowth of what is happening in society at large, i.e., the emphasis on accountability and quality improvement. A pleasant result of this emphasis is that assessment and institutional research professionals are now being sought out for assistance from some of the same people who ignored or avoided them just a short time ago. No longer are we the people to be avoided in certain departments and colleges; we are now the good guys and gals who are helping them get re-accredited with positive reviews. Similarly, those who do not listen to us and fail or are put on probation as a result end up being much more receptive to our advice the next time. There's nothing like being threatened by loss of accreditation to get the attention and cooperation of certain faculty.

INSTITUTIONAL ASSESSMENT

At the institutional level, assessment often is tied to planning and sometimes even budgeting, though again that puts it closer to evaluation than assessment. If a college or university has a comprehensive planning process, then the units within the organization must assess themselves on a regular basis to determine if they are being successful in meeting their goals and objectives. Without assessment, all that is left is a planning process devoid of useful information for planning purposes.

The two driving forces behind assessment at the institutional level are regional accreditation for all institutions and state assessment programs for those receiving direct state support. (To a lesser extent new program approval processes in some states have required assessment at private and public institutions as well.) The regional accrediting groups have incorporated assessment principles into their self studies and subsequent campus visits for over a decade in the South, and a somewhat shorter period in other parts of the country. At this point all or nearly all emphasize assessment to varying degrees. Regional accrediting bodies normally do not dictate *how* assessment is to be done, but do require that it be done in certain areas. For instance, they would not require that a certain standardized test be required to measure learning in general education. They often do require that general education be assessed, however, in a defensible manner, with results used for improvement purposes.

In recent years the accreditation standards have seemed to get more and more stringent as the accrediting agencies gain experience with assessment. The old process of gearing up for an accreditation visit and then forgetting everything for the next 5-10 years no longer is sufficient; a continuous process of assessment is now expected. Nor are the regional accreditors backing away from controversy; major universities are being put on probation as a result of non-compliance with assessment standards. As with disciplinary accreditation, this gets the attention of key people. With regional accreditation these can include the board of trustees, politicians, and the media in addition to the faculty, students, and alumni.

Probably the most attention directed to institutional assessment has come from various state governments. Beginning in the 1980s in Tennessee, a large number of states have adopted assessment requirements, most of which use institutional measures. Many have gone beyond assessment and are tying funding to achievement on various "quality or performance indicators" of institutional success, such as student retention, graduation rates, and a host of other measures. The most extreme example at this point in time is South Carolina, where all state funding for higher education is tied to as many as 37 measures. (Most states link only five percent of the funding or less to such quality indicators.) There is some evidence that state government infatuation with indicators is on the wane despite nearly half having adopted them as of 1996-97 (SHEEO/NCES Communication Network, 1998).

Perhaps the strongest long-term influence of the state assessment requirements, along with those of the regional accrediting agencies, has been to promote cultural change within institutions, private as well as public. Before the late 1980s there were no state, regional, or national meetings about assessment. AIR, as an example, had few if any papers on the topic. Without being forced by external pressures, what president or vice-president would risk the ire of the faculty and others to ask them to study themselves on an ongoing basis? Now assessment is by far the largest track in the AIR Forum; AAHE has a successful annual assessment meeting aimed at faculty as well as assessment professionals, and yet another national assessment group has met several times. These are in addition to other conferences sponsored by various institutions, the best known being the series put together by Trudy Banta and her colleagues at Indiana University-Purdue University at Indianapolis. In addition, state groups are common and are not limited to those colleges and universities receiving state support. Those who have been waiting for assessment to go away may still be waiting, but are losing hope as the years go by. By being required at the state level, by regional and disciplinary accrediting agencies, as part of new program approvals, and increasingly as part of internally- and externally-funded projects, assessment gradually is becoming part of the institutional fabric.

At the institutional level assessment normally breaks down into that of academic and non-academic units. Much of the emphasis from the various external parties naturally has been on academic units, but assessment of non-academic activities often is required as well, especially by regional accrediting agencies. Academic support and student affairs groups usually approach assessment differently than business-oriented units. The latter tend to focus more on annual reports and Total Quality Management/Total Quality Improvement (TQM/TQI) or similarly labeled processes. After all, these were developed in the business world to assist similar functions. Academic support units such as admissions or financial aid offices might use a more academic approach or a blend of academic and business, because these activities tend to overlap both types of functions.

The student affairs community in recent years has become among the greatest promoters of assessment. One reason for this is that they know that they have to prove the efficacy of what they do in order to survive in tight budget times. It's not easy to explain and prove how having student activities or a health center assists in student learning, but those of us who have read alumni surveys telling about how more was learned out of class than in class can testify to the importance of what student affairs professionals do. Because this is a well developed area of research somewhat outside of what is being addressed here, the best approach to learning more about it would be to examine Upcraft and Schuh (1996), one of the classics in student affairs assessment. Two other good sources are produced by the American College and Personnel Association (ACPA): The Student Learning Imperative and also The Principles of Good Practice in Student Affairs. The URLs for both are provided among the references at the end of the chapter.

SPECIAL PROJECTS/POLICY ASSESSMENT

Increasingly there are demands to evaluate the effectiveness of special projects or policies. No longer are new projects started or new policies implemented with the assumption that they will be successful and carry on indefinitely. Nowadays one has to *prove* the worth of something for it to continue; resources are too scarce to keep them supporting programs that are ineffective. If the information gathered from such evaluations is used to improve programs, then the process can be labeled as assessment.

Two examples of assessment of major projects that have been completed at Virginia Tech include examining the pedagogical effectiveness of a Mathematics Emporium, costing over a million dollars a year to operate, as well as looking at the effectiveness of the University's European center in Switzerland. The features in common for these two projects is that they are expensive to maintain, and therefore of great interest to senior administration, and are relatively complex situations unlike a typical department or college. They also involve a number of academic and support units.

Many issues need to be addressed in an objective way by someone from outside of the units themselves. Data must be gathered from a variety of sources; some of the data are pretty "soft" or imprecise as well. Another challenge is setting priorities: what are the most important issues to be addressed, the second most important, etc. (Sometimes it is impossible to get that question answered; sometimes those requesting the study don't know the priorities themselves.) Yet another challenge in such a study is learning about the unit, how it operates, etc., to understand it. Another major challenge is locating the necessary information. Along the way one must look out for the many pitfalls, such as learning that this is a pet project of one or another key person. An advisory committee and frequent checking of facts can assist the study to be as accurate and fair as possible. Sometimes one or more consultants are brought in to insure the accuracy of the study and to provide credibility for it as well as honest feedback to the conclusions. In the end the results may still not be what some had hoped, and the messenger can be blamed as a result.

Similar to specific projects or units of the type mentioned above, examining policies for their effectiveness is becoming more common. Here again, if the results of such studies are used primarily for improvement purposes, they might be called assessment studies. For instance, one might be asked to determine whether or not students are learning more now that they are required to purchase computers during the first year of classes. Also, how are their daily lives affected, if at all? Are graduating students better writers now that there is a Writing Across the Curriculum program? Have the new alcohol policies led to healthier lifestyles among students? The fact of the matter is that all such policies have large price tags attached to them, whether for the institution or the students or others, and so there is a strong desire to know how affective they are and how they might be improved. Lack of attention to such matters can be quite costly in a number of ways.

Related to the assessment of projects, programs, and policies is the evaluation and assessment of internally- and externally-funded projects. A need for accountability similar to that in accreditation and institutional efforts has swept research funding sources. The National Science Foundation and other federal and private agencies now must be able to prove to their own funding sources that grant money was spent wisely, that the project led to improvement in an organization or situation for which it was intended. Assessment and institutional research professionals are among those called upon to assist the people applying for the funds by developing an evaluation plan and agreeing to implement it if the project is funded. The reason for this again has to do with perceived objectivity; not being in the unit applying for the grant gives one some distance that should provide a more objective viewpoint. In addition, most principal investigators do not have the kind of expertise necessary for an objective evaluation to take place. We just happen to be in the right place at the right time!

A general approach to the kinds of studies noted above might look like the following:

- Issue identification – What is to be studied?
- Prioritizing – What is most important? Next? Least important?
- Data gathering – Where are the important data? Who has them? What form are they in?
- Data analysis – What is the best way to analyze the data? This should be determined by their form to a large extent.
- Reporting – Produce the report and circulate it among knowledgeable colleagues for correction and comment. Avoid losing credibility through small mistakes.
- External verification – Do others agree or disagree with the conclusions?

Why? Consultants can assist here if they are respected by the parties involved and have a clear sense of what they are supposed to accomplish.

- Future actions – What other kinds of studies remain to be done, such as longitudinal ones? Is there still missing information? If so, how and by whom should it be gathered?
- Resources – What will it cost to make improvements suggested in the report? What happens in the absence of those resources?

FUTURE TRENDS

Assessment as a profession in itself is relatively new, growing out of the state and accreditation requirements of the past couple of decades. Where is it headed from here?

One trend that appears clear is similar to what is happening in institutional research, at least at large universities, and that is decentralization. As administrative and academic units develop their own assessment expertise, whether out of necessity or simply a desire to control the function, it will be challenging simply to coordinate the function even in a loose way. This may be less common of a phenomenon at smaller institutions, but the centripetal forces involved will continue to operate there just the same.

Another trend that seems to be occurring is the wider range of activities in which assessment and institutional research professionals are getting involved. Assisting units in disciplinary accreditation was uncommon not so long ago; now some people are spending most of their time doing that. Likewise with evaluation of funded projects. The range of funded projects is likely to expand and may eventually include those funded by individual donors as well as governmental and private foundations.

Even within institutions, a wider range of activities seems to be beckoning – assessment of general education or educational support programs for example. The greatest challenge in most assessment offices is getting people to listen, to cooperate. Once successful, perhaps the next greatest challenge is to prioritize activities. The assessment business is one where the assessment professional wants to be successful, but not *too* successful. It's a lot more enjoyable to select from opportunities for involvement rather than having doors slammed in one's face, however.

Changing technology affects assessment as it does just about every other area of society. Increasingly the surveys and tests of student learning which are the backbone of many assessment efforts are being done on-line through Web sites. This is particularly helpful in reaching the hard-to-contact students such as those who take classes off-campus or who attend them in the evenings.

Yet another area to watch includes state and federal governments. Who knows what the next trend will be coming down the line? There is a tendency to jump from fad to fad in trying to solve what so far has been an unresolved dilemma – finding some system to better understand how the money spent on higher education is being spent and, related to that concern, guaranteeing that it is being spent in an efficient and effective manner.

What's the potential downside in future changes? Some states want to mechanize assessment so that it is easy to rank institutions in the morning like sports teams. Standardized tests and performance indicators would then be used to decide between the winners and losers. (See Burke & Serban, 1998, for a good resource on these issues.) Assessment for the sake of improvement is likely to get lost in the rush to accountability in such situations. True assessment could be damaged in the process. The signs remain good for disciplinary and regional accreditation, however. Those procedures, which are primarily driven by rank-and-file faculty and administrators, seem determined to use assessment successfully for improvement. As long as that trend continues, most of us should have plenty to do.

SUMMARY

In the past 20 years the assessment movement has come from relative obscurity to being an integral part of regional and disciplinary accreditation as well as state and federal governmental policy. The battle for the hearts and minds of the faculty, staff, and administrators continues with some successes and much work remaining to be done. Constant educational efforts are necessary in order to help convince the distrustful that this is an effort worthy of their time and talents.

The role of the assessment professional in all of this is established but somewhat precarious. How many of us will there be if the states decide to drop assessment requirements? What will happen if the regional accreditation groups shift their foci in other directions? What will happen when there is a new administration in Washington? The answers to these questions remain unknown at the moment. It will be much easier two decades from now to look back and see if this was just a passing fad driven by accountability concerns, or if assessment will be part of the fabric of colleges and universities, perhaps even to the point of not being separately identifiable. The times, at least in the near future, should continue to be interesting.

References

American Association for Higher Education. (1992). Principles of good practice for assessing student learning. Washington, D.C.: Author.

Banta, T. W. (Ed.). (1986). Performance funding in higher education: A critical analysis of Tennessee's experience. Boulder, CO: National Center for Higher Education Management Systems.

Bloom, B. S. (Ed.). (1956). Taxonomy of educational objectives: The classification of educational goals. Handbook I: Cognitive domain. New York, NY: Longmans, Green.

Burke, J. C. & Serban, A. M. (Eds.). (1998). New Directions for Institutional Research: No. 97. Performance funding for public higher education: fad or trend? San Francisco, CA: Jossey-Bass.

McLaughlin, G. W., Muffo, J. A., & Calhoun, H. D. (1995). Assessment: A collaborative model. AIR Currents, 33 (3&4), 9. Tallahassee, FL: Association for Institutional Research.

Muffo, J. A. (1996a). Lessons learned from a decade of assessment. Paper presented at the annual forum of the Association for Institutional Research, Albuquerque, NM. (ERIC No. ED 397 717)

Muffo, J. A. (1996b). Lessons learned from a decade of assessment. Assessment Update, 8 (2), 1-2, 11.

National Association of State Universities and Land Grant Colleges Council on Academic Affairs. (1988). Statement of principles on student outcomes assessment. Washington, DC: Author.

SHEEO/NCES Communication Network. (1998). Focus on performance measures. Network News, 17 (1), 1-5.

Terenzini, P. T. (1989). Assessment with open eyes: Pitfalls in studying student outcomes. Journal of Higher Education, 60, 644-664.

Upcraft, M. L. & Schuh, J. H. (1996). Assessment in student affairs: A guide for practitioners. San Francisco, CA: Jossey-Bass.

Web Sites

American Veterinary Medical Association
 www.avma.org
The Learning Imperative (ACPA)
 www.acpa.nche.edu/sli/sli.htm
National Architectural Accrediting Board
 www.naab.org
National Council of Accreditation of Colleges of Teacher Education
 www.ncate.org
National League for Nursing
 www.nln.org

North Carolina State University Internet Resources for Higher Education Outcomes Assessment
www2.acs.ncsu.edu/UPA/survey/resource.htm
The Principles of Good Practice in Student Affairs (ACPA)
www.acpa.nche.edu/pgp/principle.htm
Virginia Tech Academic Assessment
www.aap.vt.edu

Other Resources

Assessment Update: Progress, Trends, and Practices in Higher Education. (bi-monthly). San Francisco, CA: Jossey-Bass.

Banta, T. W. & Associates. (1993). Making a difference: Outcomes of a decade of assessment in higher education. San Francisco, CA: Jossey-Bass.

Banta, T. W., Lund, J. P., Black, K. E., & Oblander, F. W. (1996). Assessment in practice: Putting principles to work on college campuses. San Francisco, CA: Jossey-Bass.

Krueger, R.A. (1994). Focus groups: A practical guide for applied research. (2nd Ed.) Thousand Oaks, CA: Sage.

Suskie, L. A. (1996). Questionnaire survey research: What works. (2nd Ed.) Tallahassee, FL: Association for Institutional Research.

CHAPTER 3: ACADEMIC PROGRAM AND FACULTY ISSUES

Author: Michael F. Middaugh

This chapter focuses on issues related to curriculum; research and scholarly productivity, public service, tenure polices, program review, faculty recruitment, development, and retention; faculty flow models; collective bargaining; salary models; faculty evaluation; and decision making regarding faculty and academic programs.

Introduction

While the title of this chapter is "Academic Program and Faculty Issues," the underlying theme of our discussion will be, "How do we measure what faculty do, and how well they do it?" For what is an academic program but an amalgamation of diverse faculty activities – teaching; pure and applied research and other forms of scholarly activity; service to students, the institution, and the community; and so on? If we know the various components of faculty activity that comprise an academic program or department, why then are we presenting a chapter on how to measure them? Quite candidly, such a chapter is necessary for any volume on institutional research and policy analysis, because historically we have done an abysmal job of describing what faculty do.

For the past decade or so, higher education has been fair game to critics, both inside and outside of The Academy, who characterize faculty as largely independent entrepreneurs with little or no institutional loyalty. These faculty are portrayed as largely disinterested in undergraduate education, preferring to focus on their own narrow research and publication interests. Over the past 10 years, my favorite summary of this particular view of faculty has been that of Robert Zemsky, University of Pennsylvania, and William Massy, Stanford University, in their characterization of what they refer to as the "academic ratchet:"

[The Academic Ratchet is...] A term to describe the steady, irreversible shift of faculty allegiance away from the goals of a given institution, toward those of an academic specialty. The ratchet denotes the advance of an entrepreneurial spirit among faculty nationwide, leading to an increased emphasis on research and publication, and on teaching one's specialty in favor of general introduction courses, often at the expense of coherence in an academic curriculum. Institutions seeking to enhance their own prestige may contribute to the ratchet by reducing faculty teaching and advising responsibilities across the board, thus enabling faculty to pursue their individual research and publication with fewer distractions. The academic ratchet raises an institution's costs, and it results in undergraduates paying more to attend institutions in which they receive less attention than in previous decades. (p. 22)

Now in no small measure, much of this sort of criticism was richly deserved, particularly in the late 1980s and early 1990s, when Zemsky and Massy first started to talk about the academic ratchet. The core of the problem, it seems to me, is that we have done precious little to quantitatively and qualitatively describe what faculty do and how well they have done it in the intervening years since the firestorm of criticism first began. Instead, we have largely relied on tired old constructs to talk about faculty activity, using a language that entirely misses the point when dealing with critics of faculty productivity.

There are two prominent national studies that illustrate my point. The National Center for Education Statistics (NCES) has, over the years, established a wonderful database for studying faculty in American Higher Education. *The National Study of Post Secondary Faculty* (NSOPF), in 1998 and 1993, collected detailed data from a broad cross section of American faculty on variables such as how many hours they work, how they allocate their time by function, and how satisfied/dissatisfied they are with their working conditions. In looking at what faculty do, NSOPF enables generation of information of the sort that we see in Table 3.1. Essentially, faculty activity is described in terms of percentages of

Table 3.1
Allocation of Time by Function for Faculty and Staff in 4-Year Institutions by Program Area: Fall 1987 and Fall 1992

Program Area and Year	Full-Time Instructional Faculty and Staff	Percentage of Time Spent			
		Teaching Activities	Research Activities	Administrative Activities	Other Activities
1992					
All program areas in 4-year institutions*	405,783	50.8	21.1	13.2	14.7
Agriculture/Home Economics	9,698	42.1	30.7	13.0	14.2
Business	28,895	54.1	17.9	12.1	15.7
Education	30,127	53.8	13.1	16.5	16.2
Engineering	20,381	48.5	28.1	11.2	12.0
Fine Arts	26,874	56.5	15.4	12.3	15.6
Humanities	54,093	59.7	17.8	13.1	9.1
Natural Sciences	79,663	50.0	29.1	11.1	9.7
Social Sciences	48,030	50.5	23.6	13.4	12.2
All Other Fields	44,346	52.9	16.1	15.6	15.2
1987					
All program areas in 4-year institutions*	414,832	53.2	20.4	13.7	12.6
Agriculture/Home Economics	10,104	50.4	27.6	13.4	8.7
Business	28,630	60.3	16.0	11.5	12.2
Education	31,812	61.5	11.2	16.2	11.1
Engineering	20,915	56.2	22.4	12.3	9.1
Fine Arts	27,628	55.2	19.3	11.9	13.6
Humanities	60,781	62.2	16.9	14.5	6.5
Natural Sciences	74,852	53.8	26.7	12.3	7.2
Social Sciences	47,324	54.3	22.1	14.0	9.7
All Other Fields	29,042	59.8	14.1	14.2	11.9

* Health sciences faculty are included in the program area total but are not shown separately.

SOURCE: U.S. Department of Education, National Center for Education Statistics, 1993 and 1988 National Survey of Postsecondary Faculty, "Faculty Survey."

time spent in various categories of activity. Table 3.1 displays data from both the 1988 and 1993 data collection cycles. Comparable measures are being collected as part of the 1999 cycle as well. And while these measures are very useful for longitudinal analyses of changes in the nature of faculty work, they are absolutely non-responsive to questions about the quantity and quality of faculty productivity. They yield nothing to the individual seeking to learn whether senior, tenured and tenure track faculty spend any time at all teaching undergraduates, and if so, the outcomes of those interactions with students.

Don't misunderstand me – NSOPF is a powerful and incredibly useful database for studying faculty activity. But it deals largely with input measures – what percent of time do faculty spend in teaching, research, and service activity, without regard to the **products** of those activities. A similar approach to studying faculty is undertaken at regular intervals by the Higher Education Research Institute (HERI) at the University of California at Los Angeles. They regularly survey a different sort of national faculty sample on somewhat different measures. Their national benchmarks for the HERI Faculty Survey, like the NSOPF data, yield highly useful information on the nature of faculty work, but little on the quantitative and qualitative productivity of faculty.

Why is this an issue? There is not a college or university in the country that has not been criticized for employing that ubiquitous faculty member who is regularly seen mowing his/her lawn at all hours of the day. On the other hand, both NSOPF and HERI data suggest that faculty spend well beyond the traditional 40-hour work week engaged in activity related to the core mission of an institution. But if faculty activity is described solely in terms of inputs, it matters little whether it's 60 percent of six hours or 60 hours spent in instruction. The issue is what is the *outcome*, the *productivity* that arises from that activity.

NEW WAYS OF THINKING ABOUT FACULTY ACTIVITY

The mid-1990s brought together a convergence of analytical activities that have provided a new context for looking at faculty activity. Among the most ambitious of these was an initiative from the National Association of State Universities and Land Grant Colleges (NASULGC), the American Association of State Colleges and Universities (AASCU), and the American Association of Community Colleges (AACC). A panel of nine presidents, representing institutions in each of the three higher education associations, formed the Joint Commission on Accountability Reporting (JCAR). The Commission was created in direct response to demands from legislators, parents, and consumer groups who sought reliable and credible information on the price of higher education, and specific information on what the likely return would be on the investment in that education. For example, If a parent invests $20,000 per year in tuition, room, and board at "State University X," what is the likelihood of graduating from that institution, as evidenced by institutional retention and graduation rates? What sorts of post-graduation options await graduates of the institution, as manifested by career planning and placement data?   And perhaps most important, how do the data for "State University X" compare with those for other institutions in which the student and his/her parents may have an interest?

In order to provide consistent, stable, and comparable inter-institutional data, the JCAR developed four technical work groups comprised of faculty, administrators, and perhaps most important given the nature of their task, veteran institutional researchers with well established track records and national reputations in measurement. The Technical Work Groups were charged with developing appropriate measures and reporting methodologies for four discrete areas:

- Placement rates and full-time employment in the field following completion of a higher education degree/program
- Graduation rates, persistence rates, withdrawal rates, licensure pass rates, and transfers of students
- Student charges and costs
- Faculty activity reporting

Obviously, for purposes of this chapter, the focus will be on the work of the fourth group, i.e., reporting faculty activity. But it is important to underscore that JCAR was intended to be a comprehensive reporting project. In looking at what faculty do in terms of teaching research and service activity, JCAR expected that activity to be described in terms of outputs. If time is spent in teaching, do students who receive instruction graduate in a timely fashion? Can they pass standard licensure or accreditation examinations in the field in which they studied? Can they get jobs? Answers to these questions are crucial to any discussion of return on value for the price paid for a college education, or the actual cost to the institution of delivering that education.

WHO ARE "THE FACULTY," AND WHAT DO THEY DO?

Before coming to the University of Delaware in 1985, I spent several years working on campuses in the State University of New York (SUNY) System. In that system, all full-time librarians have faculty status and are reported as such. Since coming to Delaware, I've interacted with numerous institutional research colleagues at other research universities where they employ a discrete category of faculty called "research faculty." These are individuals hired expressly to do research, and research alone, with no expectation whatsoever of teaching or service types of activity. And, of course, we all work with presidents, provosts, deans, and other senior administrators who hold tenured faculty positions in one or more of our academic departments, but for whom teaching is, at best, a secondary or tertiary responsibility. When critics attack faculty in American higher education, wondering who is teaching our undergraduates, is this the population that they're after?

Perhaps JCAR's greatest contribution to institutional research is that it forced us to discuss those variables to be used in accountability reporting, to make certain that they were sensible, and above all, to make certain that they had consistency and credibility when used across institution types. Indeed, when talking about the faculty population at the University of Delaware (a Carnegie Research/Doctoral - Intensive institution), we want to make certain that we're using the same population parameters as applied to our neighbors at West Chester University of Pennsylvania (a Carnegie Masters I institution) or Baltimore Community College (a Carnegie Associate's College). Not that we necessarily compare the University of Delaware to a community college; the emphasis is on clarity and consistency of language when measuring and reporting data throughout higher education. That can't happen if "faculty" means one thing at Institution A, and something altogether different at Institution B.

The JCAR Technical Work Group on Faculty Activity Reporting began by adopting a common definition for what we mean by "faculty." They embraced the full-time and part-time instructional and research staff definition promulgated by the American Association of University Professors:

> ... those whose regular assignment is instruction, including those with release time for research. Additionally, faculty whose regular full time assignment is exclusively research are included. Faculty on sabbatical leave should also be counted. Replacements for faculty on leave with pay should not be reported, while replacements for those on leave without pay should be. Department heads with faculty rank and no other administrative title should be included as well. (p. 6.)

In looking at the issue of reporting what faculty do, the preceding definition leaves little ambiguity as to who faculty are for purposes of this analysis. Faculty activity was described with similar precision by the Technical Work Group through adoption of the definitions for instruction, research, and service, as contained in the AASCU publication, *An Introduction to Faculty Workloads.* Again, briefly quoting from the JCAR Faculty Assignment Manual:

- *Teaching* – includes the direct delivery as well as those activities supporting the teaching/learning process. Examples of direct delivery of instruction are lectures, seminars, directed study, laboratory sessions, clinical or student teacher supervision, and field placement supervision. Activities directly supporting teaching include class preparation, evaluation of student work, curriculum development, supervision of graduate student research including thesis/dissertation, academic and career advising, faculty training, and mentoring. Professional development geared to increasing faculty effectiveness in the activities listed above would be included also.

- *Research/Scholarship* – includes an array of activities such as conducting experimental and/or scholarly research, developing creative works, preparing or reviewing articles or books, preparing and reviewing proposals for external funding, performing or exhibiting works in the fine and applied arts, and attending meetings or conferences essential to remaining current in one's field.

- *Service* – draws on the professional or academic expertise of a faculty member and includes work within the campus community and outside the campus. Department and campus service includes work on various committees (e.g., governance, recruitment) and department administration. Community or public service includes consulting, giving speeches, and working in organizations and/or on committees related to a faculty members academic field. (pp. 6-7)

These definitions are terribly important as they are educative as well as essential to the reporting methodology. The JCAR methodology was developed primarily for reporting to constituencies outside of higher education, who may well have a limited view of the three core mission areas of colleges and universities. The foregoing definitions clarify at the outset that faculty activity associated with teaching, research, and service are not restricted to the classroom, laboratory, or cooperative extension. In measuring what faculty do, it is important to take the most comprehensive view of what faculty are expected to do as part of the effective performance of their job responsibilities. And clearly, those responsibilities are not restricted to classroom teaching, laboratory research, and public service outreach activity alone.

In describing what faculty to, the JCAR Technical Work Group on faculty activity reporting was determined to avoid the most often heard criticism of faculty data, i.e., that it is self-reported and self-serving. While the Technical Work Group certainly did not embrace the accuracy of such criticisms, they did note that such arguments are long-standing. Consequently, regardless of the accuracy of that perception, the Work Group acknowledged that it was real, and opted to avoid replicating a self-reporting strategy in gathering data on what faculty do. Instead, they shifted the focus to reporting what faculty are *assigned* to do in any given academic year, as *verifiable* through the work agreement developed between department chairs and faculty, and ratified by deans.

The JCAR productivity measure for determining what faculty are assigned to do is the *service month.*

The Service Month is a unit of work equivalent to one person working full time for one calendar month and can be allocated by function, i.e., teaching, research, or service. For example, a full time 12-month employee with half-time responsibility as the college's director of institutional research, and half time responsibility as a member of the mathematics faculty, produces six administrative service months and six faculty service months in that year. In the case of those functioning solely as faculty, service months can be distributed over the three categories of faculty work: teaching, research/scholarship, and service. Consider the full time 9-month faculty member whose assigned responsibilities include 50 percent teaching, 30 percent research, and 20 percent service. The service months for that individual would be distributed as follows: 4.5 months in teaching (i.e., 9 months multiplied by 50 percent); 2.7 months in research (i.e., 9 months multiplied by 30 percent); and 1.8 months in service activity (i.e., 9 months multiplied by 20 percent). (p. 7)

The Technical Work Group on Faculty Activity Reporting recommended that department chairs examine the assigned responsibilities for each faculty member, as defined previously, in their department. The faculty assignments would then be converted to service months using the rationale above. The output of such calculations would be assigned faculty work, measured in terms of aggregate service months, at the departmental, college, and institution-wide level. The JCAR Faculty Assignment Manual provides detailed examples of service month calculations, and a copy of that Manual should reside in every institutional research office. It is available from the American Association of State Colleges and Universities in Washington, D.C.

The Service Month is a useful way of quantifying faculty work. In the example cited above, it is far more tangible to say that a 9-month faculty appointment results in 4.5 months of teaching, 2.7 months of research, and 1.8 months of service, than to simply describe faculty in terms of "percent time spent in" teaching, research or service. Those outside of The Academy understand the concept of a month far more clearly than "x percent of" an undefined, ethereal quantity of teaching. It is important to underscore, when talking about service months, that they need not be contiguous. A faculty member does not partition his/her work such that teaching is done only in select months, while research and service are done at other times. All are essentially concurrent activities. The service months simply represent functional aggregations of how time is assigned, and what can be expected as a return on investment from the 9-month contract.

I had the opportunity to direct a national pilot study of the JCAR methodology for reporting faculty assignments. While the methodology was not without its critics within institutions (too simplistic, not comprehensive, etc.), the model was quite straightforward for those not employed by colleges and universities. It represents a step forward in that it describes faculty work in terms of output, i.e., months in service to the institution and its students. The underlying constructs in the JCAR methodology have also been viewed positively by those in Washington seeking more consistent ways to report institutional data. It is a methodology that should be refined and enhanced.

Once faculty activity is thoroughly described, as with the service month convention, it is useful to take a more detailed look at the productivity from each of the three cornerstone functions in a faculty member's professional life – teaching, research, and service. With respect to teaching, the seminal question is "Who is teaching what to whom, and at what cost?" Responding to this question goes directly to the heart of the criticism that Zemsky and Massy (1990) leveled at higher education in describing the academic ratchet. I have had the good fortune over the past decade to direct the Delaware Study of Instructional Costs and Productivity, a national data sharing consortium that collects detailed information on teaching loads, and direct expenditures for instruction, research, and public service, all at the academic discipline level of analysis. Figure 3.1 displays the Delaware Study data collection form.

Figure 3.1
1999 Delaware Study of Instructional Cost and Productivity

Institution:

Department/Discipline:

Associated CIP Identifier:

Please indicate the average number of degrees awarded in this discipline at each degree level over the three year period from 1994-95 through 1996-97.

Bachelor's:
Master's:
Doctorate:
Professional:

Place an 'X' in the box below if this discipline is non-degree granting.

Place an "X" in the box below that describes your academic calendar:

Semester
Quarter

A. INSTRUCTIONAL COURSELOAD: FALL SEMESTER, 1997

Please complete the following matrix, displaying student credit hours and organized class sections taught, by type of faculty, and by level of instruction. Be sure to consult definitions before proceeding. Do not input data in shaded cells except for those mentioned in the important note below that pertains to (G) and (J).

Classification	Faculty			Student Credit Hours								Organized Class Sections					
	FTE Faculty			(D)	(E)	(F)	(G)	(H)	(I)	(J)	(K)	(L)	Other Section Types (Lecture, Seminar, etc.)				
	(A) Total	(B) Separately Budgeted	(C) Instructional	Lower Div. OC*	Upper Div. OC*	Undergrad Indv. Instruct.	Total Undergrad SCH	Grad OC*	Graduate Indv. Instruct.	Total Graduate SCH	Total Student Credit Hours	Lab/Disc/ Rec. Sections	(M) Lower Div.	(N) Upper Div.	(O) Graduate	(P) Total
Regular faculty: -Tenured/Tenure Eligible																
- Other Regular Faculty																
Supplemental Faculty																
Teaching Assistants: - Credit Bearing Courses																
- Non-Credit Bearing Activity																
TOTAL																

In the box to the right, indicate the number of Graduate Individualized Instruction Student Credit Hours from the Total that are devote to supervised doctoral dissertation.

B. COST DATA: ACADEMIC AND FISCAL YEAR 1997-98

1. In the boxes below, enter the total number of student credit hours that were generated during Academic Year 1997-98 during terms that were supported by the department's instructional budget. (NOTE: Semester calendar institutions will typically report fall and spring student credit hours; quarter calendar institutions will usually report fall, winter, and spring student credit hours.)

A. Undergraduate
B. Graduate

2. In the boxes below, enter total direct expenditures for instruction in FY 1997-98.

A. Salaries   Are the benefits included in the number reported for salaries (Y/N)

B. Benefits   If the dollar value is not available, what percent of salary do benefits constitute at your institution?

C. Other than personnel expenditures.

D. Total

3. In the box below, enter total direct expenditures for separately budgeted research activity in FY 1997-98.

4. In the box below, enter total direct expenditures for separately budgeted public service activity in FY 1997-98.

Part A of the data collection form asks for detailed data on teaching activity at the departmental level. Departments are described in terms of the Classification of Instructional Programs (CIP) Code of the predominant course offering in that department. In looking at the "who" in "Who is teaching what to whom?," the faculty definition is somewhat broader than the JCAR definition. We want to capture teaching activity by all instructors, regardless of whether they conform to the AAUP definition for faculty. The major faculty categories in the Delaware Study are as follows:

Regular Faculty: Regular faculty are defined as those individuals who are hired for the purpose of doing teaching, and who may also do research and/or service. They are characterized by a **recurring** contractual relationship in which the individual and the institution both assume a continuing appointment. These faculty typically fall into two categories:

> **Tenured and Tenure-Eligible**: Those individuals who either hold tenure, or for whom tenure is an expected outcome. At most institutions, these are full, associate, and assistant professors.

> **Non-Tenure Track Faculty**: Those individuals who teach on a **recurring** contractual basis, but whose academic title renders them ineligible for academic tenure. At most institutions, these titles include instructors, lecturers, visiting faculty, etc.

Supplemental Faculty: Supplemental faculty are characteristically paid to teach out of a pool of **temporary** funds. Their appointment is **non-recurring**, although the same individual might receive a temporary appointment in successive terms. The key point is that the funding is, by nature, temporary and there is no expectation of continuing appointment. This category includes adjuncts, administrators or professional personnel at the institution who teach but whose primary job responsibility is non-faculty, contributed service personnel, etc.

Teaching Assistants: Students at the institution who receive a stipend strictly for teaching activity. Includes teaching assistants who are instructors of record, but also includes teaching assistants who function as discussion section leaders, laboratory section leaders, and other types of organized class sections in which instruction takes place but which may not carry credit and for which there is no formal instructor of record. For purposes of this study, do not include graduate research assistants.

Each of these faculty categories appears in the left-hand most column on the data collection form. In calculating full-time equivalency (FTE Faculty) for each of the faculty categories described above, the following conventions are recommended:

REGULAR FACULTY: Take the TOTAL FTE for <u>filled</u> faculty positions as they appear in the Fall 1998 personnel file at your institution, and report this in the "Total FTE Faculty" data field. (Column A) Be sure to report <u>filled</u> positions only. Filled positions are those that have salaries associated with them. Include paid leaves such as sabbaticals wherein the individual is receiving a salary, but exclude unpaid leaves of absence. In Column B, report the FTE portion of faculty lines that are supported by external or separately budgeted funds for purposes other than teaching, i.e., research or service. The remainder is the departmental or program instructional faculty FTE, and should be reported in the "Instructional" FTE faculty data field. That is, the FTE for Column C is computed by subtracting Column B from Column A. For example, suppose Professor Jones is a full-time member of the Chemistry Faculty. He would be reflected as 1.0 FTE in Column A. Professor Jones has a research grant that contractually obligates him to spend one-third of his time in research. The externally supported portion of his position is 0.33 FTE, which would be reflected in Column B. As a result, 0.66 FTE is the instructional faculty which would appear in Column C , i.e., 1.0 FTE (Column A) minus 0.33 FTE (Column B).

SUPPLEMENTAL FACULTY: Full-time equivalency for supplemental faculty can be arrived at by taking the total teaching credit hours (which are generally equivalent to the credit value of the course(s) taught) for each supplemental faculty, and dividing by 12. Twelve hours is a broadly accepted standard for a full-time teaching load. (If your institution assigns one course unit instead of three or four credit hours to a course being taught, use a divisor of 4) Because Supplemental Faculty generally are not supported by external funds, Column C will typically equal Column A.

TEACHING ASSISTANTS: You are asked to assign an FTE value to teaching assistants, apportioned between credit-bearing course activity where the teaching assistant is the instructor of record, and non-credit bearing course activity (i.e., section leader for zero-credit laboratories, discussion sections, recitation sections). To do this, take the FTE value for teaching assistants in a given academic department or program, as it appears in your personnel file. Then apportion the FTE as follows:

Credit-Bearing Courses: Use the same convention as with Supplemental Faculty. Take all courses which are credit bearing and for which teaching assistants are the instructors of record, and divide the total teaching credit hours by 12. The resulting quotient is the teaching assistant FTE for credit-bearing course activity.

Non-Credit-Bearing Activity: From the total teaching assistant FTE, taken from your personnel file, subtract the calculated FTE for credit-bearing activity as outlined above. The difference is the FTE for non-credit-bearing activity.

It is understood that on many campuses, the non-credit-bearing activity is not exclusively instructional, and may include activities such as grading papers. However, the decision to allow teaching assistants to do things other than teach is analogous to allowing other departmentally-paid faculty types to take reduced loads to engage in non-teaching activity. In both instances, salaries are associated with personnel, and in the interest of consistency, the personnel should be counted as a component of common practice in higher education.

Having developed the full-time equivalency for each faculty type, both student credit hours and organized class sections taught are reported on the remaining cells of the matrix for each respective faculty category. All too often, we think of instructional activity only in terms of student credit hours produced. While these are an important measure, focusing solely on student credit hours has potential for substantially understating a department's overall teaching productivity. By also reporting organized class sections taught, we get a more complete picture. An organized class section is any consistently constituted group of students that meet with an instructor at regularly scheduled times throughout an academic term. Certainly this includes the credit-bearing portion of a course that results in student credit hour production. But organized class sections can also embrace zero-credit recitation, discussion, and laboratory sections that are required components of a course, but for which no credit is received, to exclude them from an instructional productivity analysis is to significantly understate teaching activity.

The importance of this distinction is very clear when one looks at Delaware Study data over time. For each of the past four data collection cycles in the Delaware Study, we have focused on 24 academic disciplines typically found at any college or university, regardless of Carnegie classification or funding control. Those disciplines include the following:

Communications	Psychology
Computer and Information Sciences	Anthropology
Education	Economics
Engineering	Geography
Foreign Languages and Literature	History
English	Political Science
Biological Sciences	Sociology
Mathematics	Visual and Performing Arts
Philosophy	Nursing
Chemistry	Business Administration
Geology	Accounting
Physics	Financial Management

We examined teaching load data reported in each of these disciplines for research universities, doctoral universities, comprehensive colleges and universities, and baccalaureate colleges, as defined by the Carnegie Foundation for the Advancement of Teaching (1994). Specifically, we examined the following variables:

- Proportion of lower division student credit hours taught by tenured/tenure track faculty
- Proportion of lower division organized class sections taught by tenured/tenure track faculty
- Proportion of undergraduate student credit hours taught by tenured/tenure track faculty
- Proportion of undergraduate organized class sections taught by tenured/tenure track faculty

The Delaware Study produces a benchmark for each of these variables. That is, within each Carnegie category of institution, we examine the value reported by each institution for the variable in question. We take those values and compute an initial mean. In order to make certain that idiosyncratic numbers do not exert undue influence on that data pool, we take those institutional values that are more than two standard deviations above or below that initial mean, tag them as outliers, and recompute a refined mean, which becomes the national benchmark.

In the analysis at hand, we take the national benchmarks for each of the 24 disciplines in each of the four data collection cycles and arrive at an average across those disciplines. The data are reflected in Table 3.2.

It is important to underscore what these data are saying. In the first row in Table 3.2, we are not saying that 52.7 percent of all lower division student credit hours are taught by tenured and tenure track faculty. We are saying that the average proportion of lower division student credit hours taught by tenured and tenure track faculty across the 24 disciplines from the four data collections is 52.7 percent. It is important to look at the average across disciplines, as some programs, notably English, foreign languages, and mathematics typically generate a large volume of student credit hours and may exert undue influence on the data. Students do not take just English, math, or foreign language courses. They take courses across the curriculum, and it's important that these data reflect the likelihood of their encountering a tenured or tenure track faculty member across the curriculum.

Why the focus on tenured and tenure track faculty? The Delaware Study enables comparable analyses with any of the faculty categories, but it is the tenured and tenure track group that are most visible and in whom the institution has the greatest investment. These are the individuals who, once tenure is granted, are fixed costs; they are employed by the institution until they resign, retire, or die. Hence it is fair to examine this group to determine the return on investment.

99

Table 3.2
Mean Values For Selected Teaching Workload and Expenditure Variables in 24 Selected Disciplines in Four Delaware Study Data Collection Cycles Spanning Academic and Fiscal Years 1993-94 Through 1997-98

		Research Universities	Doctoral Universities	Comprehensive Universities	Baccalaureate Universities
Average Proportion of Lower Division Student Student Credit Hours Taught by Tenured/Tenure Track Faculty	Mean	52.7	54.1	68.2	74.9
Average Proportion of Lower Division Organized Class Sections Taught by Tenured/Tenure Track Faculty	Mean	46.7	51.4	67.3	72.6
Average Proportion of Undergraduate Student Student Credit Hours Taught by Tenured/Tenure Track Faculty	Mean	62.4	63.4	74.8	79.6
Average Proportion of Undergraduate Organized Class Sections Taught by Tenured/Tenure Track Faculty	Mean	60.3	63.4	75.1	76.8
Average Number of Undergraduate Student Credit Hours Taught per FTE Tenured/Tenure Track Faculty	Mean	189.5	199.6	233.7	193.9
Average Number of Undergraduate Organized ClassSections Taught per FTE Tenured/Tenure Track Faculty	Mean	1.5	2.0	3.0	3.0
Average Number of Total Student Credit Hours Taught per FTE Tenured/Tenure Track Faculty	Mean	223.2	226.5	244.9	196.2
Average Number of Total Organized Class Sections Taught per FTE Tenured/Tenure Track Faculty	Mean	2.1	2.7	3.3	3.0
Average Direct Instructional Expense per Student Credit Hour Taught	Mean	164	147	129	171
Average Total Direct Separately Budgeted Research and Service Expenditures per FTE Tenured/Tenure Track Faculty	Mean	26,337	13,932	2,001	na

Looking at the data in Table 3.2, we find that tenured and tenure track faculty teach, on average across the 24 disciplines, roughly one in two lower division student credit hours generated at research and doctoral institutions, two of three lower division student credit hours generated at comprehensive institutions, and three of four lower division student credit hours generated at baccalaureate colleges. When all undergraduate student credit hours generated across the 24 disciplines are examined, the average proportion taught by tenured and tenure track faculty are three of five at research and doctoral universities, and three of four at comprehensive and baccalaureate institutions. What these data suggest is that, since Zemsky and Massy's broadside in 1990, those faculty in whom colleges and universities have the greatest investment are generating the majority of student credit hours on average across the disciplines. This is not a trivial finding. Student credit hours are the "coin of the realm" in higher education. They determine whether a student is full-time or part-time. They measure progress toward degree. And they are, by and large, generated by regular faculty on continuing appointment.

When one looks at the organized class sections taught in Table 3.2, there is a noticeable drop off in the proportion taught by tenured and tenure track faculty, when compared with student credit hour generation. On the other hand, there is a greater convergence of proportions of both organized class sections and student credit hour generation at comprehensive and baccalaureate institutions. Why is this? The answer rests in the fact that organized class sections look at both the credit bearing sections and the zero credit recitation, discussion, and laboratory sections. These latter, zero credit sections tend to be taught by adjunct faculty and graduate assistants at research and doctoral universities, freeing up regular faculty for other activities, i.e., research and service. Interestingly enough, there are no major studies that argue that this practice is pedagogically unsound. In fact, it is intended to add to the instruction from the credit-bearing portion of the course.

The data collection form in Figure 3.1 also collects direct expenditure data on instruction, research, and service. The data in Table 3.2 confirm patterns that we already expect. Because faculty at research and doctoral institutions teach lighter loads, the cost per student credit hour is higher. It is noteworthy that the baccalaureate institutions in the Delaware Study have lighter loads and higher costs that compare with research and doctoral institutions. This is a function of sample dependency in that the baccalaureate institutions that participate in the Delaware Study tend to be highly selective, liberal arts institutions that build their reputations on small class size.

The research and service expenditures per FTE tenured and tenure track faculty mirror the missions of the respective institution types. Research universities, on average, generate twice the expenditures per faculty as doctoral universities, and 13 times that of comprehensive institutions.

All of these data become particularly powerful when the institutional researcher compares his/her own institution with each of the disciplines along each of the workload and cost variables. It enables the researcher to examine faculty activity at the home institution, and to put institutional data into context with comparable disciplines at comparable institutions. Tools such as the Delaware Study enable us to better understand the quantitative dimensions of faculty activity. Readers wishing to learn more about the Delaware Study are invited to visit the University of Delaware Office of Institutional Research's Web site at http://www.udel.edu/IR and review the Delaware Study home page.

Institutional researchers must take care when reporting data of the sort just described. As noted, these are purely quantitative analyses, and do not speak to the quality of a program. Indeed, there are programs at institutions which cost significantly more and teach significantly lighter loads than national benchmarks, and those institutions would not have it any other way for purely qualitative reasons. Those departments or programs may have national and/or international reputations for high quality, predicated on the manner in which they deliver instruction, research, and service. How, then, do we assess quality?

The University of Delaware, like most institutions across the country, is grappling with that issue. At a meeting of our Board of Trustees last year, one trustee asked a department chair the following question: "How do you *know* that you're doing a *good* job of teaching students?" The italics are mine, but they simply reflect the tonal qualities of the Trustee's question. The University's Provost, working with the Office of Institutional Research and Planning, has set about answering that question. We challenged academic departments to respond to the question of *quality* of faculty activity in *measurable* ways. Departmental faculty have been charged with identifying appropriate measures that help define the quality of a program. At the same time that the University of Delaware's faculty were addressing this issue, colleagues at other institutions participating in the Delaware Study engaged in parallel thinking.

Commencing with the 2000-01 data collection cycle, the Delaware Study will begin gathering qualitative information on faculty activity at the academic department level. The initial collection will focus on six disciplines – art, business administration, chemistry, education, English, and mathematics – and will do six different disciplines each year until the 24 core disciplines are captured that were described earlier in the national analysis of faculty productivity. Each of those disciplines will then be placed on a once-every-four-year collection cycle.

The quantitative data collection form displayed in Figure 3.1 underwent a series of revisions by the Delaware Study Advisory Committee, a group that annually provides guidance on refining and enhancing the Study's methodology. The qualitative data collection (See Figure 3.2) form will undergo comparable refinements, based upon field experience over the next few cycles, and will ultimately arrive at metrics as consistent and stable as those in the more established parts of the Delaware Study.

Many of these measures are typically collected by institutional research offices through student satisfaction surveys, post-graduation placement studies, etc. The post-graduation data in Table 3.3 is collected by the University of Delaware's Office of Institutional Research and Planning is not unlike that collected at many other institutions, and is a useful measure for looking at instructional outcomes.

Other measures of quality are more complex. The ability of students to integrate and synthesize complex ideas, to work effectively in groups, and to communicate clearly and concisely in both empirical and theoretical terms are constructs that are more difficult to measure. Certainly, we ask alumni and employers, via surveys, how well we have done institutionally and programmatically along these lines. At the same time, new teaching pedagogies are being crafted by faculty to ensure that these skills are being mastered. The University of Delaware is currently involved with the Pew Charitable Trust in a comprehensive strategy to introduce "problem-based learning" as a teaching strategy across the curriculum. Here, the role of institutional research is more limited. The cognitive testing and outcomes assessment associated with measuring the effectiveness of new pedagogies rests with offices that specialize in these sorts of psychometrics. That said, institutional research can play a supportive role in augmenting and enhancing discussions concerning the quality of faculty instructional activity.

Figure 3.2
Delaware Study of Instructional Costs and Productivity
Departmental Checklist: Qualitative Measures of Faculty Activity

Institution: _____

Discipline: _____ CIP Code: _____

FTE Tenured/Tenure Track Faculty in this Discipline: _____

1	Number of refereed faculty publications within the past 36 months	_____
2	Number of textbooks, reference books, novels, volumes of collected works authored by faculty within the past 36 months	_____
3	Number of edited volumes by faculty within the past 36 months	_____
4	Number of juried shows/competitive performances within past 36 months	_____
5	Number of editorial positions held by faculty within past 36 months	_____
6	Number of externally funded contracts and grants received by faculty within the past 36 months	_____
7	Number of professional conference papers and presentations by faculty within the past 36 months	_____
8	Number of non-refereed publications by faculty within past 36 months	_____
9	Number of active faculty memberships in professional associations and/or honor socities within past 36 months	_____
10	Number of faculty engaged in faculty development or curriculum development activity as part of their assigned workload during past 36 months	_____
11	Average graduation rate within six years for three most recent cohorts of graduating seniors	_____
12	Average proportion of three most recent graduating classes finding curriculum related employment within 12 months of commencement	_____
13	Average proportion of students over past three years passing licensing, certification, or accreditation examinations related to academic major	_____
14	Average proportion of three most recent graduating classes continuing to pursue further graduate or professional education	_____
15	Number of undergraduate students formally engaged in research activity with a faculty mentor during the past 12 months	_____
16	Number of undergraduate students engaged in internships or practica under direct faculty supervision during past 12 months	_____
17	Number of students who author or co-author with a faculty mentor, a journal article or book chapter within the past 36 months	_____
18	Number of students presenting or co-presenting with a faculty mentor, a paper at a professional meeting	_____

The focus of our discussion thus far has been measuring the instructional component of faculty activity. What about research and service? Certainly the Delaware Study measures research and service activity to the extent that such activity is supported by separately budgeted expenditures. But all this tells us is the cost of such activity; it does not focus on outcomes, although the qualitative measures are clearly headed in that direction. There are a number of public databases against which departmental and institutional data can be compared. The Institute for Scientific Information (ISI) has a Web-based data set, *University Science Indicators*, that examines for academic departments at over 100 leading universities across the nation, the number of papers published in refereed journals, monographs produced by recognized publishing houses, and the impact of publications on the field as evidenced by the number of citations. Another excellent data source is the National Science Foundation's CASPAR (Computer Aided Science Policy Analysis and Research), which, like ISI, is Web-based and in the public domain. It includes the capability to search and retrieve data,

Table 3.3
Employment and Educational Status of 1997
Baccalaureates by Curriculum Group

Curriculum Group	N[1]	F/T Major Related %	F/T Major Unrelated %	P/T Major Related %	P/T Major Unrelated %	Pursuing Further Education %	Military Service %	Still Seeking Employment %
Agricultural Sciences	78	56.4	17.9	1.3	2.6	12.8	1.3	7.7
Arts & Science								
Humanities	128	43.8	20.3	2.3	4.7	19.5	0.8	8.6
Social Sciences	317	31.5	36.0	4.1	3.2	18.3	1.3	5.7
Life & Health Sciences	86	40.7	12.8	2.3	3.5	33.7	--	7.0
Physical Sciences	67	49.3	9.0	--	3.0	32.8	1.5	4.5
Business & Economics	181	80.7	11.0	--	0.6	5.5	1.1	1.1
Education	122	83.6	1.6	10.7	0.8	1.6	--	1.6
Engineering	67	70.1	7.5	--	--	16.4	--	6.0
Human Resources	146	63.7	13.0	4.1	0.7	15.8	0.7	2.1
Nursing	88	72.7	2.3	19.3	1.1	1.1	--	3.4
Physical Education	62	43.5	17.7	12.9	3.2	22.6	--	--
1997 Total	**1,342**	**55.7**	**17.1**	**4.7**	**2.2**	**15.3**	**0.7**	**4.3**
1996 Total	1,326	52.4	17.6	5.3	3.5	14.9	0.5	5.8
1995 Total	1,457	52.7	17.7	5.6	4.5	11.2	1.0	7.3
1994 Total	1,442	48.3	18.1	5.3	4.6	14.6	0.6	8.5
1993 Total	1,431	46.1	17.6	5.8	5.0	17.5	0.8	7.3
1992 Total	1,618	43.2	19.0	4.1	4.8	15.9	4.8	8.2
1991 Total	1,529	48.2	16.4	4.3	4.7	16.7	1.1	8.6
1990 Total	1,056	58.0	17.4	4.6	3.9	13.3	0.9	0.1
1989 Total	1,185	57.6	14.4	2.5	1.7	17.4	1.0	1.5
1988 Total	1,462	58.7	13.6	1.8	0.8	18.3	1.5	0.9
1987 Total	1,487	59.8	13.9	1.9	1.5	16.3	1.8	1.5

[1] Number of respondents to the Career Plans survey.

Note: Percentage totals prior to 1991 do not add to 100. During those years, an additional column appeared in the table under the heading "Not Seeking Employment."

by institution and discipline, from the following data sources, among others:

- The NSF-NIH Survey of Graduate Students and Postdoctorates in Science and Engineering: Provides detailed information on the numbers of graduate students and postdoctoral appointments, as well as information on sources of funding support, primary mechanism for support (e.g., fellowship, assistantship, etc.), as well as basic demographic information.
- IPEDS Completions Survey: Provides information on the volume of degrees awarded annually by institutions, by degree type, by discipline

- NSF Survey of Research and Development Expenditures at Universities and Colleges: Collects data annually from roughly 500 colleges and universities that account for virtually all of the funded R&D activity in the United States. The data reflect volume of funding, by institution, by discipline, by funding source.

In addition to these highly useful data sources, when talking especially to individuals outside of higher education about the scope and worth of faculty research and service activity, we have found it particularly useful in Delaware to focus a portion of the discussion on economic impact issues. When taxpayers, and most especially legislators, understand that not all faculty research is of former Wisconsin Senator William Proxmire's "Golden Fleece" variety, attitudes change. We have effectively argued that pure and applied research and service activity at the University of Delaware not only positively impacts the quality of life in the state and region, it also creates industry, jobs, and tax revenues. These are compelling arguments for those who indirectly or directly fund research and service activity through faculty salaries. We have found success in developing economic impact models by working with econometrically savvy departments at the University. There are also a number of good economic impact models available in the ERIC database.

SUMMARY

This chapter has attempted to describe the nature and scope of faculty activity and its impact on academic programs. Institutional research plays a crucial role in measuring the quantity and quality of that activity, and in assessing program quality through systematic academic program review. Hopefully the measurement strategies outlined in this chapter will whet the reader's appetite. If so, there are excellent papers to keep you current in the practice that are delivered annually at the Association for Institutional Research Forum, and published annually in the official AIR journal, *Research in Higher Education*.

References

Joint Commission on Accountability Reporting (JCAR). (1997). Faculty Assignment Reporting. Washington, DC: American Association of State Colleges and Universities.

Joint Commission on Accountability Reporting (JCAR). (1996).Technical Conventions Manual. Washington, DC: American Association of State Colleges and Universities.

Middaugh, M. F. (2001). Understanding faculty productivity: Standards and benchmarks for colleges and universities. San Francisco, CA: Jossey-Bass Publishers.

Middaugh, M. F. & Hollowell, D. E. (1992). Examining academic and administrative productivity measures. In C. S. Hollins (Ed.), New Directions for Institutional Research: No. 75. Containing costs and improving productivity in higher education. San Francisco, CA: Jossey-Bass.

Middaugh, M. F. (1995). Closing in on faculty productivity measures. Planning for Higher Education: Vol. 24 (2). Ann Arbor, MI: The Journal of the Society for College and University Planning.

Middaugh, M. F. (1998). How much do faculty really teach? Planning for Higher Education: Vol. 27 (2). Ann Arbor, MI: The Journal of the Society for College and University Planning.

The Carnegie Foundation for the Advancement of Teaching, (1994). A Classification of Institutions of Higher Education. Princeton, NJ.

U. S. Department of Education, (1997). National Study of Postsecondary Faculty: Institutional Faculty and Staff in Higher Education Institutions, Fall 1987 and Fall 1992, Washington DC.

Zemsky, R. & Massy, W. (1990). Cost containment: Committing to a new economic reality. Change 22 (6): 16-22.

CHAPTER 4: RESOURCE MANAGEMENT AND QUALITY IMPROVEMENT

Author: Laura Saunders

This chapter focuses on resource allocation, budget and finance issues; quality improvement and cost containment initiatives; human resources/ personnel issues; allocation and expansion of capital facilities and equipment; and institutional advancement.

Institutional research offices are often involved in discussions about institutional resource management decisions. In their role of supporting central decision-making processes, they may be asked comparative questions, what if questions, or historical questions. To better provide this information, IR staff need to understand something of the economic theory behind resource management issues, as well as the terms and methods of analysis that are normally used in discussing these questions.

Introduction

Resource management is a concept used in business and economic analysis to analyze the resources required to produce a unit of output. Applying this definition to higher education, or other non-profit organizations is difficult because of lack of agreement about what the "output" is in higher education. In higher education, is the output students? Research advancement? New and improved medical knowledge? A better community? Recreation? Job training? Literacy training? Specific skill training for business? The answer is all of these and perhaps more.

Higher education institutions are not simple, focused, one-output organizations. They can be large, complex entities with multiple functions. The single-purpose institution that specializes in a few, focused activities has faded as society puts more demands on higher education. The scarcity of funding has contributed to proliferation of activities, as colleges turn to auxiliary activities to support their core mission. Some schools such as community colleges have turned heavily to contract training as a way of spreading their mission, serving their community, and not incidentally, generating income for other purposes. The growth of sponsored research in universities since World War II has dramatically changed the composition of the faculty and the orientation of the institution. Significant sized lobbying staffs in state capitals and in Washington D.C. operate as marketing and business generation arms of institutions. Most research universities have large staffs engaged in supporting research — both in directly conducting the research, as well as providing accounting, purchasing, equipment maintenance and other operational support required to obtain and hold research contracts. In addition to specialized units that only deal with research grants and contracts, many campuses have large numbers of personnel, significant space, equipment and supply costs supporting a mixture of funded research grants, as well as core institutional activities. Staffs in these areas are larger than they would be to support just teaching.

There is another aspect of higher education that makes understanding and analysis of resource allocation in higher education particularly tricky — not only are there multiple outputs and inputs, but the linkages between inputs and outputs are unclear. Supervising doctoral student education may result in a newly minted Ph.D., a significant research contribution, and perhaps the generation of more grant funds. How much of the faculty member's effort should be attributed to each of these output?

Analyzing resource allocation using a business model such as output per unit of input requires that the analyst be able to link resources with outputs. In higher education, with its multiplicity of outputs, this identification becomes complex. We will discuss some of the conventions that are used but they generally rely on arbitrary prorating, the basis for which becomes a further opportunity for debate and discussion. There are some general, loosely applicable models that can guide the analysis of resource use in higher education, but there are no universally agreed upon recipe books or cost accounting procedures that provide easy answers. The institutional researcher must draw on his or her knowledge of the higher education organization, and apply a variety of techniques to develop answers.

Notwithstanding these complexities, university administrators as well as students of higher education have all expended considerable effort in trying to understand how resources are used in higher education — descriptive studies — and whether these are the appropriate use of resources — prescriptive studies. Different techniques are required for each.

EARLY STUDIES

Some of the very early studies of resource allocation were done following World War II by James Russell and James Doi. These were faculty workload and unit cost analyses that described and measured the unit cost of teaching in terms of the direct cost of faculty time. By the mid-1960s, resource allocation had become a topic of graduate study as well as management concern. The National Center for Higher Education Management Systems, independently organized in 1971 as an outgrowth of the Western Interstate Compact for Higher Education, developed a number of resource allocation models and analyses that responded to state and federal interest in how much higher education costs, as well as how it could be made more efficient. Rand Corporation and several institutions including the University of California developed analytical studies offices that concentrated on questions of resource allocation. The Ford Foundation subsidized research in higher education analysis in the 1970s.

Presidents at state research universities were asking more questions about costs throughout the 1960s as it became apparent that governmental funding was not unlimited, and that productivity gains were limited. States also scrutinized the resources going to higher education as the burgeoning higher education enrollments resulted in many new institutions and growth in existing ones. Statewide planning agencies were created in many states to review and coordinate higher education. National data systems originating in the Department of Education collected data on enrollments, institutional finance, faculty salaries and institutional characteristics for both public and private institutions. With the Higher Education Act of 1972 and the emergence of the federal government as a leading source of financial aid for students, federal agencies began to scrutinize higher education. Institutions adopted one budgeting strategy after another, and by the mid-1990s large institutions had gone through several cycles of planning and budgeting approaches. However, institutions continue to struggle with questions of how much and what for, and for whom. Previous models for resource allocation drawn from business and military models had been tried and discarded, to be replaced by other approaches, as complex problems remained.

EDUCATION IS PART OF THE ECONOMY

The financial and political climate for higher education is strongly affected by the general economy and the questions to be answered in this arena are shaped within that context. Especially for independent institutions, the relative affluence of the target population is of concern. The ability of an institution to attract and retain its work force depends on funding availability and the general employment situation. As the key work force, faculty and their salaries are of paramount concern. Institutional researchers find themselves annually gathering data on faculty salaries and preparing comparative rankings. Institutional presidents emphasize any gains that have been made, and loudly deplore any losses. Comparing institutions, particularly with respect to salaries, has become a refined art.

General economic conditions also affect the funds available for higher education. For public institutions, state budgets are directly dependent on the health of the state economy which determines the size of the funding to be distributed. Budget limitation legislation (modeled on Proposition 13 in California) set an example for many states in changing from growth in state budgets that mirrored the economy, to constrained growth. Proposition 13 resulted in reducing the state budget available for all purposes, and this reduction was reflected in the allocations to state-supported higher education. Other needs, such as health care and prison reform, also pressed their claim for increasing their share of state support, further reducing funds for higher education.

Business & Economic Models

As the questions about higher education resource allocation continued and the demand for more and better answers about resource use grew, higher education looked to the business sector for help with analytical models. Accountants' use of unit cost analysis provided the basis for the early models that predicted resource needs; elaborate cost studies to analyze after-the-fact resource use were undertaken, and in some states tuition decisions were based on a cost model. The legislature might have reserved to itself the policy decision about the percentage of the cost that students should pay, but the cost analysis was the province of cost accountants and statisticians. Comparisons by type of institution were made, and NCHEMS sponsored intensive efforts to develop methodologies to prepare comparable costs. State coordinating agencies became the focus of much of this effort as their role was strengthened by legislatively mandated budgetary roles. Consolidated state higher education boards also developed cost and tuition analyses.

Business models had their limitations in application to higher education, and by the mid-1980s most states had moved away from formula and cost-study-based funding models. However, economic analysis continues to provide useful conceptual insights into the analysis of resource behavior. Besides traditional cost models, the work of organizational theorists such as James March and his work on the organized anarchy model for making decisions provide insights into how decisions are made in higher education.

CHANGING LANDSCAPE OF HIGHER EDUCATION

As the methodologies applied to higher education reflected changes, the underlying structure of higher education also evolved. Prior to World War II, higher education was either publicly supported through local and state government, or privately supported by student tuition payments and earnings from endowments. Federal support was largely restricted to agriculture and some support of land grant institutions. World War II and the federal decision to rely on research universities as the major engine in research and development led to a massive shift in the support for higher education. Not only did research universities increase significantly the amount of research conducted, but they also became dependent on federal resources to a far greater extent than before the war. Direct funding for research allowed staff and faculty to be added, buildings constructed and equipment acquired. Indirect funding not only reimbursed the additional costs imposed on institutions by the growth in research, but it provided a flexible cushion of institutionally-directed resources available to meet other needs. The other change in the underlying economic structure of higher education was the dependence on the federal government for student financial aid. By attenuating the link between the price of higher education and the student resources available to pay for it, institutions could be reasonably assured that students would continue to seek out higher education, even if prices continued to rise.

Two other factors changed the structure of higher education. One was the enormous growth in student enrollments and the acceptance of a higher education degree as almost a "requirement" for advancement. Prior to World War II and the subsequent baby boom, higher education and particularly advanced degree winners were a relatively small part of the population. By the late 1980s, a majority of the U.S. population had some exposure to higher education, with the percentage of bachelor's degree holders now around 25% of the working population. Sheer numbers led to a rapid expansion of higher education institutions and the growth of the peculiarly American institution, the community college.

The other significant factor altering the nature of higher education is related to the growth in other sources of income and auxiliary activities. Higher education institutions became less focused on one primary mission as they took on additional tasks. Below college level work for adults was shifted out of the K-12 school system and into higher education as returning soldiers, then immigrants and others, sought degrees. Responsibility for the education of recent immigrants was also part of the community college function. Higher education institutions run conference centers, house and feed large numbers of students, and may subsidize the development of research parks with technology originally developed in the research labs. All of these factors contribute to the increasing complexity of higher education, and pose problems for the analyst trying to determine something like "the cost of higher education."

HIGHER EDUCATION DIFFERS FROM BUSINESS

American higher education institutions can be very complex. In addition to their complexity, they differ in significant ways from the business enterprise which provides the basic model for economic analysis. These differences stem from both their non-profit status and their diffusely distributed organizational structure. Business enterprises are usually organized in a vertical fashion, in which workers are hired to produce a given output under centralized command and control. In most firms, there is a core from which leadership and control emanate.

Higher education differs in that the control of production, the interaction with students, or the production of research or other activities is controlled by the workforce itself, i.e., the faculty. A similar model exists in hospitals where decisions about how much and what kind of medical care is provided rests with the health care team. The advent of managed care and prescriptive regimens, drug formularies and restricted hospital stays have inserted a manager between the provider and the patient. No such intervening force has emerged in higher education, as the faculty member generally still has relative freedom in deciding what to teach, when and how, and almost complete freedom in deciding how and what kind of professional activity or research will be done.

Key Assumptions: Rationality

With the control of production not in the hands of management, the basic economic criterion of a rationally-organized central management structure cannot be used as a basis for analysis. Rationality is not the hallmark of decision-making in higher education. Analysts have suggested a prestige-maximizing model instead of a production-maximizing model, which may provide useful insights into hiring decisions, or the phenomenon of chasing academic stars. The nature and frequency of courses taught is decided by the faculty, often with relatively little reference to student demands. Administration at the department level is largely performed by existing faculty members who may be elected from the faculty as a whole. Except in support units, management is seldom by persons trained in management. The department chair is exquisitely sensitive to the nuances of the academic environment and serves as an interpreter of faculty preferences matched against student demand, but he or she may not be aware of vagaries in fueling streams or changing student demand. Research preferences usually remain the province of the individual, and do not reflect a group decision.

Non-Hierarchical

The department chair position as one among equals also suggests another characteristic that complicates analysis: the non-hierarchical nature of higher education organizations. Decisions about developing new fields of study may arise from individual faculty interests, a target of opportunity. Only rarely do they come from a considered decision involving more than just a few staff. Adding new staff is often a way that change takes place, and building a core of new offerings may result in the emergence of a new department in subsequent years. Because the decision-making structures are diffuse, it is rare that programs or fields of study are eliminated. In trying to apply rational decision-making processes, many state coordinating boards have adopted schemata for program review that assume that decisions about adopting or eliminating a program are rational, considered decisions. The failure of the efforts to reduce programs in this way is well documented. Program elimination does occur, but usually through repeated acts of starvation or with the retirement of a key individual.

No Bottom Line — Lack of Clear Measuring Stick — No Residual Claimant

Because there is no agreement about the bottom line, there is no residual claimant and therefore no one responsible for the overall success of the enterprise. Individual autonomous workers come and go, largely determine what it is that they will do and how they will do it, and are not concerned with the success of the institution as a whole. Decisions such as the price to be charged

112

for teaching (tuition) are divorced from an analysis of the impact of this decision on students. With no agreement on what the unit "ought" to be doing, there is no way to determine success or failure. As in the public schools, the particular success will differ with the individuals involved. Is success a winning football team? A new law school building? A training contract that attracts a new firm in the community?

Lack of Variation in Revenue Sources

A further complicating factor for the analyst and manager of a higher education institution is lack of predictability of principal revenue streams. Total tuition payments depend on student enrollments and changes can occur for reasons that are well beyond institutional control. Governmental support depends on legislative action or the ability of faculty to compete for research dollars. While this lack of certainty makes management more difficult, it also creates work for the institutional researcher. Enrollment flows, the basis for tuition revenue, and staffing decisions, have become a major workload item for most IR offices. Depending on the nature of the enrollments, these studies may involve student questionnaires, detailed studies of student preferences, and sophisticated models for predicting changes in these areas. Predicting governmental revenue decisions is more difficult with a random factor that complicates the crystal-ball gazing. Understanding the governmental structure and environment will enable better predictions. Items such as the relative taxing ability of the governmental unit, competing demands for revenue, growth and decline in population, tax base, as well as the influence of voter tax limitation initiatives, all affect the amount of governmental revenue. Predicting research revenue is very complicated because the actual success in obtaining research funds is affected by the ability of the faculty, governmental priority decisions about research areas, the amount of competition, etc.

Predictable revenue sources are usually relatively small and may be earmarked for specific uses. For instance, endowment may be designated for support of an endowed chair in Middle Eastern studies, or a named scholarship for students in particular fields of study. Large private institutions have devoted considerable attention to developing an endowment payout rate that reflects the general economy and institutional preferences for the use of their endowment. Stanford in particular has articulated models that led to institutional policy on how much to take from endowment every year for general campus support.

External Constraints

Institutional managers in public institutions face yet one more complicating factor. Governmental budgeting is typically done on a year-to-year basis. Unspent funds may lapse at the end of the fiscal period, making long-range planning difficult if not impossible. Lapsing funds leads to the "end-of-the-fiscal-year spending" syndrome where creative institutional managers see that any funds that might lapse are spent, and equally creative government accountants try to monitor this spending. Filling oil tanks or buying coal, buying equipment, or pre-obligating expenditures may all make the task of predicting the next fiscal periods needs more complicated for the analyst.

RECENT TRENDS - INSTITUTIONAL CHANGE

Not only are the institutions of higher education themselves becoming increasingly more complicated, the environment they operate in is increasing in diversity and complexity. At one time, most, if not all, postsecondary school education was dispensed through educational institutions. While there was a range of types of institution, governance structure, and markets, they were generally similar in being non-profit in nature and existing almost entirely for the purpose of education. Recently this has ceased to be the case in the United States as for-profit institutions take a larger share of the market. Distance education allows institutions in Florida to serve students in Japan who may never come to the United States. Companies offer degrees as part of their employee training program in addition to producing products. Even deciding what to include in the universe of higher education institutions becomes a quandary. Accrediting agencies operated to certify the quality of degrees and ensure certain minimum standards. They retained a powerful hold on higher education by making sure that federal financial aid was restricted to schools that were accredited by one of the regional accrediting agencies. Recent changes in the organization of accrediting and a rise in the number of specialized accrediting agencies have weakened the influence of these once powerful institutions. Some states have a centralized business registration process, which at least provides a list of those entities legally entitled to do business in the state. This may not be very helpful for purposes of actually doing analyses, though, because the institutions may have a very limited presence in the state. Washington, for instance, has six four-year public institutions with five branch campuses; 34 public two-year schools; 16 independent four-year institutions; 35 out of state authorized institutions; and another 35 religious exempt schools. The schools to be included in a research analysis obviously depend on the question being asked and the source of the question. Four-year schools are usually not interested in the average salaries or enrollment of two-year faculty, and vice versa. Schools planning new programs in management education, however, may be very interested in the universe of schools authorized to offer management training in the state.

Registration and notification vary state by state. With the growth of online degree programs, there will be fewer easy ways to determine the universe of competitors. Locating new and emerging offerings will be difficult, although searching the World Wide Web may provide a first cut.

Training offered within a business may be harder to identify, especially if its enrollees are restricted to employees or persons otherwise tied to the business. Internal business education departments were prevalent in U.S. businesses at one point, but with the overall economic pressure to downsize and become more efficient, businesses have tended to turn to specialized contract training organizations, including schools and colleges. The array of training opportunities has been greatly magnified by the growth of the World Wide Web. Specialized business training is often not degree related, no federal financial aid is available, nor is it necessary because businesses contract for exactly what they need.

FRAGMENTATION OF THE MARKET

The higher education environment has become much more fragmented than it once was. Whereas offering degrees was under the auspices of traditional residential institutions, there are now many more options for the student. Even accreditation may not mean much to students who are seeking specific training that is paid for by their employer and required to advance to the next job. Education is available in many different forms and from many different agencies, making discussion of resource use more diffuse and harder to focus. The institutional research analyst must be aware of the total market so that an appropriate arena can be defined. At the same time, there are many emerging educational providers that may become part of a more traditional institution, or may signal a change in the way a traditional institution views their students or markets.

Nowhere are the problems of the changing environment more apparent than in the hospitals and the health care industry. Medical training has long been within the purview of higher education institutions, and has usually been linked with one or more hospitals where doctors, nurses, radiologists, dental hygienists and others got at least some portion of their clinical training. Managed care has changed medical delivery — hospitals have to compete vigorously for patients and have been closed in the face of declining patient loads and inefficient operations. The market for the delivery of health care has changed dramatically in the last 10 years, and this has influenced the delivery of medical training. It is also a useful warning to higher education institutions who have not yet been affected by market forces of the magnitude of managed care. Higher education institutions have until recently controlled their own output and production processes, just as hospitals did. The analyst may find it worthwhile to review the influence of concerns about cost, the proliferation of regulation, and the effect on hospitals for interesting ways to bring the crystal ball for higher education into focus.

ANALYTICAL ISSUES - COST VS. PRICE

Price: Economists often talk about the price of a good or service. How does that apply to higher education? The first question that must be answered is the price for whom? This is particularly important in thinking about higher education and the price to students. Most institutions publish a schedule of tuition and fees to be paid by students, but, as has been recently pointed out, this is often only a starting place. What the student or her family actually ends up paying may be reduced by the amount of institutional or governmental financial aid available. Comparing tuition from one institution to another is only the beginning point of the analysis. Recent studies by large private schools have suggested that students on the whole end up paying about half of the published tuition. Prices for other aspects of higher education activity may be harder to analyze than tuition.

What is the price of preparing a research publication for example for <u>Nature</u>? Is it the amount of time the faculty member spends, times the dollar per hour rate? Is it what the National Science Foundation awarded to the principal investigator to do the research that led to the article? If price is complex for these questions, for less clearly defined transactions, price may not even be a useful concept.

Cost: A common assumption is that price is somehow related to cost. This has led to a number of fairly public debates about the "cost of higher education" where it is maintained that costs are rising because institutions are inefficient and faculty are greedy. What is being objected to as rising cost is really the level of published tuition. Institutions have responded along two fronts — one to point out the distinction between the published price and the actual average amount paid by students after financial aid is included, and the other is to point out that costs are rising because of governmental regulation and interference.

Neither of these arguments has relieved the pressure on higher education institutions to justify and defend their published tuition rates. Higher education does not function as a free market, and this also helps blur the issues. Highly selective institutions may compete among themselves for the same group of well-educated and superbly qualified students, but they do not compete by altering price. A major federal investigation into financial aid policies among a group of these institutions led to abolishing the informal practice of agreeing on financial aid awards, and there have been isolated cases of bargaining. Whether this will develop into a full-fledged practice remains to be seen, and may also reflect the underlying numbers of students vs. the number of spots to be filled. At the bottom of the high school graduation rate, colleges were more apt to try to use price adjustments to fill their enrollments, but with the burgeoning enrollments expected in the first decade of the 21st Century, institutions may end up using prices to ration student admissions.

The cost of higher education is derived arbitrarily. The reason for its complexity and essentially arbitrary nature is the joint production issue referred to earlier. If faculty effort results in more than one output, how should the institution form the basis for allocating the faculty member's salary? Several national studies have developed approaches to determining cost. Generally, a cost accounting has been used, relying on the faculty member's diary as a record of effort spent. More recent efforts have essentially given up on trying to subdivide faculty effort, (and hence costs), and have stated simply that there was a joint output known as instruction and departmental research that was produced by a faculty member. Efforts to further refine this definition have not been successful. Looking at other costs besides faculty time have been a bit more successful, because in many of these cases it is possible to say that particular inputs are only associated with particular and specific outputs. Materials bought on a sponsored research grant for a specific research project may be associated with the output of that research project, for example.

DETERMINING COSTS

Unit cost studies were among the earliest institutional research efforts, as concerns over resource use and the distribution of costs by level of student emerged. States such as Virginia and Washington mandated uniform cost studies primarily for setting tuition rates. These models were widely studied during the 1970s and 80s but fell out of favor when it became obvious that they were essentially arbitrary and of limited usefulness in comparing disparate institutions. Major differences in institutional or governmentally mandated accounting systems resulted in data that simply could not be compared across state boundaries, or between public and private institutions. The National Accounting Standards process resulted in two separate accounting standards, one for public institutions and one for private institutions. Although efforts to bring these together for higher education has started, there are still significant differences in how institutions record basic accounting data that make analysis very difficult.

Differences also exist by institutional type — large complex research universities with multiple inputs and multiple outputs found that they had to adopt essentially arbitrary conventions governing the allocation of faculty time in order to allocate costs. For a brief period of time Faculty Activity Analyses studies were the vogue in cost allocation analysis, and were in favor with state legislatures who wanted to know how much faculty were teaching.

Cost studies also exist in a political context. Legislative dissatisfaction with ever-increasing requests for support of higher education have resulted in several national taskforces on the costs of higher education. The most recent of these resulted in a vigorous defense of the costs as being reasonable for what higher education enables a student to do. This justification for current practice provided some solace to the critics of higher education by mandating reporting of cost data.

For the institutional researcher, there are several key items in conducting cost studies, and in trying to answer questions about institutional costs.

1) Understand the questions behind the questions. What are the major political and philosophical undercurrents that have led to asking for

information about costs? What does the person asking the question understand and/or assume about the nature of higher education? What will the answer be used for?

2) Understand the way the data are recorded. An institutional researcher must understand the institutional accounting system where expenditures are recorded. Are benefits recorded centrally or individually; are expenditures recorded when the item is ordered or when it is received? Are faculty budgeted in an aggregate, or by an organization unit that is the same one that is the unit of analysis? Are teaching assistants recorded by department or the college as a whole? Are salary savings (unspent amounts for salary) recorded where they were intended to be used and weren't, or are they recaptured and recorded and used for some other purpose?

3) Understand the organizational structure of the institution in order to determine what units of analysis make sense. The organizational structure usually provides the framework for recording expenditures, but occasionally may not. Some research functions may be an aggregation of individuals who are budgeted in departments, but who get together to work on projects, advise students, and even receive grants. A budget may not exist for this unit, and it may or may not be formally recognized on any organization chart. Because higher education institutions are large, complex, non-hierarchical and organic, the policies and procedures that identify inputs may be very difficult to determine. For instance, in a hierarchically-organized organization such as General Motors or Wal-Mart, it is almost always possible to say who works for whom, and what organization they are paid by. In universities, however, faculty whose salary is the major component of instructional cost may be teaching in areas where they are not paid, or organizations that do not have a budget. Where they teach may change from quarter to quarter and even within a quarter.

This is not to say that it is impossible to determine how to assign costs, just that it may be difficult, and may require a number of arbitrary allocation rules which will dramatically affect the resultant outcome. There is no substitute for the analyst knowing the institution, and understanding how the data will be used, in order to make the results as useful as possible.

Many of the problems encountered in determining costs result from trying to apply a business model to higher education, as well as attempting to disaggregate the data. At the institutional level it is possible to say how much it costs to teach all the students. Trying to break this total average cost for all students to the cost of medical students, undergraduates in electrical engineering, or majors in Far Eastern study leads to many of the intricacies, as well as the need for arbitrary conventions.

SETTING PRICES

In profit-making businesses, the concept of a price is fairly clear. Businesses set prices to allow some excess over the cost to return to the firm. This excess is then the basis for a reward to the entrepreneur or investor who has provided part of the cost of establishing the business. Profit is also a reward for taking risks. Higher education institutions do not produce one single, clearly defined product, and in particular do not relate costs to prices to generate a profit. (The recent growth of for-profit colleges such as the University of Phoenix may alter this in the future, although even here, price or tuition seems at first blush to be linked to comparative prices rather than costs.) The closest analogy to prices in traditional higher education is tuition charged to students. The fairly steady increase in tuition has resulted in national attention, and in 1996 a presidential panel to review the Cost of Higher Education was established. The focus was on price; the cost to the parent and student of attending college. The Commission's report was a vigorous defense of the value of higher education, and suggested that contrary to the popular impression of the high cost of higher education, most students did not pay full cost because of financial aid. The Commission also pointed out that the value (to an individual) of going to college far outweighed the tuition cost. The report was not entirely satisfactory to the critics of higher education, and the national debate continues. A separate but related study is still underway. Calls for the National Center on Higher Education Statistics to conduct a study of costs and develop some actual numbers to report to Congress by 2002. Whether these will be any more successful in answering critics and defusing the argument remains to be seen.

Tuition and the sensitivity of students to different prices is a field of ongoing study for institutional researchers. Colleges and universities have experimented with altering prices to attract students, or freezing tuition at a certain level to encourage students to remain enrolled. Students' preferences for a given college seem only loosely related to the cost of attending; most studies suggest that students define their choice domain for college based on where their friends or family are going or have gone, or where a particular field is taught. In many cases the more expensive the college, the more sought after it is, so in that sense, the price of attendance may be related in an inverse fashion to attraction.

The relation of tuition level to attendance may be crucially important to sub groups of students, and here the institutional researcher can help develop a careful analysis. There is widespread tuition discounting through financial aid in many forms. Knowledge of the availability of financial aid may not be widespread, particularly among target groups, and institutional researchers can help assess the impact of this information.

As in many other aspects of the study of higher education, comparative data on tuition is extremely important, particularly in the crucial time period where tuition levels for the next year are set. Tuition is determined in a variety of ways — some places set it at the institution level, others by the state. Individual tuition may be derived almost after the fact so that total tuition revenue is enough to fill the gap between other sources of revenue and the total budget required. Private schools may determine tuition levels after setting an overall budget, and after determining what other available sources of revenue will generate. State sponsored schools, even those that determine their own tuition, may determine total revenue and only then set the institutional budget.

ANALYZING EFFICIENCY AND PRODUCTIVITY

Institutional research expertise is often called for by resource managers who are trying to understand whether there can be improvements made in the allocation of resources. How do we know whether this is the right amount to spend for undergraduate instruction in English? What does it cost to field a basketball team and what other uses might these resources be put to? The National Association of College and University Business Officers have devoted considerable attention to the use of benchmarking in an attempt to help institutions analyze their own resource uses. Benchmarking calls for organizations to compare their policies, practices and performances against other highly-ranked organizations, and adapt those that promise meaningful results. Coming from the total quality improvement movement, there are clear applications to the business and support activities of higher education. The most difficult aspect of benchmarking is trying to find out where the exemplary organizations are. The network of interinstitutional connections that institutional research officers maintain can be very helpful in locating them.

COMPARATIVE STUDIES

Perhaps one of the major jobs of an institutional research office, and one that makes it extremely valuable to institutional decision-makers, is their ability to gather and analyze information on what other institutions are doing. Conventions of interinstitutional analysis and appropriate use of comparisons are described in works by Brinkman and Teeter in The Primer for Institutional Research (AIR, 1992, pp. 63-72). Analysis that is useful to institutional resource decision-makers must be based on a thorough understanding of the ways entities can be compared. Comparing dollars per FTE student makes almost no sense at all unless there is a detailed understanding of what elements enter both the numerator and the denominator. Legislative and governing boards are very fond of using broad brush comparisons, such as $/FTE, because they appear to suggest that some institutions are more efficient than others. However, the numbers should be viewed with skepticism.

Some states have developed highly articulated comparison models upon which to base funding requests. Kansas in particular has a funding model that involves collection of data from a number of states, and preparation of recommendations based on the relative standing of the Kansas institutions.

Because the numbers that are used in summary form are derived after painstaking analysis and collection, they have gained credibility.

Another very common use of institutional comparisons is in the area of faculty salaries. Because competition over faculty is an important part of the academic workplace, identifying what average salaries at institutions send faculty to an institution are extremely important to decision-makers. Salaries at institutions seeking to hire faculty away are equally important. Where institutions have flexibility in determining salary increases, the relationship of salaries here and elsewhere may preoccupy the decision-makers in allocating new money. Richard Howard, Julie Snyder and Gerald McLaughlin present an overview of salary analysis with respect to competition, compression and equity in the Primer, and examples of typical analysis and sources of data are shown. Because faculty salaries are a large portion of the total costs of an institution, and since the well being of the faculty is of crucial importance to the institution, this analysis is usually a major function of the institutional research office.

Not only are comparative average salaries important, but entry-level salaries are of particular concern. While entry salaries are only one element of a total package that is needed to attract faculty to a given institution, it is a crucial one. Other elements of this "package" may include work space, lab equipment, teaching course load, access to graduate students, opportunities for release time and entrepreneurial activity, and, of course, traditional insurance and other benefits, including employment for a spouse or partner.

TECHNOLOGY

Acquiring and funding technology has become an increasing worry for campus administrators. Relatively few schools have had the luxury of providing an ongoing technology reserve that replaces hardware and software on a regular basis. Funding flows are often fully committed (if not over committed) and earmarking significant amounts of money for technology replacement has been difficult. Enterprise-wide administrative support systems are an even bigger worry, as older main frame systems cannot provide the support required by distance education and other instructional activities. Many of the larger campuses initially developed administrative support systems in the 1970s and 80s, and only now are beginning to realize that they are inadequate. Turning to the commercial sector for enterprise-wide integrated systems that handle financial, personnel, facilities and student systems has not been a success. Higher education institutions, while not large compared to some businesses, have significant complexities arising from their non-hierarchical nature, distributed decision-making power, and intricate structure. The ideology of collaborative decision-making pervades higher education even on the administrative side, making it ponderous and slow. Modern administrative systems may require significant changes in the way institutions have grown accustomed to doing business, and this adds to the complexity. In addition, because many institutions have lived with basically the same administrative systems for many years, staff have customized them to provide the features that they want. Learning to go with a "plain vanilla" system, while it may hold costs down, may put burdens on staff that they are unable to absorb without significant dislocation.

An additional complicating factor in technology planning has been the recent and widespread introduction of technology into the instructional process. Computing has been supporting administrative functions for many years, but its presence in technology was much more limited until very recently. With the growth of distance education and the use of mediated instruction in classrooms, technology expenditures have increased dramatically. Instructional technology, unlike administrative technology, continues to evolve relatively rapidly and is spread among many vendors with specialized applications. With each faculty member acting as their own technology expert, there is little standardization. In this environment, expenditures for instructional technology can be expected to grow relatively rapidly for a number of years.

CAPITAL

Managing resources for capital expenditure is a relatively specialized area. The amounts involved are usually somewhat less than for operating expenditures. The capital budget may run between 10 and 20 percent of the operating budget. Particularly in public institutions, capital budgets are separated legislatively from operating budgets, with limited opportunities for crossover. The growth of deferred maintenance that is well documented in the physical facilities literature reflects increased pressures on operating budgets, reducing the funds available for day-to-day maintenance. Increasingly, campuses find themselves facing a wholesale capital renovation of a facility simply because routine maintenance has not kept up with building deterioration. Changing building usage, increasing environmental and safety concerns, and changing academic programs have also resulted in buildings that are obsolete. Prioritizing limited maintenance budgets may also be an issue; frequently projects blend between true maintenance and the need to meet academic program demands. Capital is "lumpy" — that is, it is not a continuous rate of expenditure but rather is associated with physical entities that come in fixed quantities. Building renovations are difficult when only partially done.

High technology research facilities located on university campuses are very expensive. Institutions increasingly have been exploring partnerships, use of gifts and grants, and joint developments as ways of providing these resources. Pressures on institutional budgets have led to the development of extremely creative arrangements, and a blurring of any distinction between institutional/ commercial and institutional/private resources.

ECONOMIC IMPACT

Institutions of higher education have a significant impact on their surrounding communities. A specialized study of these impacts is often requested of institutional research offices in the form of an economic impact study. Several formats for these studies have been developed, and they often include an estimate of a multiplier effect of local expenditures. Economic impact studies depend for their results on how this multiplier is estimated. Multipliers are often borrowed from regional economic studies rather than developed at the institutional level. Economic impact studies may become part of an institution's marketing and outreach activities as the institution establishes its importance to the local or state marketplace.

AUXILIARY ENTERPRISES

Higher education institutions have varied support functions; many mirror activities in the community. Police, fire, purchasing, deliveries, utility system operation, banking, payroll, etc., all have institutional counterparts. Managing resources for these entities have many similarities to their operation in the community. Benchmarking, quality improvement, and just-in-time inventory all are examples of techniques that started in private enterprise and have been applied to higher education. The National Association of College and University Business Officers (NACUBO) annually sponsors a contest for most effective cost saving ideas. Recent winners provide many more examples of the application of good business management practice to higher education. However, the complexity of the educational institutions may make application of these techniques difficult, and the presence of a decentralized, non-hierarchical decision system further complicates implementation. Student housing and food services have been affected by many of the market trends that affect the community. For example, students growing up in smaller families are less willing to share dormitory rooms and they expect rooms to be fully wired for television and computer use. Accommodating these changing social demands has imposed significant cost burdens on institutions. There are also swings in the popularity of on-campus versus off-campus housing, and misjudging the cycle can leave campuses over-built or over-subscribed.

TOOLS

Budgeting

Forecasting, control, and management in higher education are all summarized in the institutional budget. The NACUBO handbook, <u>College and University Budgeting: An Introduction for Faculty and Academic Administrators</u>, defines the budget as serving seven functions. It is a mechanism for setting priorities, an institutional plan of action, an institutional contract, a control mechanism, a gauge of risk, an instrument of communication, and a political device. The budget is the place where decisions are reduced to definite resource implications, where new directions are identified and where reductions are indicated. Budgets cover several time periods, are usually not updated against expenditures, and may have arcane local conventions whereby institutional realities are conveniently ignored. One prominent research university never formally budgeted graduate student teaching appointments on the grounds that these were always temporary and could go away at any time. The college deans paid for GSA's by generating salary savings from regular faculty appointments on leave or with time bought out by research grants.

Institutional budgeting may be constrained by the institutional governance — public institutions may have the form of their budgets specified by state or local government. Budgets and the processes that lead to them may be public or closely held, and individual salaries may be disclosed or not, depending on the institution. While conventions in displaying budgets have increased over time, there is little uniformity from one institution to another. Particular areas for the analyst to observe include how benefits are budgeted (centrally or to the individual), how salary vacancies and savings are treated, and how the various funding sources are treated in the budget. An institutional research analyst must learn to read the budget, and also to ask in each case whether the budget or expenditure record is better for the particular use in question.

Setting the annual institutional budget provides a clear opening into the internal operations and balance of power on the campus. Particularly important is the role of the faculty, either as decision-makers or in consulting institutional priorities and determining how any new funds are allocated. There may be a formal budget decision-making process and an informal one. The analyst must be aware of both in order to understand how decisions are made.

A Special Case — Responsibility Centered Management

A recent development in institutional management has grown from the experience at several private schools where each organizational unit was made responsible for its own budget. Pioneered and widely publicized at the University of Pennsylvania, responsibility-centered budgeting set fees that each college paid for central services, and provided for a system of transfers of resources from profit-generating schools (professional schools largely), to the undergraduate colleges. Because of governmental and institutional constraints, responsibility-centered management has not been widely applied.

Services

Some services are provided on a fee-for-service basis. Particularly in the case of services provided to externally-funded research projects, it has been feasible to develop a cost, analogous to a cost in private business, and apply this to the service. Analysis of these costs can often suggest ways in which resources can be reduced and service increased.

STATE BUDGET PRACTICE

Institutional budgeting for public institutions has often been shaped by the budgeting practices of the state governing agencies. When states adopted PPBS in the late 60s and 70s, institutions developed parallel program budgeting systems. Allocation formulas used by legislative budget offices showed up in campus budgets when formulas were in vogue. Performance budgeting is the latest budgeting strategy used by states in an effort to improve accountability. Colleges and universities are awarded funds based on how well they perform on certain measures. South Carolina has developed a full range of 37 different measures of performance, and is planning to allocate all institutional funds based on performance. Other states have instituted variations on performance measures. The recent *New Directions in Institutional Research*, (Performance Funding for Public Higher Education: Fad or Trend, No. 97, Spring 1998) summarized many of the recent developments in performance funding.

These state budget procedures have had relatively little effect on actual budgeting practices of institutions except for the work required to create a parallel format. Much institutional practice reflects the realities of institutional decision-making, concentrating on funding for faculty positions, (either replacements or new), salary increases, and the occasional new initiative. Institutional budgeting tends to be based on existing budget levels, while some schools in the wake of the PPBS and Zero-based budgeting schemes adopted a decision package approach to budgeting. There has tended to be a fairly clear dividing line between the justifications used to obtain funds from central authorities and that used to allocate funds within the institution.

Understanding resource allocation in an institution requires an understanding of the political and decision-making structure of the institution. A somewhat dated but still useful analysis of different styles of university decision-making is in Leadership and Ambiguity by James G. March and Michael D. Cohen. In describing metaphors of leadership with respect to the presidential role, they name eight distinct styles: competitive market, administrative, collective bargaining, democratic, consensus, anarchy, independent judiciary and plebiscitary autocracy. Each of these leadership descriptions translates into an organizational and decision-making style that can shape resource decisions. Cohen and March favor the term "organized anarchy" to describe higher education institutions, and this description has some creditability among students of higher education.

The institutional researcher must not be satisfied with printed budgets and rows of numbers. To make effective use of these data, answers must be found to questions of "how" and "why." Observing the formal and informal decision processes of an institution will provide information, as does watching how decisions are altered, whether they stay final or are adjusted as individuals express themselves. In public institutions there may be formal priority announcements, especially before legislative sessions. Private institutions may have a more guarded and hidden process. Resource analysis in the absence of organizational analysis may not yield useful predictions, and the institutional research office's knowledge of internal structure will sharpen the analysis.

In addition to understanding the formal and informal organizational structure, knowing something about the nature of prestige in American higher education may be helpful. There is a definite "pecking order" to traditional higher education — graduate school rankings, awarding of research dollars and presence of Nobel Laureates among the faculty, are all evidences of prestige among institutions. Knowing which school your institution aspires to be will be helpful in presenting analysis. Incorporating a comparison to these aspirant peers may be more helpful to decision-makers than relying on in state institutions or local neighbors. Institutions that compete for student enrollment may form another comparison group that guides decision-making.

BEST PRACTICES

Another type of comparative analysis that originated in the quality improvement movement deals with the identification of best practices. Private industry uses benchmarking as a way of measuring the difference between existing and ideal states, and higher education can do the same thing. Trying to determine what the best practice relates to may be difficult. Institutions where student satisfaction is high, institutions that are efficiently run, or institutions that attract faculty expertise all may provide some examples of how to do things better. Because traditional higher education has been relatively static compared to the more rapidly changing industrial sector, changing practices can be threatening. Institutional researchers, by serving in their intelligence gathering mode, may be a good source of information on places where improvements may be copies or good practices shared.

SOURCES OF INFORMATION

There are a number of resources available for information analysis, including national databases such as those at the National Center for Educational Statistics or the National Science Foundation. The American Association of Community College's Web site has a number of reports comparing and analyzing community colleges. The advent of the World Wide Web has made searching for data easier in many respects. The AIR Web site maintains a list of resources, as does the Society for College and University Planning. Formal publication programs also provide a ready source of information. Listservs that link educational technology planners, community college administrators, registrars, and IR analysts all exist and can be a good source of quick responses to queries or as guides to further resources.

There have been several national commissions and national reports that contribute significantly to resource allocation analysis. The American Association of State Colleges and Universities, the American Association of Community Colleges, and the National Association of State Universities and Land Grant Colleges sponsored the Joint Commission on Accountability Reporting (1997) which has released reports on faculty activity, student charges, student advancement and student employment. With many institutions facing increasingly probing questions about what they were doing, the three associations developed a number of reporting conventions and report formats that could be used to present information in a way that could be understood by the general public, and even compared across institutions.

Another ground-breaking study on institutional productivity originated out of the institutional research office at the University of Delaware, where for a number of years Michael Middaugh has prepared information at a discipline level on productivity ratios. Unlike some of the more mindless attempts to compare dollars per FTE, lengthy comparative analysis precedes data collection. Analysts envisioning working with these data should carefully review the conventions and cautions that are behind these studies.

OTHER RESOURCE ANALYSIS FUNCTIONS OF THE IR OFFICE

Because institutional research analysts serve as general support to decision-makers, they can provide early information on the efficiency of resource use within an institution. Having comparative data helps in drawing these conclusions, but an equally valid approach is simply to look at variations within an institution and ask the question "why?" Why are social sciences less expensive to teach than performing arts? By how much? Is this an institutional desirable ratio? How big should the programs get? Colleges and universities are an intricate web of cross subsidies, in addition to joint production. Large undergraduate classes taught by graduate student appointments may allow tenured full professors to specialize in their own research and guide the doctoral work of graduate students. Reviewing the distribution of teaching effort by various kinds of teachers will provide some indication of the subsidies. Growing use of part-time faculty, now in all institutions, not just community colleges, provides another measure of the relative importance of preserving lighter teaching loads for permanent staff.

Uncertainty and risk are part of the decision-maker's world. The institutional research analyst may be able to help in identifying the sources of risk, and with careful predictions, indicate the range of risk. Studying the variation in revenue streams and potential funding sources may indicate the exposure due to changing enrollment demand. Analysis of rate of return from an endowment portfolio will also help the analyst recommend a pay out rate that will preserve the bulk of the endowment, yet provide much needed supplemental funding. (Private institutions have developed the analysis of an appropriate payout rate.)

Using market intelligence gained from familiarity with the national higher education landscape, institutional research analysts may be able to identify targets of opportunity that would serve to increase funds, or develop new sources of funding. Targets of opportunity may come from careful scrutiny of the local community, along with familiarity with local business. Environmental scanning is useful in a formal planning process, but it is also part of the daily life of the institutional researcher. The biggest part of the environment for higher education is what other higher education institutions are doing.

LOOKING TO THE FUTURE

Higher education in the late 20th Century has undergone rapid change internally, with the impact of changing governmental support, technology, increasing external unfunded mandates, and changing student bodies. Externally, there are many more providers of higher education outside the traditional institutions than there were 10 years ago, and traditional schools no longer have a monopoly on providing training and education. While degree conferral, particularly at the graduate level, is largely still held by traditional institutions, undergraduate level education is now available in a variety of formats. Further, the consumer has changed as the growth in the market-priced entrepreneurial institutions, such as the University of Phoenix, have shown. Working adults are willing to pay near the top of the market range to take classes taught by practitioners at times and locations that are convenient to them.

This growth in non-traditional, unaccredited and entrepreneurial organizations presents enormous competitive challenges for higher education. Increasingly, students are voting for convenient education, putting less emphasis on the four-year campus experience. While there will always be room for some of these institutions, public support for any expansion is dubious. Institutions that want to remain viable will need to adapt some of the techniques of their competitors.

References

Burke, J. C. & Serban, A. M. (Vol. Eds.). (1998). New Directions in Institutional Research: No. 97. Performance funding for public higher education: Fad or trend? San Francisco, CA: Jossey-Bass Publishers.

Caruthers, J. K. & Wentworth, C. L. (1997). Methods and techniques of revenue forecasting. In D. T. Layzell (Vol. Ed.), New Directions for Institutional Research: No. 93. Forecasting and managing enrollment and revenue: An overview of current, trends, issues, and methods. San Francisco, CA: Jossey-Bass Publishers.

Cohen, M. D. & March, J. G. (1974). Leadership and ambiguity: The American college president. New York, NY: McGraw Hill.

Doi, J. I. (1961). The proper use of faculty load studies. in Studies of College Faculty. Berkeley, CA: Western Interstate Commission for Higher Education and Center for Research and Development in Higher Education.

Foster, E. (1989-90). Planning at the University of Minnesota. Planning for Higher Education. Vol. 18, (2), 25-38.

Haberaecker, H. J. (1992). Cost analysis. In M. A. Whiteley, J. D. Porter, & R. H. Fenske (Eds.), The Primer for Institutional Research. Tallahassee, FL: Association for Institutional Research.

Hanson, G. R. & B. R. Price. (1992). Academic program review. In M. A. Whiteley, J. D. Porter, & R. H. Fenske (Eds.), The Primer for Institutional Research. Tallahassee, FL: Association for Institutional Research.

Heyne, P. (1994). The economic way of thinking. New York, NY: Macmillian College Publishing Company.

Hollins. C. S. (Vol. Ed.) (1992). New Directions in Institutional Research: No. 75. Containing costs and improving productivity in higher education. San Francisco, CA: Jossey-Bass Publishers.

Howard, R. D., Snyder, J. K., & McLaughlin, G. W. (1992). Faculty salaries. In M. A. Whiteley, J. D. Porter, & R. H. Fenske (Eds.), The Primer for Institutional Research. Tallahassee, FL: Association for Institutional Research.

Jedamus, P. & Peterson, M. W. (1980). Improving academic management: A handbook of planning and institutional research. San Francisco, CA: Jossey-Bass Publishers.

Katz, R. N., & Oblinger, D. G. (1999). Renewing administration: Preparing colleges and universities for the 21st century. Bolton, MA: Anker Publishing Company.

Middaugh, M. F. & Hollowell, D. E. (1992). Examining academic and administrative productivity measures. In C. S. Hollins (Vol. Ed.), New Directions for Institutional Research: No. 75. Containing costs and improving productivity in higher education. San Francisco, CA: Jossey-Bass Publishers.

Morgan, A. (1984). The new strategies: Roots, context, and overview. In L. L. Leslie (Vol. Ed.), New Directions for Institutional Research. No. 43. Responding tonew realities in funding. San Francisco, CA: Jossey-Bass Publishers.

Rooney, P. M., Borden, V. M. H., & Thomas, T. J. (1999). How much does instruction and research really cost? <u>Planning for Higher Education</u>. Ann Arbor, MI: Society for College and University Planning.

Russell, T. D. (1946). Service loads of faculty members. In <u>Problems of Faculty Personnel. Proceedings of the Institute for Administrative Officers of Higher Education</u>. Chicago, IL: University of Chicago Press.

Symposium on the economics of higher education. (1999). <u>The Journal of Economic Perspectives. Vol. 13</u>, (1).

Teeter, D. J. & Brinkman, P. (1992). Peer institutions. In M. A. Whiteley, J. D. Porter, & R. H. Fenske (Eds.), <u>The Primer for Institutional Research</u>. Tallahassee, FL: Association for Institutional Research.

Trainer, J. F. (Vol. Ed.). (1996). <u>New Directions in Institutional Research: No. 89. Inter-institutional data exchange: When to do it, what to look for, and how to make it work</u>. San Francisco, CA: Jossey-Bass Publishers.

CHAPTER 5: PLANNING AND POLICY ANALYSIS

Authors: John D. Porter, Robert H. Fenske, and Jonathan E. Keller[1]

This chapter focuses on planning and policy analysis related to the major governance and executive functions of an institution. Issues include policy and management analyses, strategic and tactical planning processes; operations research; and decision support.

The policy and management analyses, strategic and tactical planning requirements, and institutional mission development activities of the institutional researcher are influenced significantly by the governance structures present in the state and institution. The uniqueness and complexity of the governance mechanisms that characterize each institution has a direct bearing on the institutional researcher's activities. Because planning and policy-making at all levels requires data collection and analysis, the institutional researcher is usually the one called upon by many stakeholders to respond to a broad and complex array of needs. For the institutional researcher to succeed, he or she must be cognizant of the intricacies of the governance structure, the history and traditions of the institution, the deeply held values of the stakeholders, and how the bureaucracy of the institution works.

This chapter discusses how these structures impact the policy analysis and planning activities performed by the institutional researcher. Additionally, policy analysis often leads to planning as policies are implemented. Therefore, the interconnectedness of governance, policy analysis, and planning is demonstrated. Where appropriate, examples are used to illustrate the activities that the institutional researcher may be asked to perform. Also, potentially helpful resources are identified whenever possible.

GOVERNANCE

The system of governance has a significant impact on the requirements made of the institutional researcher. The more governing agencies or levels of oversight, greater is the complexity and potential for political influence. The institutional researcher must understand and navigate this environment if he or she is to be successful. Often, multiple and at times conflicting demands are made for research to support decision-making on a diverse range of issues at both the internal and external levels of authority. Internally, faculty and administrators require data and analysis related to funding requests, curriculum decisions, admissions policies, hiring practices and other areas of institutional policy and planning. Coordinating agencies, governing boards and legislatures also seek data and analysis concerning issues that faculty and administrators are interested in, but from the standpoint of external oversight. These multiple layers of governance utilize the services of the institutional researcher for varying purposes, expectations, and to support levels of perceived and actual influence over institutional policy and practice.

Over the years, the structure and focus of governance in American higher education has expanded greatly. For example, development of statewide coordinating boards added another layer of external governance; growth of faculty senates and unions added complexity to internal governance. Yet, no single model for balancing power and authority has emerged. Some systems of higher education have broadly shared oversight capacities, while others are more narrowly focused under a single authority. The level to which governance should be shared is the subject of continuing debate, and has a direct influence on the activities of the institutional researcher. The greater the sharing of authority within the system, the more uncertain are the requirements on the institutional researcher. This uncertainty is a reflection of what Baldridge referred to as the "goal ambiguity" of the college/university mission (Baldridge, et al., 1977, p. 3).

> What is the goal of the university? This is a difficult question, for the list of possible answers is long: teaching, research, service to the local community, administration of scientific installations, support of the arts, solutions to social problems . . . . .

The broad-based mission of a university is an expression of the diverse values and preferences of its leaders. Through the exercise of power and influence, certain values and preferences may gain ascendancy, but often for only a temporary timeframe. As in most other areas of public and private governance, the priorities of higher education management are transitory, influenced by changing conditions, power structures and perceptions.

The locus of control and influence in higher education governance has historically shifted, based on fluctuating levels of empowerment among the various layers of oversight. In more recent history, the locus appears to have shifted away from institutional self-governance and toward external coordinating and governance boards (Hearn, et al. 1994), although the power of the university president generally remains strong. For public higher education institutions in the United States, these external boards tend to be centralized at the state level, making for a governance scenario that differs widely among the 50 states. In most other countries around the world, higher education is overseen by a single ministry of education which governs all of the nation's institutions. In contrast, the U.S. federal government exerts only circumspect influence over the policies and practices of higher education institutions, despite the significant federal revenues that are provided through research grants and student financial assistance. This unique aspect of American higher education oversight is the outcome of its unusual history and evolution.

Historical Antecedents of Governance

The earliest institutions of higher education in America were the colonial colleges, which functioned mainly as theological seminaries for young men preparing to enter into the clergy. The first of these was Harvard, founded in 1636 by Puritans. By 1776, there were eight church-affiliated institutions: Harvard, William and Mary, Yale, Princeton, Columbia, Brown, Dartmouth, and Rutgers (Domonkos, 1977). Lay boards, often dominated by prominent clergy, had authority over every aspect of these early institutions. The notion and practice of oversight by a lay board was adopted from the northern European model of lay control over Protestant churches (Kauffman, 1983). Separate lay board control is still a common feature of American higher education, even though the predominance of church-based colleges gradually gave way to public and private secular institutions. The public lay boards are primarily composed of either elected officials or gubernatorial appointees, and often reflect the political leanings and social philosophy of those who selected them. They tend to serve for limited terms, affording periodic fluctuations in the prevailing attitudes and preferences of the board as a whole. Private lay boards also have members that are elected or appointed, usually by alumni or distinguished members of the university community, for widely varying terms of service. Because the private boards tend to be self-perpetuating, they are more insulated from changing state-level interests and expectations.

The President

Throughout the nineteenth and early twentieth centuries, powerful lay boards directed the activities of colleges and universities with almost unfettered control. However, as American higher education began to show significant growth in both scope and complexity, lay governing boards started to delegate substantial levels of authority to college presidents. This was especially true in the period following the Civil War (Carnegie Commission, 1976). College presidents were given decision-making power over a wide variety of matters related to the day-to-day functioning of the institution. Today, the remnants of the "strong president" model of organizational dominance can be clearly seen in American higher education. While the president shares power with many other stakeholders in governing the institution, the "presidency" has authority and influence far beyond that of any other single group. Furthermore, the president is the most important point of contact between the external board and the institutional administration. At times, the president serves as both a buffer and a bridge between these two entities. In many ways, this is similar to the role public boards fill as a buffer and bridge between the legislature and the institution.

The Academy

The academy also performs a major role in college and university governance. Kauffman suggests that one of the crucial events which helped to create a shift in the relations of boards, presidents and the faculty was the establishment of the American Association of University Professors (AAUP) in 1915 (1983). The founding of the AAUP was triggered by the dismissal of an eminent Stanford economics professor because the wife of the university's founder did not like the beliefs embodied in his teachings. Professors felt that they were powerless to resist the whims of the lay boards and presidents (Brubacher and Rudy, 1968). Although the original mission of the AAUP was primarily to defend the principles of academic freedom, the organization eventually expanded its mission to include advocating "collegial governance."

Faculty Senates

Many of the early European universities emerged as alliances of scholars who greatly valued autonomy and were able to create self-governed associations. Paul Westmeyer asserted that in Europe, the faculty was the university in its entirety and not simply employees (1990, p. 5).

American institutions never actually got off on the same foot. From the very beginning, except for those institutions where the college president was a member of the board...faculty were seen as employees. And even if the president...was on the board he still served at the pleasure of the board.

In certain instances, faculties were not interested in gaining governance responsibilities that might be burdensome, especially for areas of oversight beyond the specific realm of their own departments and disciplines. However, some faculty yearned for a greater voice in decision-making at the highest levels, particularly with regard to the appointment of deans, vice presidents and presidents. In the late 1940s and 1950s, faculty senates began to emerge as a viable means to expand the power and influence of the faculty as a whole. The relative authority of the faculty senates varies greatly from institution to institution and rarely remains constant over a course of years. This relative level of power and influence is dependent on the initiatives taken by the senate and the ongoing conflicts between the institution's internal layers of authority and control.

Shared Governance

The "collegial" or "shared" forms of governance that are common in American higher education today involve multiple layers of management. These multiple layers may be found both internally and externally to the institution. The external layers include legislatures, coordinating boards, and governing boards. Although these external layers retain significant legal authority, they share decision-making responsibilities with a complex and uniquely dichotomous structure of oversight within the institution. Birnbaum asserts there are two primary types of authority exerted over the internal aspects of decision-making: administrative and professional (1991).

Administrative authority tends to follow traditional lines of management (i.e. from president to vice-president to provosts to vice-provosts to deans) and reflects the corporate model of management. The foremost focus of this form of authority is on the clearly delineated chain of command, which starts with a single authoritarian figure and flows down to the many. Professional authority, on the other hand, begins with the many and ends with limited power in the hands of the few. The most important stakeholders in the professional authority model are the faculties who, through academic or faculty senates, promote academic autonomy and the affirmation of academic freedom and tenure. One possible way to visualize the nature of institutional shared governance is to imagine a six-pointed star composed of one triangle with the vertex facing up and an equal overlapping triangle with the vertex facing down. The triangle with the vertex facing up represents the administrative hierarchy, with the president at the narrow apex. The opposite triangle represents the professional power structure, in which widespread coalitions of faculty form the highest level of authority. The overlapping area is the realm of the faculty representatives, department chairs, deans, provosts, vice-presidents and other administrative or quasi-administrative staff. This unique bipartite structure is one of the key features of higher education governance in America. While it has within it certain ambiguities, it serves to enhance inclusion and a sense of belonging in a shared enterprise. The key for anyone, including the institutional researcher, to function successfully in this type of organization is recognizing the need to foster collaboration and consensus in the institution's decision-making processes.

Faculty Unions

The idea of shared or collegial governance is not always accepted as a given in higher education oversight. For example, some university faculty may feel that the extent of their involvement in institutional management is inappropriately or unfairly circumscribed. Although most higher education institutions engage in some form of shared decision-making, the specific structure of power and influence can range from a broadly inclusive collegial model to a more narrowly defined hierarchical bureaucratic model. Also, in the multi-layered and political environment of higher education, key players may form special interest groups that are able to leverage power and influence over the process of oversight. In a variety of American higher education institutions, both public and private, this complex and potentially adversarial milieu of governance has been a fertile ground for the establishment of faculty unions.

Baldridge asserts that if university governance is viewed in terms of a political context that promotes the building of alliances through special interest groups, then the emergence of faculty unions appears quite logical (Baldridge, et.al., 1977). After all, unions conventionally operate as a special interest group. However, unions may seem less logical with regard to the notion of collegiality. Some faculties perceive unions as the unnecessary partition of key players into competing and perhaps contentious factions. On the other hand, some faculties believe that the principal practices of unions, namely collective bargaining and contract negotiation, enable them to be better partners in the governance process. Baldridge states "the best way to guarantee shared decision making, according to the union viewpoint, is to mandate it in a legally binding contract" (1977). In other words, the formation of a union does not necessarily stand in the way of collegiality, and the benefits derived therefrom.

On the national level, The AAUP was established as one of the first interest groups to specifically address the concerns and needs of faculty. Founded in 1915, the AAUP is a strong advocate of academic freedom and collegiality in higher education governance. The American Federation of Teachers (AFT), founded shortly after the AAUP, was established as a trade union by a small group of school teachers. Although the AFT is primarily made up of K-12 teachers and non-education public employees, there are currently more than 100,000 higher education faculty and professional staff who are affiliated with this union. The AFT affiliates are most prominent in states with long histories of effective unionization. The National Education Association (NEA) is the oldest and largest organization in America that focuses on the interests of teachers. Founded in 1857, the NEA includes members from all levels of education, including higher education. The approach of the NEA falls somewhere between the shared governance emphasis of the AAUP and the powerful unionization of the AFT.

The presence of a union does not necessarily negatively impact institutional quality, even though it may remove some of the discretionary power exercised by the administration and governing board. The union can be an effective advocate for improved academic quality and standards, and foster better policies and processes for employees. An example of a positive relationship between the faculty union and the administration is Nassau Community College. Nassau's president and the union leadership have consistently worked toward mutual objectives for many years to the benefit of the institution, and its academic programs and students. Trust, collegiality, and a respect for the interests of the other side characterize the relationship between these two governing forces.

Other Stakeholders

In addition to boards, the administration, and the faculty, there are a variety of other influential stakeholders who may affect the process of decision-making and institutional governance. In private institutions, the trustees or overseers are often a self-perpetuating group, but even they must answer to ecclesiastical stakeholders, alumni groups, student councils, and a variety of benefactors. Also, many private institutions receive some public funding and must meet the requirements of the public granting agencies.

By comparison, public institutions of higher education have a more extensive list of stakeholders and constituencies with influence over decision-making. These include the governor, the legislature, civic and community organizations, alumni groups, student councils, public and private granting institutions, and the general public.

Another influential external stakeholder is the institution's accreditation agency. Accreditation agencies are entities that routinely evaluate, assess and endorse institutions and/or programs. Although they are non-governmental bodies, their endorsements are sometimes utilized by government agencies to legitimize the disbursement or withholding of public resources. Also, although higher education institutions generally volunteer to be accredited, the choice to be accredited is sometimes viewed more as an imperative or imposition than a purely voluntary decision. There are basically two forms of accreditation, broad-based institutional and specialized. Institutional accreditation is usually granted by one of several regional agencies following an investigation and evaluation of the overall quality and integrity of the institution. The specialized accreditation agencies tend to be associated with professional associations or field-specific organizations. The focus of these agencies is the professional college or an academic department or program.

In some cases, the process of obtaining and retaining specialized accreditation is considered to be very cumbersome and demanding. It is not uncommon for a specialized accreditation agency to deny or withdraw its "stamp" of approval from a program or department. Such an action may have far reaching consequences in terms of prestige, funding, leadership, and student enrollment. Furthermore, the agency may require changes that involve committing additional resources for new equipment and/or faculty. The alternative to making such a commitment may be the loss of accreditation, a veritable "death sentence" for any program. Although the accreditation function is apart from traditional governance, its influence pervades all levels of institutional organization and activity.

Diversity in Structures and Characteristics

The current forms and functions of lay boards vary significantly among states, sectors, systems, and institutions. This inherent diversity is one of the primary characteristics that distinguish how American colleges and universities function from universities in other countries. Higher education oversight in many other nations tends to be much more uniform as a result of centralized governmental authority, e.g., a national government ministry. American forms of oversight reflect both the sovereignty of the states and the relative independence of individual institutions. With the exception of military service academies, the federal government has relatively limited control over higher education. This is true notwithstanding the fact that the federal government substantially funds higher education, at first primarily through grants to institutions, and later, through financial aid to students (Brubacher and Rudy, 1968).

For the most part, private boards are usually referred to as "Trustees" and public boards are frequently called "Regents" (Kauffman, 1983). However, there are no specific rules of nomenclature for governing boards. State oversight of public four-year institutions falls primarily into two categories, coordinating boards and governing boards. Coordinating boards do not have governing authority, with the possible exception of certain specified duties. For example, some coordinating boards can approve or disapprove budgets, but do not have the authority to implement specific programs within the institution. Coordinating boards generally operate at the system and/or state level and almost never have direct control over specific institutions and their functions. Governing boards, on the other hand, have broad oversight duties that include setting policy, appointing the president, allocating fiscal resources, and exerting final approval over most major actions. Also, governing boards often act as both advocates and buffers between the state legislature and other constituent groups. Board members, often called Regents, are elected, or politically appointed, or administratively appointed.

Public community colleges frequently have lay boards at both the state and local district levels. However, state-level governing boards tend to have broad responsibilities, usually involving the state budget and financial aid programs. By comparison, oversight boards at the local level tend to be much more involved in the ground-level operations of the institutions. For example, Arizona has both state and local or "district" governing boards. The local board has more direct influence over the institution than the state board. In fact, in most states where multiple governing boards exist, there is often tension among the boards creating a unique and complex balance of power. This environment is further complicated by the fact that most community college board members are elected and/or politically appointed (Ingram, 1998). In contrast to this multiple oversight approach is the Utah model, in which a single state board of regents governs all public postsecondary education. The single state board system does not necessarily obviate the possibility of power struggles or political tensions within the system, but it may allow for a more cohesive and focused oversight.

The boards of trustees of private colleges and universities are usually composed of distinguished alumni, prominent members of an affiliated group or corporation, and other individuals who are respected by the institutions and their constituents. As stated earlier, since boards of trustees are usually self-perpetuating, they tend to be less affected by changes in the political landscape of state or national politics. However, many private institutions of higher education have become increasingly interested in addressing public concerns about important and timely issues, such as the under-representation of minorities in higher education. Although the trustees are not publicly appointed, they are generally aware of and sensitive to public interests and concerns. These concerns are usually balanced with the unique mission of the institution.

Two Examples of Governance: Ohio and Wisconsin

The State of Ohio follows a model of higher education governance that exists in less than a quarter of the states. This model allows for some of the more senior public universities to have their own institution-specific governing boards, which are not merely adjuncts of the overarching state-level board. For example, Ohio State University has its own Board of Trustees, which is separate and distinct from the Ohio Board of Regents, a statewide coordinating agency. However, the membership of these two types of boards tends to be somewhat similar, because they are both primarily composed of gubernatorial appointees. One advantage of the dual board structure is that it may be effective in promoting institutional autonomy.

The Ohio model of higher education governance has led to a unique system in which both the institutions and the state board have significant power. On the statewide level, the Ohio Board of Regents coordinates all higher education institutions, both public and private. While the jurisdiction over private institutions is considerably less than that of public schools, there are certain activities and programs for which the private institutions must seek the Board's sanction. The head of the Ohio Board of Regents is referred as the "Chancellor." The members of the Board appoint the person who fills this position. The head of the institution-specific Board of Trustees carries the title of President of the Board. Similarly, the CEO of each higher education institution is referred to as President of the University. The Ohio model affords multiple levels of institutional advocacy, while still retaining an overarching coordination that promotes inter-institutional cooperation and a sense of mutual purpose.

The Wisconsin model of governance contrasts greatly with the Ohio model. The University of Wisconsin System (UW System) is what is referred to as a "true system," in the sense that each of its 26 institutions are part and parcel of a highly integrated structure. There are three types of institutions in the UW System; research universities, four-year comprehensive institutions and two-year colleges. All three types of institutions are named "University of Wisconsin-" followed by name, location, city or county (UW System Fact Book, 2000). The UW System was established in 1971, by legislative act, when the previously divided public university systems were merged into one umbrella structure under a single board of regents. It is interesting to note that, in contrast to the Ohio model, the person in the lead post for the entire Wisconsin System is given the title of "President," whereas the CEO's of the institutions are called "Chancellors." The Board of Regents appoints the President of the UW System, as well as the chancellors of the universities. The head of the Board of Regents is also referred to as the "President of the Board."

The UW System has a 17-member Board of Regents. The governor, with the exception of the ex-officio members, appoints the Board. The Board has a broad range of decision-making powers and responsibilities that impact many aspects of the higher education enterprise. These include budgeting and finance, curriculum and program, admissions, human resources, physical plant, degree requirements, and other aspects of university oversight and administration. The centralized structure in Wisconsin does not imply intrusion into the institutions or weakening of institutional autonomy. Additionally, there may also be certain benefits to centralization, including state-level cohesion, coordinated planning and collegiality that reaches beyond the boundaries of the institutions.

Several other models could be used to illustrate the diversity that exists in higher education governance structures today. Certainly, the three-tiered system of governance in California has had a significant impact on American higher education. However, given the need for seamless articulation between community colleges and universities, the separate system model may result in unwarranted barriers for the transfer student. The impact of the transfer student has grown in recent years; forcing many institutions to put in place articulation mechanisms to remove barriers along the path to baccalaureate attainment.

An interesting part of the oversight and governance drama is currently unfolding in Florida. Florida's move to eliminate system boards in favor of local boards of trustees coupled with a single state coordinating board has the attention of governors and legislatures everywhere. The new "super board" will oversee all sectors of education in Florida, including the trustees of each institution. Although this decentralization of control may increase the ability of Florida's institutions to self-govern, some believe that the new structure will ultimately diminish local autonomy, as statewide standards of reporting become mandated, e.g., a statewide course taxonomy. Also, some are concerned that the Florida Legislature will expand its oversight role in the vacuum created by the absence of system boards.

A Key External Issue: Accountability

In recent years, the oversight of public higher education has increasingly emphasized accountability through the measurement of institutional performance. Moreover, this measurement sometimes has been assigned to groups external to the institution, usually representing the legislature or governor. In the 1980s, institutional performance was measured primarily through self-assessment. In the 1990s, there was a distinct shift toward state level accountability based on externally established performance indicators (Ruppert, 1994).

University administrators favor the model of institutional self-assessment that was prevalent in the 1980s, in which the universities were given significant autonomy with regard to every aspect of accountability. However, most governing boards assert that on-going self-assessment efforts do not satisfy the growing public demand for rigorous oversight. The most influential voices in the demand for more stringent accountability often come from members of the state legislature or the governor's office. Both have been the sources for wide spread support for new ways to hold higher education accountable. Sometimes to maintain control or sometimes acting as an advocate of the governor or legislature, governing boards will exercise even more stringent levels of oversight by putting in place externally-driven mandates for accountability and performance. In some cases, the accountability or performance mandates are even used as the basis for funding of the institution. Universities frequently view this as an unwarranted intrusion, opening the way to external micromanagement.

Case Study # 1

Institutional researchers are sometimes caught between external oversight groups and their own institution. Because the institutional researcher has access to or knows how to get the data upon which most accountability and/or performance measures are based, their position in this process can be extremely delicate.

An institutional researcher experienced this when a member of the institution's board of regents made a direct contact to obtain data for inclusion in an accountability measure under consideration by the board. The board was reacting to concerns expressed by the governor to establish increased oversight over higher education in the state.

The institutional researcher's position in this process was exceptionally sensitive because the institution's administration viewed the external mandates as micromanagement, and was attempting to influence the measures and benchmarks being considered. The institutional researcher properly referred the regent to the president to make his request. This brought the administration back into the picture, but did not earn the good will of the regent.

A Key Internal Issue: Tenure

In American higher education, micromanagement is not solely an external governance issue. Due to the dichotomous internal power structure of colleges and universities, micromanagement may be exercised from within as well as from without. Presidents, provosts, deans and department chairs at times seek to increase the scope of their oversight, potentially limiting the individual autonomy of the faculty. Also, decisions may be made at the external board level that effectively alter the internal balance of power. In recent years, there is a growing debate both internally and externally over the validity and efficacy of faculty tenure. Tenure, which ostensibly immunizes faculty from the threat of dismissal from their employment, was originally established as a means to protect academic freedom. The concept of tenure gained valence in the 1960s, in reaction to the firing of faculty who expressed radical views in the classroom. Without the protection of tenure, many academics fear that senior university administrators or departmental heads will assert control over the curriculum. However, in recent years, the need to re-invent higher education due to the emergence of new technologies and sciences, and the concomitant impact on pedagogy and curriculum, has lead many to question whether tenure is an outdated structure preventing the institution from adapting to core changes in the environment.

Case Study # 2

The board of regents, in response to concerns that the institution's tenured faculties were no longer current or productive, put in place a post-tenure review process. The purpose of the process was to review all tenured faculty at 10-year intervals. If it were determined that a faculty member was no longer current or productive in their discipline, they entered a probationary period to demonstrate currency and productivity. If they still failed to demonstrative sufficiency at the end of the probationary period, tenure could be removed. Obviously, the academy of the institution and the faculty senate were concerned about the policy, and the process and information upon which the review was to be based.

The institutional researcher was called upon to assist the institution in preparing the packets for review, and summarizing the instruction, research, and institutional service of the faculty members being reviewed. Because the institutional researcher used many of the databases containing this information for other reporting purposes, the administration viewed this as a logical extension of the institutional researcher's duties. However, because of the importance of the review to the individual, the institutional researcher found that involvement in the process was difficult and at times tedious. Many groups within the institution, such as the faculty senate, wanted information concerning the review and the institutional researcher at times felt caught between the faculty senate, the administration, and the governing board.

POLICY ANALYSIS

The institutional researcher, in response to the external or internal governance issues, often becomes involved in policy analysis. In this section of the chapter, policy analysis is considered as a general approach within the context of institutional research. The various settings where policy analysis is performed, the most useful techniques the novice institutional researcher should know, and the pitfalls and prospects for policy analysis are all discussed. The section concludes with a review of useful resources on policy analysis.

Definitions and Origins of Policy Analysis

Policy analysis is a fairly recent development as a sub-discipline in the social sciences, and as an approach to providing information that is of assistance to decision-makers. Some scholars point out that the general concept of analyzing pertinent information to possibly influence the decisions of policy makers dates back to at least the time of Machiavelli (Garson, 1986). Definitions of policy analysis in their variety reflect the dualism between viewing this activity as a sub-discipline versus informational support for decision-making. Geva-May (1997) lists 14 such definitions (pp. xxii-xxiii) in her highly prescriptive book based on the work of Aaron Wildalsky. Of those the author lists, the most pertinent to this chapter are those of Macrae and Wilde (1979): "The use of reason and evidence to choose the best policy among a number of alternatives," and of Cochran and Malone (1995): "Investigations that produce accurate and useful information for decision makers."

Origins of policy analysis as a distinct way of examining issues include the influential writing of Harold Lasswell in the early 1950s and 1960s (Lerner and Lasswell, 1951; Lasswell, 1963). Lasswell predicted that policy analysis would grow into a theoretically-based disciplinary approach important to understanding social issues, as exemplified by Gunner Myrdal's epic study of social problems titled An American Dilemma (1944). Lasswell foresaw that policy analysis would emerge as a discipline in its own right based on the theory of choice in decision-making. Policy analysis would become a chief approach embedded in many established social sciences disciplines, such as political science, sociology and public administration. It is evident that by the turn of the century, policy analysis had been adopted by these fields, including education, but mainly as a methodology or conceptual framework rather than a co-discipline.

Policy analysis achieved considerable notoriety in the 1960s and 1970s when scholars and researchers in many disciplines used it to examine the role of government at all levels in dealing with social issues. In the late 1970s Aaron Wildavsky coalesced the current thinking around policy analysis in Speaking Truth to Power (1979). He viewed policy analysis as a value-laden "art and craft, not a narrow science" (Garson, 1986, p. 17). But whether an art (method) or a science (discipline), the question of identity remained, and through the 1970s and 1980s policy analysis vacillated between an "ivory tower" discipline and a methodological "tool" for decision-makers. Influential scholars such as Quade (1977) favored the latter identity and defined policy analysis as an effort to serve the information needs of decision-makers. Even though policy analysis has not achieved the disciplinary vision of Lasswell, it has emerged with a clear identity as a ubiquitous and well-accepted approach in many fields. Policy analysts identify with each other through professional associations, such as the Association for Public Policy and Management, and journals, such as the Education Policy Archives, a peer-reviewed electronic journal.

Policy Analysis in Institutional Research

In the context of institutional research, it is clear that policy analysis is simply one of a number of ways in which the information needs of higher education decision-makers are met. Specific applications of policy analysis to institutional research activities began to be of interest in the early 1970s. The Eleventh Annual Forum of AIR in 1971 had "Institutional Research and Institutional Policy Formulation" as its theme. Several conference papers, including the AIR presidential address by Sidney Suslow, focused on policy analysis. The paper titled "The Role of Institutional Research in Support of Policy Formulation" by Bernard Sheehan (1971) is still relevant as an overview of policy analysis in institutional research. Sheehan points out a crucial factor that pertains to the role of the institutional researcher as a support function to policy makers: "University policy formulators are usually professional scholars and teachers, and amateur managers" (p. 21). Sheehan predicted over a quarter of a century ago that institutional research would grow into an interactive partnership with policy makers. The partnership Sheehan saw was one where consultation on problems and issues would, as often as not, originate with the institutional research office as with policy makers. That vision has not developed except in a few places, and in these instances, the relationship between the institutional researcher and the policy decision-maker is ad hoc or on a spontaneous basis, rather than a regular on-going relationship. However, even though Sheehan's vision did not fully materialize, the role of the institutional researcher in providing the data to drive policy analysis is paramount.

There is considerable variation in concept and practice by which policy analysis in institutional research can be viewed. Nagel (1986, pp. 254-5) offers a relevant continuum of four levels of utilization of policy analysis that can be applied to the context of institutional research. His lowest level is "Not Even Referred To," the second level is "Referred To," the third level is "Reinforces Values or Decisions" and the highest level is "Converts Values or Decisions." It is probable that most institutional research veterans have experienced the first level, often in the setting of a public governing board meeting. In this setting, decisions are reached through an often-heated dialectic that has no time or place for facts, even though the institutional researcher may have prepared an analysis.

Most institutional research veterans have experienced the second level either positively or negatively; i.e., their policy analysis is "Referred To" but perhaps as often criticized as praised. In the former case, the institutional researcher may be comforted somewhat by knowing that at least their work was acknowledged.

The third level is the norm for most institutional researchers – their analysis "Reinforces Values or Decisions." This often results from studies commissioned by a wise administrator who has achieved longevity in her or his position by knowing how and where to do battle. Often, the senior administrator and institutional research director over time learn from each other to distinguish winnable issues and to avoid or postpone confronting the others. One of the greatest validating experiences of institutional research is when one achieves Level Four and finds that his or her analysis actually "Converts Values or Decisions" on an important issue. It is truly a highlight of a career when an institutional researcher learns their analysis was the persuasive influence on an important decision.

These four levels of utilization of the institutional researcher in policy analysis refer to the normal origins of their work, namely, the analysis was commissioned specifically by the decision-maker. An even more exalted level occurs when an institutional researcher takes the initiative (as foreseen by Sheehan) to identify an important issue and then designs and completes an analysis that is accepted and actually changes an established policy. An example of this most satisfying level of institutional research work is described in the following case study.

Case Study # 3

In a state where new funds for the public university system are allocated by a funding formula based on full-time student equivalents (FTE), an institutional researcher at one of the universities was completing an instructional cost study. He noted a dramatic difference in the per credit hour costs of lower and upper division. The institutional researcher expected a significant difference between undergraduate and graduate costs, but the analysis revealed that upper division was twice as costly as lower division. Yet, the state did not recognize this difference in the formula used to compute full-time student equivalents. The formula only recognized a difference between undergraduate and graduate education (undergraduate FTE being based on 15 credit hours and graduate FTE based on 10). The implications of this finding were crucial because the majority of the institution's undergraduate students transferred from the local community college into an upper division program. A quick analysis of the other universities in the system revealed that most had more traditional distributions of student credit hours (i.e., larger enrollments at lower division than upper division). The impact of the current funding formula was clear. The state's FTE formula was creating a growing disparity in resources between the institutional researcher's institution and the other universities that served fewer transfer students.

The institutional researcher prepared a graph of the distribution of student credit hours at the three universities. He then scheduled a meeting with the president's key advisor. Presenting the graph to the advisor he said: "We will never have the resources to compete with the other universities as long as the funding formula fails to recognize our unique instructional load distribution." Immediately, the advisor took the institutional researcher and the graph into the president's office. Several policy changes resulted from the researcher's presentation. First, the institution convinced the state legislature to revise its funding formula. Lower division FTE is still based on 15 credit hours, but upper division FTE was changed to 12 credit hours. Second, the institution set a goal to increase the size of the freshmen class relative to the other classes. In the intervening years, the institution has achieved its goal of becoming a research university with a more traditional distribution of student credit hours. The impact of these changes can be measured in tens of millions of dollars of new funding and continues to grow.

Formulating Policy Analysis in IR

Radin (1996) has commented on the "frustrations experienced by policy analysts who have not been able to convince contemporary decision-makers of the wisdom of their recommendations" (p.1). The root cause of such frustration may often lie in the way the goals and scope of the analysis are formed. The administrator commissioning the policy analysis knows the problem to be addressed, but may not know if it is feasible to study given the availability or lack of data, the amount of time and resources available to the institutional researcher, and the "political" pitfalls that await. Radin postulates that the success or failure of policy analysis is often determined by the quality of discussions held between the institutional researcher and the "decision-maker client." This process may be especially crucial in the higher education setting given the dispersion (or sharing) of institutional governance described earlier in the chapter.

Ideally, the policy analysis will be formulated in a thorough interactive dialogue between the decision-maker client and the institutional researcher. This dialogue should clearly define (1) the problem, (2) the research questions that can be answered given the available data, (3) the time and resources available to complete the analysis, (4) the political sensitivities impacted by the analysis, and (5) the type and scope of recommendations that will be useful as a product of the analysis. Such a formulation enhances the chance of success but almost presupposes a track record of trial and error by both the researcher and the decision-maker client. If either is a neophyte in the process, success is much less assured. A novice researcher can bring little to the commissioning dialogue except willingness and a naïve hope or expectation that the data are available and that the time and resources available are sufficient for the task. A novice decision-maker client may be so naïve as to preclude conversation and simply memo the researcher: "Here's the problem. I don't care how you get the job done. Just have the recommendations and supporting findings on my desk by tomorrow!"

A substantial (and sometimes stressful) learning process is necessary to develop the mutual understanding that underlies successful formulation of policy analysis in higher education. The process will be enhanced by examining and using resources like Radin's work (a presidential address to the National Association for Public Policy Analysis and Management in 1996) and the book by Geva – May (1997). The latter work is highly detailed and prescriptive concerning the mutual input necessary by both the researcher and the decision-maker client. Geva–May is explicit in her advice to the policy analyst: "It is your duty to help your client clarify what his/her needs actually are" (1997, p. 15, emphasis in original). She further advises that the analyst not "accept the user's formulation of a problem uncritically. It is your professional responsibility to probe the assumptions implicit in a client's statement of a problem" (p. 17). By doing so the researcher and the decision-maker client will begin the project with a clear and mutual understanding.

Policy Analysis Models in IR

Several institutional researchers have developed distinctive approaches to policy analysis. Hanson (1999), for example, describes policy analysis as a process that is neither a self-contained discipline nor a "handmaiden to policy makers." He states "Policy analysis is the design, collection, analysis and dissemination of data or information for the purpose of creating or modifying educational policy" (p. 47). He identifies five basic steps in policy analysis:

(1) The primary decision-makers must identify the purpose and goals of the research. This requires clear specification of the parameters of the policy to be analyzed.

(2) Data sources must be located in order to build the working database on which the analysis will be performed.

(3) The nature of the working database and the policy parameters determine the appropriate statistical techniques to be used.

(4) The next step of data manipulation and policy simulations requires interaction and dialogue with the primary decision-makers. This dialogue helps the researcher "fine-tune" and shape the analysis in the direction of policy goals and purposes defined in the first step.

(5) The final step "validates" the policy decisions based on the research. It answers the question "did the research help produce a desired and workable policy?"

Hanson relates these steps to the critical issue of knowing when the analysis is completed. Attainment of "closure" in policy analysis is helped by careful specification of each of the five steps.

In 1992 Judith Gill and Laura Saunders published "Conducting Policy Analysis in Higher Education," a chapter in a *New Directions For Institutional Research* sourcebook that remains the best "cookbook" resource available on methods of policy analysis in IR (Gill and Saunders, 1992). These authors, both seasoned higher education administrators, postulated a two-stage research design that focuses on the initial statement of the problem as the central core of the process. They describe how the core statement is modified by accommodation to an iterative diagnosis of the problem as it relates to the availability of time and policy and financial constraints. They contend that the policy analyst uses three main tools: (1) the iterative process, because the initial problem statement rarely encompasses all of the relevant factors involved, (2) intuition and judgement, and (3) the advice and opinions of others. Note that their approach emphasizes interactive dialogue and presupposes the required technical expertise and availability of data and necessary resources. Gill and Saunders' Second Stage focuses on "Decomposition" in which they emphasize consideration of policy issues, the setting or environment and the implementation of strategies, procedures, and recommendations. Finally, they note that outputs include not only the report, but also "ongoing iterative analysis" (p. 16), suggesting at least the potential for evaluation of whatever programs or policies that may result from implementation of the recommendations.

Parker and Fenske, in a 1982 AIR Forum paper, describe specific models for undertaking policy analysis in institutional research. They note that the information and recommendations produced are "almost always situation – and time-specific" (1982, p.1). In terms of the "ivory-tower" versus "handmaiden to decision-makers" dilemma posed earlier, their discussion places institutional research policy analysis squarely in the latter category. However, they emphasize the importance of the work to institutional well being, and discuss the value of improving policy analysis effectiveness through professional interchanges such as at the Annual Forum of the Association for Institutional Research and through publications.

Timothy Sanford has succinctly described what he calls the "policy analysis/ technology dilemma" (1995, pp. 85-6). The dilemma comprises the tension that occurs when the institutional researcher is increasingly recognized for her or his technological expertise and, at the same time, called upon to do policy analysis for decision-maker clients across the institution. The former function is valuable and certainly politically "safer," but it may undercut the valuable contributions that can be provided by the latter function. Obviously, choices have to be made to resolve the tension, and the tendency of the institutional researcher toward one or the other function may well depend on the personality and perceived job security of the various roles the institutional researcher has the opportunity to fill. Policy analysis holds the promise of a professional level of contribution to the institution beyond that of repository and purveyor of institutional data.

Contexts of Policy Analysis in IR

By its nature, policy analysis will typically involve the institutional researcher with constituencies beyond the direct purview of the decision-maker client who commissions the work. The policy in question may involve the faculty senate or academic units, the student association, the alumni group, or any of a number of other institutional components, including administrative domains other than the one in which the decision-maker client is located. Obviously, the researcher should be aware of the political pitfalls inherent in tensions that naturally exist among units that compete for scarce resources or prestige in the institution.

Beyond the involvement of various components across campus, policy analysis often involves external constituencies. These could include other campuses in a multi-campus institution, other institutions in a multi-institution system, or colleges in a consortium. The analyst may interact with counterparts located on the institution's governing board staff or the statewide coordinating agency. The research may involve policy issues relating to a regional higher education organization, an accrediting agency, a professional association or even the federal government. Policy issues usually have blurred boundaries. For example, any policy analysis concerning the undergraduate program will likely include the high schools or community colleges that feed students into the institution. The decision-maker client should be made aware of the potential for widespread effects of any possible changes resulting from the study.

A familiar context for policy analysis in institutional research concerns policies that impact students. Often the heart and soul of an institution's "portfolio" of policies, policies that affect students may be categorized as enrollment management (including marketing and admissions), retention and degree completion, student and parental satisfaction with the college experience, and achievement of institutional and political goals (e.g., diversity and service to the larger community). The following two case studies illustrate many of the concepts of policy analysis.

Case Study # 4

Hanson (1999) describes a case study where an institutional researcher performed a policy analysis that dealt with sensitive and controversial issues of equity, affirmative action and the goal of increasing ethnic diversity in a large university system. The need for a policy analysis was triggered by the 1996 decision of the Fifth Circuit Court in the Hopwood case. That decision and a subsequent ruling by the Texas Attorney General prohibited the University of Texas at Austin from continuing its use of race-based scholarships aimed at increasing ethnic diversity in the student body. Prior to 1996, the university had offered two scholarship programs to academically meritorious African-American and Hispanic applicants. The academic criteria used resulted in scholarship offers mainly to minority applicants from middle and upper-income families. After the Hopwood decision, university decision-makers asked an institutional researcher to explore how a policy could be framed that identified and financially supported students "from socio-economically disadvantaged backgrounds who may have attended an academically inferior high school" but also found ways to nonetheless excel academically (p. 53).

According to Hanson: "Policy analysis research begins with the researcher meeting the individual or committee responsible for the policy development to define and clarify" the policy goals of the research (1999, p. 53). Key terms must be defined during the interactive dialogue. For example, what is meant by "socio-economically disadvantaged background" and "academically inferior high school?" Research design and data gathering cannot begin until such definitions are fully identified and understood. As the dialogue between the researcher and the policy makers proceeded, it became clear that it would be possible to develop an index to measure the type and number of impediments overcome by the target group of students. The result was an "adversity index" to gauge these impediments. A usable index was achieved through use of many iterations of data analysis that simulated the projected policy goals. Hanson states "these policy simulations form the heart of policy analysis research because the results of 'applying' the policy to a particular group of students could be evaluated, adjusted, and reapplied before having to make a 'final' decision about the policy standards" (p. 57). The simulations resulted in a new non race-based scholarship program based on the "adversity index." The final step was to validate and monitor the program to determine how well it meets the policy goals established to guide the analysis (p. 58).

Case Study # 5

Another example of a policy analysis involving institutional research concerned the retention and degree completion rates of women and underrepresented minorities in science, engineering, and mathematics. Concerns included the level of academic preparation of such students for success in these fields, and whether institutional resources and other financial aid programs were sufficient to support success in these fields.

Interest in these issues was not limited to a single campus. The institution's governing board, as well as state agencies such as the legislature and the governor, was also interested. This concern was often expressed at the national level by the professional associations in the field and the federal government. The National Center for Education Statistics had developed data sets, such as the Beginning Postsecondary Students (BPS) Survey, with the specific potential to investigate such issues.

A research grant, co-sponsored by the Center and the Association for Institutional Research, explored this issue at a large, public research university. The institution's institutional researcher collaborated with a faculty member to study the retention and degree completion of women and underrepresented minorities majoring in science, engineering, and mathematics. The grant enabled the analysts to develop an institutional data set that paralleled BPS. The parallelism allowed for comparison between the institutional situation and the national one. Analysis of the data sets produced findings that influenced campus policies directly, and have become of interest to similar institutions elsewhere (Fenske, Porter and DuBrock, 2000). In this case, the findings from this analysis provide baseline data against which the institution and the state can measure progress in meeting the goals of these initiatives in the future.

PLANNING

In this section of the chapter, planning is considered within the context of institutional research. The various settings where planning occurs, the most useful approaches to planning that the novice institutional researcher should know, and the pitfalls and prospects of planning activities are illustrated. Planning is considered as a general approach; however, the governance structures and the policy issues present will influence the planning requirements encountered by the institutional researcher.

A Brief Overview

Two basic forms of planning exist in higher education (although the literature is replete with many "flavors" of planning). For purposes of this chapter, they will be called tactical planning and strategic planning. Tactical planning is a "nuts and bolts" type of planning that occurs throughout the institution, and focuses on the near horizon. Because of its connection to the coming operating period, tactical planning is often linked with budgeting. Strategic planning, on the other hand, focuses on the distant horizon, and attempts to change the organization in a fundamental way.

Planning, of course, has been around a long time. Throughout history, civilizations that learned to plan survived and thrived. However, for purposes of our discussion, planning in higher education begins in the 1950s and 60s when most existing campuses were expanded and many new campuses were built. Because many disciplines are represented in the academy, the institutional researcher should not be surprised to find a blending of many disciplines represented in the planning structures present in their institution.

The Master Plan

In the post World War II period, America was building public schools, colleges and universities, freeways, and suburban communities. This effort was based on a "public-oriented" form of planning that relied on census data to support large projects paid for by the public. In higher education, this period could be called the era of the "Master Plan." The Higher Education Facilities Act of 1963 provided federal resources to colleges and universities for campus development. In order to qualify to receive support, institutions needed a master plan. Master plans are documents that combine an architectural view of campus development, intermingled with a statement of institutional purpose. Often the conception of the campus was grounded in the demographics of the region and/ or clientele the institution aspired to serve.

Lyman Glenny was the archetypal master planner and was instrumental in developing California's master plan for higher education. Probably the best example of master planning, this plan is still in use today and has been copied by many other states. The California master plan conceived of a differentiated system of higher education with three distinct tiers, i.e., the California Community College System, the California State University System, and the University of California System (UC). Each system was designed to serve a different clientele. Architects wanting to create unique environments also exerted a significant influence on the physical environment through the master plan (Glenny, 1959). Two interesting examples are UC - Santa Barbara, a beautiful campus by the ocean, and the circular wheel design of UC - Irvine.

The impact of master planning was so great that most institutions developed master plans to guide the development of the physical campus by 1965. Today, most of these plans will be found in the institution's archives. Because enrollments in higher education have stabilized along with the need for new buildings and campuses, master planning is not the central issue it once was. However, institutions building campuses today will find the master plan very much alive. During the 1980s Arizona State University built a campus in western Maricopa County on 325 acres. At the inception, a traditional master plan was created to give the institution an identity, and guide the physical development of the campus. This plan included a vision of the clientele to be served. The result was an upper division campus serving the educational needs of working adults. While the history of the institution did not follow the vision, the physical plant does reflect the original master plan.

Program, Planning, Budgeting (PPB)

Another form of planning was also gaining acceptance in higher education during the era of the master plan. Known as "program, planning, budgeting" (PPB), this planning model was implemented in the Department of Defense by Robert McNamara in 1961 to support America's involvement in the Cold War and Vietnam (Keller, 1983). PPB attempts to express every aspect of the organization in quantitative or measurable terms. The purpose is to direct the allocation of resources to critical areas so that programs are completed on time. PPB focuses on the relationship between resource inputs and workload.

PPB quickly found its way into higher education when consulting groups, such as the National Center for Higher Education Management Systems, attempted to model higher education to allocate resources to academic and administrative areas of the institution. An example of a PPB is the Induced Workload Matrix (IWLM). The IWLM was developed by institutional researchers to direct course workloads from academic departments to academic programs. Other examples of PPB are the funding formulas many states use to funnel resources to campuses based on full-time student equivalent workloads per FTE faculty.

Management by Objectives

During the 1960s a new planning theory, Management by Objectives (MBO), was gaining favor in business, and soon notable attempts were made to apply these concepts to higher education. MBO focuses on the goals or objectives of an organization. Critics argued that PPB's focus on inputs and workload resulted in a loss of focus on the organization's stated and/or actual goal. Allocating resources to achieve organizational objectives was a concept that governing boards readily adopted. In 1979, the National Task Force on Accountability of Higher Education to the State called for a "process that involves setting goals for higher education, measuring progress in relation to those goals, and reporting to the people of the state, through the responsible state authorities, the degree of attainment of [those] objectives" (Education Commission of the States, 1979, p. 2).

Rogers and Van Horn proposed a "goal-oriented resource allocation" model for higher education in 1976. However, this model presupposes that the goals of the organization are known and measurable. The model is interesting because each unit within the organization earns income (either directly or indirectly through attribution) and pays expenses in achieving its goals. In effect, the model combined the goal-oriented concepts of MBO with the financial model utilized in business and industry by applying a mechanism to attribute revenue and expense to each unit within the organization. The mechanism to attribute revenue and expense was purely a PPB concept.

The vestiges of MBO are seen today in the charge back procedures some institutions use to control costs. For example, some institutions require departments to "pay" for central computing and technology. The charge back is a form of re-distributing resources within the institution while granting organizational units the autonomy to meet certain objectives and control costs. In this model, the computing center collects "revenue" (a transfer of budgeted resources) to cover the expenses of providing central computing support. Another example of MBO today is the "report card." Most governing boards are assessing the performance of higher education through a series of performance-based measures. The performance measures, in effect, express the surrogate goals of the institution. These are simply applications of MBO using PPB mechanisms applied to outcomes rather than inputs.

"Fuzzy" Goals

As governing boards and institutions struggled to implement MBO concepts, institutional researchers engaged in studies to determine what the goals of the institution are or should be. This may seem strange, but governing boards and institutional presidents quickly realized that college and universities served many different constituencies – each with differing views of the institution. To try and institutionalize this, goal inventories were developed and ranked using "Delphi methods" to prioritize the importance of various goals.

The fundamental problem with both PPB and MBO is that colleges and universities are too complex to be described by formulae or by a set of definitive goals. PPB proved to be too complex in implementation and lacked credibility because the underlying assumptions implicit in the formulae were easily challenged. Further, many areas of the university simply could not be adequately described through a mathematical expression. With MBO, the primary problem was achieving a consensus about the institution's goals, except in the broadest of terms. Finally, there are problems with measuring many goals, e.g., increasing the level and quality of public service.

In 1980 Fenske registered strong doubts about the efficacy of MBO and the validity of models borrowed from business and applied to higher education (in Jedamus and Peterson, p. 177). When MBO was first being considered for higher education, Brandl commented on the difficulty of applying the planning techniques of business, with its single-minded profit motive, to colleges and universities. He observed that

Higher education is many things to many people; it is impossible to compile a self-consistent . . . list of goals of a university. Existing techniques were designed for organizations with an incentive to produce efficiently an agreed-on product. A university is in many ways a nonorganization, where there is no agreement on its product, the independence of the . . . . faculty is highly valued, and there is . . . no goal to maximize.

Nevertheless, many of those who governed higher education became infatuated with MBO. In business during the 1980s, this theory evolved into "total quality management" (TQM) where the objective became improving the production process. Here the focus shifted from inputs and outputs to the intervening processes. In the 1990s, higher education's response to TQM was an attempt to re-engineer the institution's business processes. Probably the most significant contribution of MBO thinking in higher education is the mission statement. Virtually every institution has one and it is the first document the regional (institution-wide) accrediting association wants to see. Indeed, accrediting groups, such as the North Central Association of Colleges and Universities, have fully adopted this thinking in accrediting or re-accrediting an institution.

Case Study # 6

Tactical planning is usually grounded in MBO and PPB concepts. This type of planning occurs primarily in the middle and lower managerial levels of an institution. Institutional researchers are often called upon to provide data for tactical planning activities. Everything about tactical planning is usually well understood, including the objective and measures of success.

The governance structures internal and external to the institution usually dictate the information and analysis required by the institutional researcher in a tactical planning situation. For example, in an effort to eliminate non-productive programs, a governing board wanted to establish degree-production standards for programs. One of the institution's senior academic officers asked the institutional researcher to serve on a system-wide committee to recommend the standards by looking at degree production over the past 10 years. In this situation, the measurements were well understood, and once the board saw the data, they determined what the standards would be. The following case study illustrates how tactical planning activities often shift to implementation.

Case Study # 7

A public university was trying to improve student retention from one term to the next. The institutional researcher was asked to document the relationship between pre-registration and term attendance. Once the institution's enrollment management council digested this information, the institutional researcher was asked to identify ways to improve the progression of students from term to term. Various ideas were considered. In the end, the most effective approach was a simple one. The institutional researcher identified students in good academic standing who had not pre-registered for the next term. The institution contacted each student, and on a case-by-case basis attempted to resolve any impediment keeping the student from pre-registering. This solution, though simple, resulted in an improvement in retention. It is also a good example of how tactical planning often shifts from planning/policy analysis to implementation.

Strategic Planning

During the 1980s, the focus of planning theory shifted to the distant horizon. Until this time, most planning theory was tactical in orientation, focusing on the next operating cycle. However, planners began to realize that another type of planning was needed if the fundamental character of the institution was to change. For example, in 1980 Peterson observed that planning was "a conscious process by which an institution assesses its current state and the likely future condition of its environment, identifies possible future states for itself, and then develops organizational strategies, policies and procedures for selecting and getting to one or more of them" (Peterson, p. 114, in Jedamus and Peterson, 1980).

In 1983, George Keller published a seminal treatise where he articulated the theory of strategic planning for higher education. Keller's strategic planning was an open-ended process designed to move the organization to a desired future state. He saw strategic planning as the basis for re-inventing higher education and making fundamental changes in the institution (Keller, 1983). Keller recognized there were benefits from both near and distance planning when he observed: "organizations have both localized, short-term, and bottom-line demands, and all-organization, long-term, and investment-strategies-for-the-future demands. They must live for the familiar today, yet also must be forever looking out for how to live in a very different tomorrow" (Keller, 1983, p. 116).

Because strategic planning attempts to alter the future of the institution, this form of planning primarily involves the institution's senior executives and governing boards. The antecedents of strategic planning have been around for a long time and were originally known as "long term" planning in 1960's business literature. However, as Rowley, Lujan, and Dolence (1997) note, there is a fundamental flaw in strategic planning because the future environment cannot be known or predicted, as many institutions learned the hard way during the 1980s (p. 31). For example, the Arizona Board of Regents contracted with a consultant to build an enrollment projection model to help planners prepare for an anticipated influx of students that were believed to arrive by 2000 and 2010. The model was based on population demographics and local and national economics (i.e., a PPB-driven model). As the years passed, it became clear that the enrollment projections from the model exceeded the true rate of growth significantly. Failures such as this influenced many presidents and boards to shift the focus of planning efforts back to near horizon, which was more reliable and easily understood, rather than commit resources to a new tomorrow that may never materialize.

As a result, some writers observe that strategic planning can only occur where there is low turbulence in the environment, meaning that the future is reliably predicted (Pisani and Filkins, 2000, p. 479). Strategic planning is an inherently more difficult activity than tactical planning because (1) there are no rules, (2) ambiguity and uncertainty are fundamental to the process, and (3) the participants are forced to think outside their normal contextual framework (i.e., "think outside the box") which they may or may not be able to do. Consequently, conflict and lack of consensus are often part of the process.

Rowley, Lujan, and Dolence (1998) observe: "Conventional planning tends to be oriented toward looking at problems based on current understanding or an inside-out mind-set. Strategic planning, however, requires an understanding of the nature of the issue and then finding an appropriate response, or an outside-in mind-set (pp. 35-36)." It is the outside-in mind-set that is so challenging in strategic planning. Yet, it is clear that this form of planning is the most powerful and potentially critical to the future viability of any system or institution.

Case Study # 7

In Arizona, before the state was willing to support additional resources for postsecondary education, the governor established a "blue-ribbon" task force to chart the future course of higher education in the state. Both university and community college representatives were included on the task force, but the chair and the majority of the representatives were business leaders. At first, the universities and community colleges postured back and forth, trying to protect what they perceived to be their "turf." The business leaders where frustrated with the apparent unwillingness to "think outside the box."

When it was apparent that neither the universities nor community colleges could control the situation and that the governor would not support any increase in resources without the task force's recommendations, the community colleges and universities set differences aside and adopted the "outside-in mind-set." In the end, a report was prepared that was forward thinking, comprehensive, and supported by the governor and the business community. During the process, several institutional researchers supported the work of the task force by providing data, responding with more information as the task force's dialogue continued, and drafting the final report.

"Eyes Wide Open" Planning

In considering the above discussion, institutional researchers should keep in mind that planning theory and higher education are like lovers' perpetually in search of each other, but somehow never coming together. In this drama, the institutional researcher plays a major supporting role in whatever planning processes exist in his or her institution.

Part of the problem stems from the fact that most governing boards and senior executives believe there is a perfect planning model that will make their institution efficient, effective, and vital to society and the new economy. Yet, in application, mistrust by faculty, tenure, faculty unions, naivete on the part of inexperienced academics who become senior leaders, and a large dose of organizational bureaucracy and politics make it all but impossible to get the same result from planning as seen in business and industry. To further complicate matters, in higher education, planning theories are applied to organizations inherently more complex and diverse than any business organization of comparable size, budget, and organization. The key difference is that business has a single unifying goal (profit), whereas postsecondary institutions have a multiplicity of often-conflicting goals. In this challenging environment, the institutional researcher is well advised to remain flexible and ready to adapt, especially when involved in strategic planning.

While the above discussion may lead some to question whether planning should be avoided, in actuality, the opposite is the case. The institutional researcher can help her or his institution by providing accurate and timely information. Indeed, the institutional researcher's work will help drive the process, and most planning activities will have positive benefits. Planning necessarily leads the institution to reflect on its purpose within the context of its environment. Even when applied at the margin, planning helps the institution implement new programs, initiatives and policies.

A good example is the current trend to rank colleges and universities, develop report cards, and hold institutions accountable for key performance indicators. No one really likes doing this or believes these measures capture the essence of the institution. Still, each of these efforts encouraged leaders to better understand their institutions as they search for answers, and in the search, make qualitative improvements. Two good examples have been the recent focus on faculty workload and student graduation. As a result, many institutions have made substantive improvements in both areas. While one could question whether these improvements have changed the character and quality of the institution, the changes are positive. And most importantly, institutional researchers played an integral role in the process, helping their institution to capture the data and track progress toward achieving its goals.

RESOURCES IN GOVERNANCE, POLICY ANALYSIS AND PLANNING

As illustrated throughout this chapter, institutional research issues can be complex, challenging, and delicate depending on the internal and external governance structures within the institution (not to mention the skills, experiences, and personalities of the key decision-maker clients). To help the institutional researcher work through this difficult environment, there are many resources available. The first source that should be consulted is the Association for Institutional Research. The aptly named "Internet Resources for the Association for Institutional Research" (www.airweb.org/links/) lists over 300 associations that can be directly accessed from the Web. Most of these associations are involved in various aspects of governance, planning, and policy analysis related to higher education. And most of the materials of the associations are available free of charge.

Also listed are numerous publications including journals specifically focused on governance, policy analysis, and planning including several issues of *The New Directions in Institutional Research* quarterly sourcebooks, the *Research in Higher Education* journal, and especially the AIR *Professional Files* that focuses on specific topics. Occasional publications such as the *Handbook on Higher Education, Strategies for the Practice of Institutional Research: Concepts, Resources and Applications,* and the *Primer for Institutional Research* are other valuable resources.

Apart from the institutional research field, many other organizations have valuable resources available to the institutional researcher. Foremost among these are the professional and institutional associations, most of which are headquartered in Washington, D.C. for lobbying purposes. A primary example is the American Council on Education (ACE) that provides synopses of many of its policy studies. The full reports can be obtained directly from ACE. An association that deals exclusively with policy analysis is the Association for Public Policy and Management (www.qsilver.queensu.ca/appam/). An association that deals exclusively with governance issues is the Association of Governing Boards (www.agb.org). Their Web site includes membership of boards in public and private higher education. Another resource in the governance area is the state Higher Education Executives Offices (www.sheeo.org). This group focuses more on representing statewide coordinating boards and agencies. An association that deals exclusively with planning is the Society for College and University Planning (www.scup.org) or SCUP. SCUP's Web site lists many resources that all planners will find exceptionally useful.

Perhaps most important is the information to be obtained from colleagues, especially through attendance at the Annual Forum of the Association for Institutional Research. The Forum, and the papers presented that are available on the Web afterwards, provide timely examples of excellent policy analysis in higher education, and interested persons can contact the authors for more detailed information.

References

Andrade, S. J. (1998). How to institutionalize strategic planning. Planning for Higher Education, 27 (2).

Balderston, F. E. (1974). Managing today's university. San Francisco, CA: Jossey-Bass Publishers.

Balderston, F. E. (1995). Managing today's university: Strategies for viability, change, and excellence (2nd ed.). San Francisco, CA: Jossey-Bass Publishers.

Baldridge, J. V. (1971). Academic governance: research on institutional politics and decision making. Berkley, CA: McCutchan Publishing Corporation.

Baldridge, J. V. & Riley, G. L. (1977). Governing academic organizations: new problems, new perspectives. Berkley, CA: McCutchan Publishing Corporation.

Brandl, J. E. (1970). Public service outputs of higher education: An exploratory essay. In B. Lawrence (Ed.), The outputs of higher education. Boulder, CO: Western Interstate Commission on Higher Education.

Birnbaum, R. (1991). How colleges work: The cybernetics of academic organization and leadership. San Francisco, CA: Jossey-Bass Publishers.

Boyle, T. P. (1995). Good questions for sound decision making. In D. Woodward (Vol. Ed.), New Directions for Student Services: No. 70. Budgeting as a tool for policy in student affairs. San Francisco: Jossey-Bass Publishers.

Brubacher, J. & Rudy, W. (1968). Higher education in transition, a history of American colleges and universities, 1636–1968 (rev. and enlarged). New York, NY: Harper & Row.

Carnegie Foundation. (1976). The state and higher education: A proud past and vital future. Report by Carnegie Foundation for the Advancement of Teaching. Washington, DC: U.S. Department of Education.

Cochran, C. L. & Malone, E. F. (1995). Public policy perspectives and choices. New York, NY: McGraw-Hill.

Cohen, A. M. (1998). The shaping of American higher education: Emergence and growth of the contemporary system. San Francisco, CA: Jossey-Bass Publishers.

Cutright, M. (1996). Can chaos theory improve planning? Planning for Higher Education, 25, (2).

Cutright, M. (1997). Planning in higher education and chaos theory: A model, a method. Paper presented at Education Policy Research Conference, Wolfson College. Oxford, England: Oxford University.

Dolence, M. G., Rowley, D. J., & Lujan, H. D. (1997). Working toward strategic change: A step-by-step guide to the planning process. San Francisco, CA: Jossey-Bass Publishers.

Domonkos, L. (1977). History of higher education. Encyclopedia of higher education. San Francisco, CA: Jossey-Bass Publishers.

Education Commission of the States. (1979). <u>Accountability and academe: A report of the National Task Force on the Accountability of Higher Education to the State</u>. Denver, CO: Education Commission of the States.

Ewell, P. T. (1999). Borrowed management techniques in higher education. <u>Change: The magazine of higher education</u>. Washington, DC: American Association of Higher Education.

Fenske, R. H. (1980). Setting institutional goals and objectives. In P. Jedamus, M. W. Peterson, & Associates (Eds.), <u>Improving academic management</u>, San Francisco, CA: Jossey-Bass.

Fenske, R. H., Porter, J. D., & DuBrock, C. P. (2000). Tracking financial aid and persistence of women, minority and needy students in science, engineering and mathematics. <u>Journal of Research in Higher Education, 41</u> (1).

Garson, G. D. (1986). Policy science to policy analysis: A quarter century of progress. In W. N. Dunn (Ed.), <u>Policy analysis: Perspectives, concepts and methods</u>. Greenwich, CN: JAI Press.

Geva-May, I. (1997). <u>An operational approach to policy analysis: The craft</u>. Boston, MA: Kluwer Academic Publishers.

Gill, J. I. & Saunders, L. (1992). Conducting policy analysis in higher education. In J. I. Gill and L. Saunders (Vol. Eds.), <u>New Directions in Institutional Research: No. 76. Developing effective policy analysis in higher education</u>. San Francisco, CA: Jossey-Bass Publishers.

Glenney, L. G. (1959). <u>Autonomy of public colleges</u>. New York, NY: McGraw-Hill.

Hanson, G. R. (1999). Policy analysis research: A new role for student affairs research. In G. D. Malaney (Vol. Ed.), <u>New Directions for Student Services: No. 85. Student affairs research, evaluation, and assessment: structure and practice in an era of change</u>. San Francisco, CA: Jossey-Bass Publishers.

Hearn, J. C. & Griswold, C. P. (1994). State-level centralization and policy innovation in U.S. postsecondary education. <u>Educational Evaluation and Policy Analysis, 16</u> (161).

Hobson, J. E. (1965). A case study in institutional planning. <u>Long-range planning in higher education</u>. Boulder, CO: Western Interstate Commission for Higher Education.

Ingram, R.T. (1998). <u>Rethinking the criteria for trusteeship</u>. San Francisco, CA: Jossey-Bass Publishers.

Kauffman, J. (1983). <u>Governing boards: Higher learning in America</u>. Baltimore, MD: The Johns Hopkins University Press.

Keller, G. (1983). <u>Academic strategy: The management revolution in American higher education</u>. Baltimore, MD: The Johns Hopkins University Press.

Keller, G. (1997). Planning, decisions, and human nature. <u>Planning for higher education, 26</u> (2).

Kotler, P. & Murphy, P. E. (1981). Strategic planning for higher education. In R. Birnbaum (Ed.). <u>ASHE reader in organization and governance in higher education</u>. Lexington, MA: Ginn Press.

Lasswell, H. D. (1963). The future of political science. New York, NY: Atherton.

Lerner, D. & Lasswell, H. D. (1951). The policy sciences. Stanford, CA: Stanford University Press.

MacRae, D., Jr. & Wilde, J. A. (1979). Policy analysis for public decisions. North Scituate, MA: Duxbury Press.

Myrdal, G. (1944). An American dilemma. New York, NY: Harper Brothers.

Nagel, S. S. (1986). Conceptualizing public policy analysis. In W. N. Dunn (Ed.), Policy analysis: Perspectives, concepts and methods. Greenwich, CN: JAI Press.

Norris, D. M., & Poulton, N. L. (1991). A guide for new planners. Ann Arbor, MI: Society for College and University Planning.

Parker, J. D. & Fenske, R. H. (1982). Policy analysis: The new reality for institutional research. Paper presented at the Annual Forum of the Association for Institutional Research. Denver, CO.

Peterson, M. W. (1980). Analyzing alternative approaches to planning. In P. Jedamus, M. W. Peterson, & Associates (Eds.), Improving academic management, San Francisco, CA: Jossey-Bass.

Pisani, A. M. & Filkins, J. W. (2000). Strategic planning in a transitory higher education environment: Building on historical foundations and industrial parallels. In Higher education: Handbook of theory and research (Vol XV). New York, NY: Agathon Press.

Quade, E. S. (1977). Analysis for public decisions. In S. Nagel (Ed.), Policy studies review annual. Beverly Hills, CA: Sage Publications.

Rabin, J., Miller, G. J., & Hildreth, W. B. (Eds.) (2000). Handbook of strategic management (Second edition). New York, NY: Marcel Dekker, Inc.

Radin, B. A. (1996). The evolution of the policy analysis field: From conversation to conversations. Presidential address, 18th Annual Conference, Association for Public Policy Analysis and Management. Pittsburgh, PA.

Rowley, D. J., Lujan, H. D., & Dolence, M. G. (1997). Strategic change in colleges and universities: Planning to survive and prosper. San Francisco, CA: Jossey-Bass Publishers.

Rowley, D. James, L., Herman D., & Dolence, M. G. (1998). Strategic choices for the academy: How demand for lifelong learning will re-create higher education. San Francisco, CA: Jossey-Bass Publishers.

Rogers, F. A. & Van Horn, R. L. (1976). Goals-oriented resource allocation for university management. In R. H. Fenske (Ed.), Conflicting pressures in postsecondary education. Tallahassee, FL: Association for Institutional Research.

Ruppert, S. (Ed.). (1994). Charting higher education accountability: A sourcebook on state level performance indicators. Denver, CO: Education Commission of the States.

Sanford, T. R. (1995). Higher education and institutional research: What lies ahead. In T. R. Sanford (Vol. Ed.), New Directions in Institutional Research: No. 85. Preparing for the information needs of the twenty-first century. San Francisco, CA: Jossey-Bass Publishers.

Sheehan, B. S. (1971). The relationship of institutional research to general issues of policy formulation. In C. A. Stewart (Ed.), Institutional research and institutional policy. Tallahassee, FL: Association for Institutional Research.

Shulock, N. & Harrison, M. E. (1998). Integrating planning, assessment, and resource allocation. Planning for higher education, 26 (3).

Slaughter, S. & Leslie, L. L. (1997). Academic capitalism: Politics, policies, and the entrepreneurial university. Baltimore, MD: The Johns Hopkins University Press.

Suslow, S. (1971). Present reality of institutional research. In C. A. Stewart (Ed.), Institutional research and institutional policy formulation. Tallahassee, FL: Association for Institutional Research.

University of Wisconsin System Office. (2000). U W System fact book 2000. Madison, WI: University of Wisconsin.

Watkins, J. F. (1999). Reflections on the value of strategic planning. Planning for higher education, 27 (4).

Westmeyer, P. (1990). Principles of governance and administration in higher education. Springfield, IL: Charles C. Thomas.

Whiteley, M. A., Porter, J. D., & Fenske, R. H. (Eds.). (1992). The primer for institutional research. Tallahassee, FL: Association for Institutional Research.

Wildavsky, A. (1992). The new politics of the budgetary process (2nd ed.). Berkeley, CA: Harper Collins Publishers.

Wildavsky, A. B. (1979). Speaking truth to power. Boston, MA: Little, Brown and Co.

CHAPTER 6: THEORY, PRACTICE, AND ETHICS OF INSTITUTIONAL RESEARCH

Authors: Gerry McLaughlin and Richard Howard

This chapter focuses on the role, scope, and evolution of institutional research in support of planning and decision-making. Topics include surveys of institutional research practice; evaluation models for assessing the research function; techniques for managing the institutional research office; and the ethical and political dimensions of practicing institutional research.

Introduction

Logically, we should begin this discussion with some precise
definition of what is meant by the term 'Institutional Research'.
I can only say I wish we could. (Lyons, p. 1)

John Lyons in his Memorandum to a Newcomer to the Field of Institutional Research, (1976) begins his discussion with this comment which still reflects the reality of many institutional researchers when trying to define their work and what they do.

Institutional research as a profession is a rather new phenomenon in higher education. In fact, some of the founders of the modern institutional research office still attend the annual AIR Forum. During the past 40 years, the profession has developed and matured into a vital function in higher education. This development has occurred in an environment of rapidly changing expectations of higher education that have been characterized by expanded capabilities of technology and increased demand for its services, shrinking resources, and vocal demands for accountability. As higher education has reacted to the changing demands of society, institutional research has become a key player by providing reliable data and valid information, responding to accountability demands, assessing the effectiveness and efficiency of institutional processes and programs, and preparing for future challenges.

In the other chapters of this book, specific topics and activities that, cumulatively, define the broad spectrum of institutional research as it is practiced today are addressed. In this chapter, we intend to look at the profession in terms of its past and present. Building on the thoughts of our predecessors, we try to provide a "picture" of the early thinking about what institutional research should be. With this as background, we then address the practice of institutional research from a theoretical perspective and then from the perspective of practicing institutional research. In all honesty, we found it difficult to separate these two ways of looking at the profession. Institutional research has as its base a very practical reason for being—talking about it from a theoretical perspective is bounded by pragmatism. In fact, in many instances, we found our notion of theory to be that of conceptual models and used these models to illustrate the points of our discussion about the practice of institutional research.

Since the early days of institutional research, higher education has passed through several phases which have had direct influences on the practice of institutional research. Generally, the broad phases of the development of institutional research operations fall into three major timeframes. The first phase was the decentralized operations of information creation and inquiry occurring, arguably, in the late 50s and 60s. In these years, institutional research tasks were often completed using tally sheets, stand-alone databases which were not computerized, and Monroe and Freeman calculators to complete calculations. With the advent of mainframe computers, the centralized institutional research office came into being with many institutions consolidating the institutional research tasks in a specific organizational unit. This second phase also reflects the creation of the identity of institutional research, allowing it to begin developing as a profession. Again, arguably, in the mid-to-late 80s, the second phase of centralized institutional research activity began to move into a third phase. In this phase, the function began to be distributed across the campus. A code of ethics and professional practices came into being. Institutional research is now in this third phase. It has become a complex organizational function driven by technology and the resulting impact technology has had on the infrastructure of our colleges and universities.

BACKGROUND OF THE "PROFESSION"

Brackett (1983) has reviewed the earlier history of institutional research and the following are some of the definitions and discussions that she highlights.

As one reads the following efforts to describe the activities of institutional research, it is amazing, at least to these authors, that in general, these writings are still relevant when describing the profession. While the conduct of institutional research is much different than it was 40 years ago, the purpose and intent of institutional research today is consistent with the basic tenets described by our founders. In terms of their persistent relevance, some might well consider these concepts as part of our "theory" grounded in persistence.

It was not, however, a straightforward task to describe institutional research. As a relatively new function on most campuses in the late 60s, the founders of institutional research struggled to develop a "precise definition" that was both inclusive in describing the institutional research activities and founded on the scientific principles of disciplined inquiry. As illustrated below, the discussions revolved around the "purposes" of institutional research in relationship to "how" it should be conducted.

In 1960, John Dale Russell defined institutional research as "...a form of applied research. The initiation of a research project of this type is nearly always stimulated by the desire to find an answer to some practical problem." (p. 19) At a national institutional research forum that preceded AIR, Hubbard had a definition in terms of the institution. "Why do institutions engage in institutional research?

Perhaps the simplest and most direct response is that institutions expect institutional research to provide data which will improve their operations." (Hubbard, 1964, p. 7)

In the early thinking about, and the development of, institutional research, Hugh Stickler went into more detail when he indicated, "Institutional research refers to research which is directed toward providing data useful or necessary in the making of intelligent administrative decisions and/or for the successful operation, maintenance and/or improvement of a given institution of higher education. It includes the collection and analysis of data used in appraising the environment or "setting" in which the institution operates, in preparing the budget, in planning new buildings, in assigning space in existing buildings, in determining faculty loads, in admitting students, in individualizing instruction, in planning the education program, in keeping abreast of student progress, and the like." (1968, p. 3) Even the concept of "and other duties as appropriate" is rooted in our formation as a profession.

Saupe and Montgomery, talking about the institutional researcher, indicated that "the institutional researcher should be as objective, detached, thorough, and systematic as any other research. His problems should be as well defined, his methods as appropriate, his analyses as logical, and his conclusions as uninfluenced by pre-conceptions, as those of any scholar. In the process of his work he should develop or redefine a clear philosophy of higher education to serve as a catalyst for his efforts." (1970, p. 5)

In 1971, Sidney Suslow in the first presidential speech to the Association for Institutional Research defined institutional research as ".... an attitude of critical appraisal of all aspects of higher education, which has as its primary purpose the assessment and evaluation of the expressed goals of the institution and the means used to achieve those goals, and that this assessment and evaluation are guided not by purposes higher than the goals themselves, but simply by the estimated efficiency of the processes and the probable utility of the results." (p. 1)

Lyons (1976) discussed the dual nature of institutional research—scholarly research or management analysis. He concluded that most institutional research offices find themselves somewhere in the middle, focusing basic research on issues of importance to the institution, while being responsive to immediate concerns of efficiency. He suggested that this dichotomy may be more imaginary than real, as all are working to bring "greater rationality to bear on decision processes." (p. 3) Lyons quotes the Association for Institutional Research's definition of institutional research as "...a multi-disciplinary profession that draws on the relevant techniques and insights of modern management science and educational psychology, welding them into a new analytic approach to institutional governance and the general problems of higher education." (p. 3) This dual nature of the profession resulted in discussions around questions like: "Are we an art to be practiced or a science to be refined?," "Are we academic and scholarly or are we administrative and managerial?," or "Who makes our rules?"

The conclusions drawn in response to these and other questions became the basis that determined the nature of a profession that was thriving without a coherent conceptual core.

What then do these writings tell us about the "reality" of institutional research as it was conceived early in the evolution of the profession? The function was described as a form of applied research that used the tools and techniques of other disciplines to address issues important to the institution. Key to the difficulty in precisely defining institutional research was the fact that each institutional research function tended to take on roles as defined by its institution's needs, desires, and the particular skills and interests of the institutional researcher. We used a large number of methodologies from educational research, operations research, systems analysis, evaluation research, computer modeling, program budgeting, policy research, outcomes assessment, and planning models (Fincher, 1985; Saupe, 1990; Stecklein, 1970).

This range of methodologies has varied in prevalence as the issues at our institutions have varied. This ebb and flow became so strong that in 1986 we created a track system for the AIR Forum to prevent exclusion of topics that were ebbing in the face of "financial accountability" issues. The lack of science in the management of colleges and universities greatly limits our ability to think of what we do as a rigorous science. Even if institutional research did not achieve scientific status in our earlier years, the conclusion was that as an art, craft, or practice, those in institutional research have developed a set of problems to be worked on and functions to be performed. In many ways, this is still the situation in which we find ourselves. The prevalence of the institutional research function or office in discussions of its role by accreditation agencies, national and regional government agencies, and in discussions of the management of higher education has brought increasing focus to who we are and what we do at an institutional level.

Unlike those functions dealing with finance or human resource operations, institutional research as an organized function has not had externally defined "rules" of operation such as one might find from a profession that is also accepted as an academic discipline. Nor did specific guidelines exist to define the profession because of the unique role the institutional research function played in support of its institution's planning and management. Instead, much of the literature written about institutional research in the early days of the profession were efforts to describe the profession, mixing conceptual models with established scientific theory. Finally there was no group of academic scholars that taught institutional research as their primary discipline or who concerned themselves with the boundary of our profession or even the best way to conduct our business. While these various efforts have provided important insights about best practices and the role(s) that institutional research plays in higher education, it has been, and continues to be, the responsibility of the individual institutional research professional to put these models and theories into the context of the institutional researcher's particular job, at the institutional researcher's particular institution.

Our profession went through the transition with higher education in the early 80s that came from the anticipated downturn in the college-age cohort of traditional students and the actual decrease in funds provided many institutions by various states. Often, institutions tried to improve their management, restructured themselves, and then "retrenched." Our direction changed to include more focus on the efficiency of managing the institution as many external groups looked for the return on their investments. Fincher (1985) traces the basic methodology of institutional research from the early years, when we were involved in educational research, to the crisis years (1968-1973), when we sought to support a push to institutional management.

In this second phase we turned to planning, operations research, and financial analyses. In these later years, the profession has become more mature with its methodologies and the concerns for a balanced or more consistently defined methodology emerged. As outlined above, it was during the mid-70s and early 80s that institutional research began to redefine the profession. Others put the crisis years a bit later and the first transition of the profession in the early 1980s. (Peterson, 1985) Regardless of the specific time, our institutions went through major stresses between the golden years of the 60s and the initial accountability demands of the 80s.

The 70s also represent a point when the founders of institutional research hired many of us to support their institutional research offices and functions. We brought the analytic and computer skills required to program computers and use emerging statistical software, which enhanced the offices' ability to conduct a broader array of institutional research studies. With this came the maturation of data management, giving us more confidence in the reliability of our institutions' operational data. As we moved through the 80s, desktop computing supported basic analyses and offices began to emerge from the smaller "family" businesses into entrepreneurial functions, supporting a set of activities that had an impact across the campus. We broadened the base of institutional research, settled on a professional identity that had diversified foci (as identified through the Forum tracks), and through the Association for Institutional Research and its regional and other affiliates established an aggressive professional development program to broaden our skills and develop new institutional research professionals. In this second transition, we have integrated the use of communication technology into our analytic functions and reached out to other professions.

During the past decade or so, increasingly we have seen these same communications and analytic capacities distributed throughout the organization. With this has come an increasing demand for the data and information that in the past was the purview of the institutional research office. However, even more than previously, in this environment the value added to our campuses' information by the institutional research function has remained consistent with the thoughts of Suslow, Montgomery, Saupe', and Lyons. The tools and methodologies we use have changed dramatically and our role has often shifted to the person who conducts, coordinates, and facilitates institutional research rather than the person who does all the institutional research within an institutional research office.

To understand this most recent transition, it is necessary to consider the context in which institutional research is practiced within colleges and universities. Institutions of higher education tend to have multiple purposes and missions, internally conflicting interests and goals, and are dynamic, ever-changing complex organizations. There are over 3600 public and private institutes, colleges, and universities in the United States and tens of thousands worldwide, their missions ranging from doctoral instruction, research, and outreach, to small single-purpose institutions offering certificates of completion. The diversity of postsecondary education is as great as the number of institutions. And, while unique in structure and processes, all postsecondary institutions are political in nature (Saunders, 1983). The political nature of higher education has become increasingly apparent as external forces (regional and national agencies) exert more influence on what and how higher education does its business. This has been reflected through increased external demands of accountability. Accountability has come in the form of increasingly detailed reports about the institution's operations and outcomes required by governing and funding agencies. In addition, specific requirements for evidence of programmatic and institutional assessment from accrediting bodies reflect an increasing pressure from society for higher education to demonstrate its value to our communities, the country, and the world.

These increasing demands for "proof" of our postsecondary institution's value to funding agencies and society have often resulted in conflicting priorities within the institution. In general, the conflict revolves around the notions of efficiency and quality. Within the institution, there is a demand for quality. We see this in the policies developed by faculty that govern promotion and tenure, graduation requirements, and other academic activities. Calls for accountability are often seen as demands for efficiency—a requirement that in the minds of many in the academy is an oxymoron to the institution's academic concern for quality. In this context, institutional governance and management has, for self-preservation in many cases, turned to institutional research to provide them with reliable data and information to support institutional planning and decision-making. Responding to this context, institutional research has become a part of organizational processes on campuses of every kind and mission.

All of this has resulted in a general move away from the centralized management of "business as usual" toward a focus on the management of data and information that supports the explanation and evaluation of the processes and outcomes of our institutions. As the profession of institutional research moves through this second transition, our use of technology has evolved to the point where data marts and warehouses are being created to provide users access to institutional data across the institution. Desktop and handheld computers have brought users together campus-wide, with software that is specifically designed to support the conduct of analyses on institutional data specific to their unique institutional research needs. In this transition, we are seeing the distribution of the ability to do institutional research to not only other central administrative offices, but also to more distant offices, individual faculty, and faculty committees. Some news media are now obtaining data under Freedom of Information laws so they also can do institutional research. In this environment, institutional research offices must be prepared to work with all organizational entities toward improving organizational intelligence and supporting organizational learning.

To support this latest shift, we need to educate a large number of individuals in the basic skills of institutional research. The realization of this requirement has caused the Association for Institutional Research to develop a book series, *Resources in Institutional Research*, that parallels *NDIR*, *The Handbook on Research in Higher Education*, and the *Professional File* series in publishing conceptual models and best practices for the membership and others in higher education. If we are to pursue the notion of broadening the knowledge and skill base of those in our institutions who can support distributed institutional research, then we need to strengthen our conceptual models and place more demand on having workable theories. These theories not only support the training and professional development of our colleagues, but they also provide an opportunity for the profession to refine its methodologies and the practice of institutional research. The following illustrates several of the concepts that we see as theories. They are only selected to be representative of the beliefs that have relevance to our profession. Exclusion of other "theories" is based on space limitations rather than their quality.

THEORY

Theory is a frame of reference that helps humans to understand the work and to function in it. Theory is crucial in research. Theory provides not only guidelines for analyzing a phenomenon but also a scheme for understanding the significance of research findings. (Chen, p. 17)

It was this frame of reference that Fincher was concerned about in 1985 when he noted that, "The efforts of Institutional research to solve institutional problems and to study internal processes are not guided by a conspicuous network of hypotheses and conjectures that could be called theory." (Fincher, 1985, p. 28) The presence of theory grounded in the reality of our work could provide a framework to explain our values to our stakeholders and provide a reference for improving and generalizing our methodologies.

In thinking about theory in relation to institutional research, we have the same challenges that other evaluation researchers have faced. As a profession, our focus on methodology has limited communication between those of us who use different methodologies. The methodologies have become difficult to communicate and strategies are narrowly focused. The thoughts that follow about theory are designed to assist in providing an opportunity to support communication between those who focus on different methodologies and approaches in the conduct of institutional research.

Institutional Research: What it Should Do and What it Should Value

Theory has two major roles for the profession. It should tell us what to value and it should tell us what to do. One of the stronger institutionalized statements about what institutional research should do, and how it should be done, comes as a set of standards for institutional research developed by the Southern Association of Colleges and Schools, Commission on Colleges (2000):

Institutional research must be an integral part of the institution's planning and evaluation process. It must be effective in collecting and analyzing data and disseminating results. An institution must regularly evaluate the effectiveness of its institutional research process and use its findings for the improvement of its process.

The institutional research process may be centralized or decentralized but should include the following activities: ongoing timely data collection, analysis and dissemination; use of external studies and reports; design and implementation of internal studies related to students, personnel, facilities, equipment, programs, services and fiscal resources; development of data bases suitable for longitudinal studies and statistical analyses; and related activities in support of planning, evaluation and management.

Institutions must assign administrative responsibility for conducting institutional research, allocate adequate resources, and allow access to relevant information. (Section 3.3, SACS)

The performance of institutional research involves a full range of activities from collecting data, the analysis and restructuring of these data into information, and the dissemination of the results of its activities to key constituents. The data reflect internal operational activities, special studies, and external comparative data. Specific activities include studies about students, personnel, facilities, academic programs, services, and financial resources. These studies include trend analyses, comparative analyses, and point-in-time studies that address specific issues or institutional concerns as previously noted. Our methodology also includes the broadest range of content areas (Muffo and McLaughlin, 1987; Whitney, Porter and Fenske, 1992)

These activities provide support to planning, managing, and evaluation of programs and processes at the institution. In addition, the institutional research office or function itself needs to be effectively managed. It needs goals and a mission consistent with its responsibilities and the character of the institution. There needs to be measurement of the impact of the institutional research efforts. These measurements need to be included in the regular and systematic evaluation of a campus institutional research office or function. Where appropriate, changes should be made based on the results of the evaluation of these measures. These improvements can range from changes in the mission, the data and other resources available for conducting institutional research, the capabilities of the institutional research office or function, or the process(es) of communicating the various products and outcomes of the institutional research effort(s) (SACS, 1997, Section 3.3).

As a profession, we have also generated a great deal of discussion about what we should value in conducting institutional research. As noted earlier, some of this discussion has questioned our values and others have attempted to describe what to do in order to be successful. The following reflects an accumulation of thoughts from some of our earlier writers such as Dressel (1971), Saupe and Montgomery (1970), Suslow (1972), Sheehan (1985), and others who have written about the aspects and values of our profession.

Our projects need to be initiated, shaped, and framed based on values. We should set standards for our work and move toward those efforts that are feasible within our means, suitable for who we are, necessary for our institutions, and can be accomplished with efficiency and quality. Into these efforts, we need to bring a representative set of views and the ethic of fairness.

We help solve problems by being able to obtain and analyze essential data and then generalizing the results of our efforts to the situation of concern. This requires that institutional research efforts are timely. If we are unable to produce data and information until after it is needed, then we will have very little worth to the organization. It is also necessary that we provide sufficient data and information to deal with the issues. This often involves educating users on the proper use of the results of analyses. We should produce relevant data. Also the focus of our efforts must be on key concerns, thus reducing the confusion that can come from excess information. This requires that institutional researchers engage in learning about our customers' or stakeholders' needs. Finally we should produce reliable data that are stable, objective, and consistent.

Approaches should be systematic, factual, analytical, and consistent with the common values of higher education and the culture of our institution. As we examine our activities and responsibilities, we should formulate general programs and processes for the production of information required to study and inform decision-makers about institutional effectiveness. We should actively engage our constituents in learning about key issues.

In our institutions, we should be sufficiently separated from the operational responsibilities of administrative processes to maintain the needed objectivity, credibility, and focus. Those who become entwined in operational responsibilities are likely to become defenders of political positions and have a reduced ability to present a balanced response to institutional needs. While the office should not have heavy operational responsibility, it needs to occupy a support position where the institutional research professional can stay abreast of what is going on and what is important.

In terms of management information systems, the institutional research office or function should help develop these systems. However, it should be cautious in becoming involved in the operation and maintenance of these systems. Likewise, an institutional research office should become involved in supporting policy discussions and decisions, but hesitant about continuously promulgating or implementing policy. It is extremely difficult to look objectively at one's own policy and offer viable alternatives.

As a group of individuals, the institutional research office should serve as moderator between the technical aspects of the institution and the managerial and administrative aspects. This broker role should include forming active relationships with faculty in disciplines germane to the needs of the institution. In general, these disciplines include the behavioral sciences and education to study student retention and learning processes, business and management science to support studying the business side of the institution, and computer and information sciences to support the link to technology. Within these domains, the various key areas will depend on the situation. For example, marketing can support admissions and enrollment management; planning and strategic management can support the ability of the institution to anticipate and prepare for future challenges; statistics can help with the more sophisticated investigations requiring the use of multivariate or stochastic processes; and, computer science can help develop the data mart.

Institutional research should solve important problems for the important people in the institution. Most institutional research efforts should have this type of practical approach. The projects selected by the office will be driven by the needs of key individuals in the institution. As much as possible, the projects should have utility for the entire institution.

One of the most important institutional research activities involves providing feedback to various key individuals and groups through the evaluation of programs and processes. We can help determine if programs are meeting their objectives. This requires the description of the program, the identification of its outcomes, and the comparison of those outcomes against the intended outcomes. A second form of evaluation is to determine if the outcomes of a program or process have sufficient utility for the institution. Are they meeting a sufficiently important need? The third type of evaluation is to look at current processes and see if there are other important needs that are not being met.

These forms of evaluation must be put within the timetable of the management of the project. While information must be sufficient to answer the key questions and relevant as to not overwhelm the decision-maker, above all it must be timely. This involves knowing when the information is needed and what decisions the data/information are going to support. If the need is to frame alternatives to the existing program, the information must come before the implementation decision has been made. If the intent is to provide support for a decision that has been made, the information must come after the decision is made.

Suslow summarized the nature of what we should do when he wrote:

Only a collection of characteristics can adequately define the mission

172

of institutional research so as to distinguish it from other activities. For purposes of discussion, here is one such collection: pursuit of goals neither mundane nor perfunctory, detachment from day-to-day policy formulations and implementations; active assessment of the long-range effects of existing or proposed policies in their implementations; enthusiasm for proposals made by others for new methods and new utilizations, but a vigilant skepticism for partisan, mediocre, or reputedly consummate solutions; willingness to assume a spectrum of responsibilities and request to provide assistance to academic and administrative functions of the institution. (1972, p. 17)

Managing Institutional Research

With the earlier look at concepts for doing our activities within the institution, we also need to consider how to do institutional research. This extends the discussion to the strategies of a managed activity. The first issue is to understand how the transitions of institutional research discussed above are related to how institutional research is done at our institutions. Initially, institutional research was a decentralized set of activities conducted in numerous offices using a broad range of methodologies. The function then centralized in the form of an institutional research office that used one or more mainframe computers to conduct analyses and create planning and decision support information. The third wave of institutional research activities has seen the distribution of the function across the campus. In this distributed mode, the office serves as a data and information distributing and coordinating function that supports many individual institutional research operations conducted in other operational and support offices across the institution.

The strategies presented below identify institutional research as being a change agent with the support of senior executives but without a massive amount of formal authority. The authority is derived from the situation and must be accepted by those in the organization it influences.

Function and Office

The presence of an institutional research office varies from institution to institution. The size of such an office also varies with a tendency to be small in many institutions. Because of this variability, the following looks at managing the function rather than directing the office.

As a function, institutional research needs to take a strategic view of the institution and its role. Its relevance comes from adding value to data and information and improving institutional intelligence. As such, the institutional research function must position its information infrastructure in such a way that its activities enhance the value of information that is produced. The information production and distribution capabilities of the institution must be assessed relative to its needs. From this analysis, gaps for the services of institutional research

173

should be identified along with the important stakeholders. Developing prototypes for these services, the institutional researcher should monitor customer responses and make appropriate adjustments. With these services, the institutional research function can create a positive belief about the importance of information in planning and decision-making. Advertise institutional research services and products as value-added items; and, for the services that seem to be most profitable in terms of robustness and expandability, build participant communities of information users and data suppliers.

A strategy should be implemented to increase the quality of the institutional research function or office, both in terms of effectiveness and efficiency. This initial strategy should be used to share a vision of institutional research that supports the institution; attract and develop the best people, keeping in mind the continued uncertainty about the specific skills that will be needed; also identify and share credit for accomplishments. This should include those accomplishments that maintain group processes and that communicate with internal and external constituencies; focus resources and services that sustain the function; and position the function to have capabilities for future central information needs.

In the office, where one exists, always keep the objectives of the institutional research function in mind. The office is the custodian of the function as it is responsible for the function's accountability, accessibility, and availability in the institution. The strategic goals for the office need to be adjusted to fit management information needs, the level of resources available to the office, and the information needs across the institution. Adjust the ends to fit the means and always have an awareness of the technological situation. With the continued changes in all institutions, maintain flexibility of plans and resources. Have several sustaining core activities such as a fact book. Develop annual reports that reinforce the core competencies and accomplishments of the office and use these same competencies to do short, effective projects for key individuals. Presley (1990) extends these concepts into the broader domain of office issue, particularly on the issues of organizing for various activities. Also see Middaugh, Trusheim, and Bauer (1994) who discuss the broader aspects of operating an IR office.

Projects

As projects are focused on an area of specific interest, the office should be aware of services provided across the institution by other units and avoid duplication. Strategies should be developed that avoid major conflicts with other units, turf battles, and other forms of resistance. It is important that key individuals know what is feasible with the resources that are available and be able to identify appropriate resources that will be needed for specific tasks. Often having an office process that measures the time spent by office staff on major activities will facilitate this.

In addition, activities should be developed to bring customers with similar needs together. This ability to form "user groups" improves the efficiency of the office and pursues activities that meet multiple objectives. For example, those who are responsible for marketing the institution have some of the same concerns as those concerned about retention and student satisfaction with services. One project that involves both types of customers will often do double duty. As projects are developed, office staff should help the customers frame questions in order to identify the essential information needed to answer the questions. This includes suggesting methodologies that are most effective and efficient, both from the perspective of the individual customer and also from the perspective of the office and the institution. Such approaches should include making sure that "off-the-shelf" products are used to the fullest extent feasible before additional information is developed.

Where current products and processes do not meet an important need, scan the situation and make key stakeholders aware of potential problems before the project starts. As a project is considered, use your professional network to find out what other institutions have done when facing a similar situation. Develop a general agenda for the product, including where it fits with other projects. The purpose of the process is to negotiate the timelines and resources required to complete the project with identified deliverables. Sometimes the best way to do this is to go through a project negotiation cycle. Brainstorm the situation with the key stakeholders and include those who are the sources of the data as well as the customers. As the focus of the negotiation turns to what will be produced by the successful completion of the project, tie the development of products to decisions and when they will be made. This helps to frame relevant questions, such as: What are the likely outcomes of the institutional activity under study and how desirable are they? What are anticipated causal relationships? What is the best strategy for proceeding with the project? The next step is to clarify the project by developing required actions and feasible milestones. Finally, identify individuals responsible for different components of the projects and milestones to be met within specific timeframes.

Finally, as the project is initiated, develop interactive processes that involve the interaction of the research process along with the provider of the data and the intended user of the results. Space the results of the project to support institutional learning. Include reflective processes that cause participants to consider best strategies for the remainder of the project. These in-progress reviews should be fairly well spaced throughout the project and should involve the ability to capitalize on unanticipated good things as well as deal with unanticipated bad things. Use an agenda and post-meeting memorandums to document and maintain progress. Celebrate successes throughout the life of the project. However, also be willing to have walk-away events where the project can be terminated or substantially modified. (McLaughlin and McLaughlin, 1989, McLaughlin and Snyder 1993)

The Information Support Circle

While the preceding discussion of concepts has dealt with considerations of our strategies and the issues related to managing our function, we still have to deal with a general operational process, or methodology, for doing our projects. At one level, each project has its own methodology. The specific disciplines from which we acquire our techniques have their own set of values, beliefs, purposes, and methodologies. We return to the concern by Chen that to focus on these specific methodologies divides our efforts and decreases our focus, and in some significant ways can weaken our profession.

With this concern in mind, the following is provided as a generalized method for thinking about the practice of institutional research. This general paradigm says that facts start in the form of disaggregated and detached data. These data become information when they are restructured and analyzed within a specific context, resulting in increased understanding of the issue or situation under study. Most frequently, this understanding involves reducing the complexity of the issue and focusing on the specific aspects under consideration. The information is then delivered and used to shape beliefs, make decisions, support strategies, and to generalize increased understanding to other situations. At this point, information is converted into the increased intelligence of the individual, and organization learning has occurred.

In a very general sense, the transformation of the facts as described above represents adding value to the organization; the transformation of facts to intelligence is part of the core competencies of information professions such as institutional research. As the paradigm represents the context of improved value of information, it also then represents a way for us to frame our strategies and to use our techniques and methodologies.

The Information Support Circle (Figure 6.1) has been presented as a process by which the organization converts data into information and then uses that information to increase organizational intelligence. In this conceptual model, three primary roles and five steps are defined, which are required to create information that effectively supports decision-making. The roles are those of the supplier or custodian of the data, the broker who converts the data into information, and the customer or manager who uses the information as increased intelligence. The functions include the activities of identifying the situation, developing the data, focusing the data on the situation, providing the resulting information to the manager, and the use of this information in the context of the problem. The circle comes from the continuous identification of issues based on the previous decisions, and the continuous nature of the learning process. The theoretical basis behind the Information Support Circle can be found in CAUSE/ EFFECT. (Howard, McLaughlin, and McLaughlin, 1989, vol. 12, no. 2) The components are briefly elaborated in the following.

In this model, three roles are defined as the custodian, the broker, and the user. In general, the custodian obtains and stores those operational data, which result in the creation of an asset or resource to support planning and decision-making. Data from the custodian are then restructured and integrated, or converted to information by a broker. The person in this role then communicates the information to the user, thus supporting decision-making in the institution. Numerous individuals hold these three roles across the campus, and key to quality of the resulting information is the coordination of the roles in an institution-wide data administration function. In the book, *People, Processes and Managing Data* (McLaughlin, Howard, Balkan, and Blythe, 1998), the specific responsibilities of these roles are defined and discussed in relation to data administration. Below, these roles are defined specifically in relation to the practice of institutional research.

The five functions in the Information Support Circle represent a sequential set of tasks that are typically associated with institutional research. Specifically, data are identified as relevant, captured, stored, restructured, analyzed, and integrated to form information. This information is then delivered or communicated in a form that can be integrated into the knowledge base of the decision-maker. This process develops in increased intelligence for the user, answering some questions and raising others. This then initiates the next cycle, illustrated by the Information Support Circle. As such, effectiveness of the institutional research function is dependent upon its involvement in, and the integration of, the three roles and five functions.

In recognizing the three roles and the five-step decision support process, institutional research has an opportunity to add value to the institution's management by putting into place systems which effectively manage data, information, and its interpretation. When data are needed, the institutional researcher must function with, or sometimes as, the custodian of the needed data. When information is needed, the institutional researcher often must function as both the creator and broker of that information. When facts are being interpreted to increase organizational intelligence in order to better understand a situation, the institutional researcher functions with and as the user who needs those interpretations. These three roles are further explored below.

The Custodian

The custodian acts as a source of internal and external data. With census files with the advent of data warehouses and data marts, institutional research is becoming involved as a secondary source of data and, as such, of "the secondary data custodian." This is a natural extension of the institutional research role evolving out of our responsibility to obtain, maintain, and retain reliable and valid data for key surveys such as the NCES IPEDS reports. By obtaining and combining data from various operational sources, institutional researchers have historically created census-type databases. In this role, institutional research has demonstrated appropriate activities for the custodians at the institution. In creating these census-type databases, the institutional research function has acted as a steward of the data, not as an owner of the data. Using this experience, the institutional research function or office must help establish, audit, and share the definitions and descriptions of the data to other users. The function must balance access and security, and must be concerned with the overall management of institutional data.

A second type of data that requires custodial activities are those data from external sources. Frequently, the institutional research office is the custodian of such data. This responsibility includes documenting and developing distribution methods and protocols for accessing the data. The role also includes being the conduit for such data that may be made available on CD, the World Wide Web, and other sources.

Figure 6.1
Information Support Process

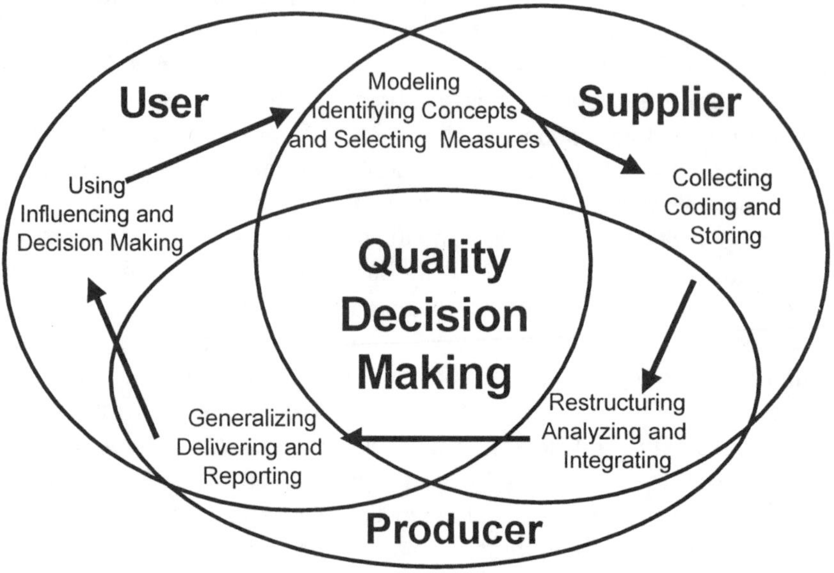

The Broker

The broker acts to restructure, analyze, or integrate the data to create information. This frequently involves interpreting the data within the context of the data collection process and the primary focus of the decision to be made. Statistics, and other analytic tools are critical in reducing the amount of data and making it more usable for decision support. Success is heavily dependent on the institutional researcher's knowledge of various technical skills requiring the use of computers, software, networks, spreadsheet techniques and quantitative tools, such as statistics, operations research, and econometrics. Also needed are qualitative analytic skills that support case studies, situation assessment, and content analysis. Such skills must be integrated into the organization at the strategic, managerial, and operational levels. In this role, the institutional researcher must strive to better understand the relevance of observable events and from that understanding structure the information derived from the analyses of institutional data to meet the decision-makers needs.

The User

To increase the usefulness of information at the strategic level, the institutional researcher needs to anticipate the future needs for information by institutional decision-makers as well as correctly defining the institution's current situation. This requires insights and a keen understanding of the decision-making process as implemented by the institution's managers. Increases in organizational intelligence of the information users require that the institutional researcher have, or develop, political skills that will allow him to anticipate and interpret the decision-maker's situation. In addition, the institutional researcher must be able to assess the value of information to the user.

Finally, communication of the information at that point-in-time, where it can make the greatest contribution to the decision-making process, enhances the value of the information to the decision-maker. This requires an individual to act, not only as an office or unit manager, but also one who interfaces with others at the boundary of the office, simultaneously structuring institutional research projects to make them manageable, doable, and relevant. In other words, the capable institutional researcher must be a qualified manager who has access to, and knowledge of, proper tools; who can develop appropriate policies and recommendations; and, who has the interpersonal and organizational skills to involve required staff in projects.

The Five Functions of Information Support

Understanding the functions of institutional research begins with the understanding of those who ask questions, including those who make decisions at the operational, managerial, and strategic levels of the institution. Data and information needs at these different levels are significantly different in terms of timing, scope, and detail. Often decisions at the strategic level are long-term and concerned with the future direction of the institution. Decisions at the managerial level are more likely to be concerned with how the institution will position itself relative to other competitive institutions over the next two years. Decisions at the operational level are more likely to focus on day-to-day operations of the institution. The institutional research function needs to manage its data resource in such a way as to provide a sufficient base for reporting, research, and related activities that support all levels of decision-making. This requires that the institutional research function or office be involved with, and gain an understanding of, those functions that provide the raw materials for data analysis and research, information technology, and data management. If the needs of different customers are properly identified, and the quality of data maintained, analyses can produce descriptive, comparative, or projective results that will meet the information needs of decision-makers at all levels across the campus.

The strategic application of the skills and abilities that add value to the data, information, and organizational intelligence provided by institutional research can be described by the following five sequential functions:

Problem Identification

In this initial step, the problem is defined. What is the situation? What are the primary characteristics of the problem? How do you know it is a problem? What is it that the decision-maker really needs to know? The definition of the problem comes with the exploration and clarification of the situation. From this, crystallization of what needs to be done to deal with the situation occurs. If the situation of concern requires that a decision be made at a known point, organization of the project must be taken into consideration when the decision needs to be made. In cases where a set of sequential events lead to a decision point, a realistic timeline needs to be considered, as the collection or creation of quality data and analysis (the conduct of effective institutional research) take time.

Following this situation assessment, appropriate measures must be identified and incorporated into a parsimonious model. While the measures may be framed as performance indicators or critical success factors, more typically they take the shape of data that can help decision-makers understand "what causes what" and to anticipate the outcomes resulting from specific decisions. If the need is to develop a model to monitor or anticipate specific events, a good starting point may be to identify six or seven key components of the situation and then select two or three measures that define each of these components. The resulting measures can then be organized to create a conceptual model of the event or situation that allow data collection and analyses of manageable size, creating the specific information that will support the decision-making process.

Data Acquisition

What data are available? Are available data sufficient to create the needed information? While some data that define key measures are usually available for any problem, the institutional research professional must determine if the data are sufficient to address the problem. Key data issues include timeliness and reliability.

The second concern to be addressed is the availability of resources for securing the data. In general, a well-developed understanding of the situation helps the institutional research function anticipate needed data, usually resulting in the production of better data and information at reduced costs. If the data are external to the institution, obtaining them may involve the identification of resources required to purchase the rights to use the data. In other cases, substantial monetary resources may not be required and secondary databases, such as those supported by NCES, may be available. Often there will be tradeoffs of time versus comprehensiveness that must be factored into the data collection process.

When using secondary data, political issues concerning perceived believability, value, and appropriateness of source may need to be addressed. If the data are for internal uses only and not to be made public (as is often the case in data exchanges), then agreement about masking the data sources and the public release of information need to be discussed and agreed upon at all levels of the decision-making process. If collecting primary data to establish an internal database, the institutional research function needs to establish its own ability to manage the resulting database - data administration.

Data Restructuring and Analysis

What do the data mean? Converting the data to information involves the analysis and restructuring of the data within those parameters defined in the problem assessment phase, and analyzing the data to focus on the situation. The key is to understand that detailed data must be restructured in ways that keep the important detail, while simultaneously simplifying and summarizing "noise" in the data.

To accomplish this, the institutional researcher should consider the use of multiple data sources where possible, because the same indicator coming from multiple sources results in a stronger argument. In addition, the institutional researcher, when conducting the analysis, needs to consider the perspective of those using the resulting information. The analysis should include some conceptual components, some empirical components, and some experiential components. These three basic types of evidence typically result in information that individuals find compelling. The process of successfully converting data into useful information must include the integration of data from multiple sources, making sure that interpretations are consistent, and to determine when sufficient data are available for making interpretations with adequate confidence.

Information Reporting

To whom do the results need to be delivered? How should the findings be interpreted? Interpretation and integration of information into the context of the situation occurs when the results are delivered to the manager/decision-maker. Putting the information into the context of the user increases the level of organizational intelligence about the situation.

The key focus for institutional research is to interpret and generalize the results from various analyses to specific situations. Conditions under which the data (supporting the information reported) were collected must be reflected. Understanding changes in primary influences in the environment, which might affect the data, will assist the user in interpreting the implications of the information for his or her situation. Additional information that should be provided includes estimates of the confidence that can be placed on the findings and conclusions of causality, if appropriate. Discussing the desirability of those specific outcomes which most likely can be achieved from specific decisions may or may not be included, depending on what the manager or decision-maker needs. Access to the data and information must be provided in various forms. The more technically savvy customer may want to conduct additional analyses. The administrator may want to check indicators to see if reality is consistent with his/her belief structure.

Information Use

What actions do the data, information, and interpretation support? What are the next steps? After the interpretation is provided the user, there is an increase in the organizational intelligence related to what is known about the situation. In other words, the users' knowledge base has been expanded. However, the reduction of uncertainty further depends on the timeliness, sufficiency, and relevance of the information provided. The information must be available before the decision is made to have value. If the results are provided after the decision has been made, it will be a waste of the customers' time and can introduce further uncertainty. The sufficiency of the conclusion determines whether the customer is made aware of all key issues affecting the situation. The relevance of the conclusions determines whether the information focuses the user on key issues without including a large number of surplus facts that have little bearing on the situation. When the information adequately increases the intelligence of the decision-maker, appropriate actions will more likely be taken and the focus of the custodian, broker, and use will shift to the next issue affecting the situation. Beliefs about the situation are changed at this point and the next set of questions will require a refined set of definitions that may result in the need for different data and information.

An Example

The following is an example of how the five-step model works. The example is for a retention study. The first step is the development of a conceptual model of the area of concern — retention. This includes a determination of the factors to be measured. Studying retention, we would very likely start with the work discussed in Pascarella and Terenzini (1991). From the models discussed by these two, it might be decided to measure engagement in key activities, resulting integration or functionality of outcomes, and satisfactions with primary services. As producers, we would involve the customers or users of our study and also the custodians of the student data in this step. In the second step, we have to identify data that define these measures and capture and store these data so that they have the needed reliability. In the third step we access the data from the domain of the input event and restructure it to conform to the needs for evaluating outcomes. Also in this step, we need to analyze the data to reduce its complexity and to highlight the key aspects of the information that relate to the concerns of the specific situation and purpose for which it was developed. This might involve summarizing performance of students in primary academic areas such as social studies and natural sciences, and then modeling the expected performance using regression analyses. In the fourth step of the process we need to deliver the information to the customer, making sure that a sufficient amount of information and data are included to deal with the questions as identified in the conceptual model. In the final step of the process, the information needs to be integrated into the knowledge of the user so that it can be used to influence the activities, values, and priorities of the community. This usually results in increased intelligence about the organization.

The value of the information to reduce uncertainty depends on its relevance to key concerns around the decision to be made and its timeliness in the use sequence, often referred to as the decision-making cycle. It is important to recognize that in the development of information support, the use of the information will require a change in the conceptual model that defines the situation under study. As a result of the information, new questions will be asked and new measures will become more important. Providing information support requires the sequence to be circular in order for continuous organizational learning.

The other characteristic to consider is that in the cycle of creating decision support information, the value of the information is limited by the quality of the outcomes of the preceding step. If reliable data are not collected, analyses can have no value. If the information is interpreted incorrectly, then it cannot add value to the decision-making. Improvement of the weakest step improves the value added at every step. Based on this dependency, it is possible to produce the greatest amount of information improvement by identifying the weakest point of the information process and improving it. This enhances the value of the following steps until the next limiting issue is encountered.

It is also important that individuals in the three roles understand and interact with each other. This is becoming increasingly important as enterprise information systems bring to the organization a new context of opportunity and also a new fog of uncertainty. Functional users are implementing much of these systems. As the custodians and stewards, they can bring a tremendous knowledge to the discussion of how to best measure the issues in the conceptual model and also in how to generalize results from a specific set of data to other situations.

ISSUES IN THE PRACTICE OF INSTITUTIONAL RESEARCH

Practicing institutional researchers who have read thus far can perhaps be forgiven for being depressed....good analysis and good decisions are not necessarily related, and the seemingly straightforward process of providing for sound information for decision-makers is layered with complexity. (Ewell, 1989, p. 85)

Ewell continues to explain that the practice of the profession requires the ability to fully understand the institutional context of a request for information and being able to keep the request in the sequence of knowing. He identifies the questions of:

1. Who's asking?
2. What for?
3. What's the proper medium? and
4. What happens now?

This perspective of pragmatic inquiry was reinforced by Suslow (1970) who said:

The successful practice of institutional research depends upon the individual who has a broad knowledge of diverse disciplines, an intense understanding of his institution, and, above all, an attitude which commits him to the value of these institutions purpose in society. (p. 1)

Why Would an Institution Value Institutional Research?

If institutional research is to add value to facts, then we in institutional research must have a feel for their use. As noted earlier from Hubbard, Suslow, and others our role is to provide data and information that have value in their use within our institutions. This use can be viewed from two primary lenses: Why are the facts valued? How are they used? These two topics are also considered as the paradigm being used and the style of the decision-maker. The following is a brief overview to illustrate their importance in the practice of institutional research.

One of the more balanced views of alternative ways to establish truth is given by Guba (1991). These different approaches determine much of what facts a person wants, when they want them, how these facts are seen in establishing reality, and how the facts are best used. In other words, the paradigm from which a person works is a primary context that determines the value of information. Guba identifies three basic ways in which individuals approach their reality: the positivist, the constructivist, and the critical theorist. In considering these three ways in which individuals establish truth, it becomes obvious that effective institutional researchers use a combination of these approaches to support decision-makers.

The positivist identifies truth through a procedure that many consider the scientific method. This method, when extended to the decision-maker, is often referred to as a rational decision model, and has given rise to disciplines such as scientific management. Using this paradigm, the institutional researcher seeks to be scientific and rational. Problems are identified and causes are analyzed. Alternative solutions are considered. Proof is provided, often with numerical representations of reality. A decision is made based on the facts, the results are measured, and the process continues. If in using the Information Support Circle (Figure 6.1) the process starts with a research question that is followed by the testing of a hypothesis, then the five steps in the Circle are similar to the scientific method as defined by the positivist paradigm.

In the critical theory paradigm, the person has a personal grasp of the truth and the best way to deal with various decisions. The use of facts is to persuade and prove to others as to the correctness of the perspective. In terms of institutional research, we are often asked to identify weaknesses in the argument of the opposition and document the correctness of the position held by our stakeholder. In the constructivist model there is no way to be scientifically neutral, and it is also foolish to look for proof. The situation is considered to be so complex that it is appropriate only to observe, document the observations (collect data), and attempt to draw insights from the observations. This paradigm often produces vignettes and other qualitative outputs. As noted earlier, there are some strategies for describing reality that seem to integrate these perspectives. For example, grounded theory and case study approaches seem to integrate the positivist and the constructivist paradigms.

Decision-Making Models

While the discussion of paradigms sounds a bit theoretical, the combination of the logic of these paradigms in the context of time and space produce what can be referred to as decision models. The following discussion is based on four types of decision-makers. They were developed from work done by Peterson (1985) and are more fully discussed elsewhere (McLaughlin, McLaughlin, and Howard, 1987).

Decision-makers use various decision-making philosophies in the management of the institution. It is critical that the institutional researcher, in supporting decision-making processes on his or her campus understands the decision-making philosophy being used, the primary context of concern that drives the philosophy, and the characteristics of the information support required. In Figure 6.2, four primary decision-making philosophies are identified. Each philosophy reflects its own context of concern and requires a different form of information support.

In the **Political Decision-Making Philosophy**, others' perceptions are of primary concern. Usually key executives dealing with external and internal constituents use this type of decision-making philosophy. As these individuals are typically busy individuals, the most effective information support often is discrete bits of information, focused on a specific topic or concern. This might be a single enrollment figure or the average salary of full professors. The desirability of outcomes and the causes of these outcomes are of lesser value to these decision-makers, as typically, decisions are based on a complex set of relationships and influences that are often political and/or situational.

In the **Autocratic Decision-Making Philosophy**, the decision-maker's personal agenda relative to an organization such as a college or major research

Figure 6.2
Characteristics of Decision-Making Philosophies

Decision-Making Philosophy	Context Primary Concern	Information Requirements	
		FOCUS	BREADTH
POLITICAL	OTHERS' PERCEPTIONS	DISCRETE	FOCUSED
AUTOCRACTIC	PERSONAL AGENDA	CONTINUOUS	FOCUSED
MANAGERIAL	PROGRAM QUALITY	CONTINUOUS	BROAD
COLLEGIAL	"CORRECTNESS" OF PROCESS	DISCRETE	BROAD

center is the primary focus. The decision-maker often prefers or wants a continuous flow of information as it relates to his/her agenda, but often likes to have it delivered in focused bits. They are less concerned about the desirability of different outcomes, because their preferences are focused on their personal agenda. They are, however, very interested in the best ways to cause a specific outcome.

The **Managerial Decision-Making Philosophy** occurs where there are a large number of issues and often some requiring unstructured decision-making. Often there is the need to be persuasive and participatory in the decision process. The primary concern is for program quality where both effectiveness and efficiency are important, such as in an academic department or program. In general, these decision-makers are interested in a broad and continuous flow of data/information that describes the quality of their programs. They often use some form of the positivist or rational decision model and greatly value the types of information that institutional research can provide. They are interested in both the causation of outcomes and the desirability of the outcomes.

Finally, the Collegial Decision-Making Philosophy is one that resides on virtually every campus. In this type of decision-making process, the primary concern is "correctness" of process. In supporting this type of decision-making, the institutional researcher needs to provide discrete bits of information or data covering broadly the issues under consideration. Virtually every aspect of the situation that the decision-maker thinks "might be" relevant needs to be examined. Great care is often taken to ensure that all perspectives are considered. Often, many of the initial discussions revolve around the desirability of various outcomes and less on the causation of the outcomes.

The Broader Context

In addition to being aware of the context of the decision-maker, the focus of institutional research efforts and the resulting value to our organizations is heavily dependent on the culture of our institutions and the context of the society in which they find themselves. For example, Fincher doubted that we could ever become a science because there was no science in the management of institutions of higher education. Peterson (1999) refers to the phases of higher education as being the driving force behind what we in institutional research do and the types of problems we need to help our institutions solve. Volkwein (2000) continues with a current discussion of the role of the context of our studies.

Overcoming The Barriers to Success

Even though information should be of great value to any rational decision-making process, much of our information is:

- Gathered and communicated but has little decision relevance;
- Used to justify a decision and is created after the decision is made;
- Gathered for a specific decision, but not used for that decision;
- Requested even though there is enough information to make the decision;
- Not used even though people complain that there is not enough information;
- The relevance of information is not as important as just having information. (Tetlow, 1983)

It is obvious that there are limitations to the value that our services have for our institutions. For example, some of the most often mentioned limitations in a survey of institutional research practitioners included heavy demands for routine data that limits time for significant research; institutional research is not seen as part of the leadership team; and, campus politics interfere with the appropriate use of the information. (Knight, Coperthwaite and Moore, 1997) Another perspective was provided by Billups and DeLucia (1990) who saw the primary limitation as institutional research not being integrated into the institution's management and planning processes. Barriers that limit the ability to accomplish this integration seem to be primarily people problems. Hackman (1989) provides advice on the management of projects and the presentation of results as part of seven maximums for effective institutional research. In terms of information use, barriers that limit the value of our information can occur in regards to any of the five functions in the previously noted Information Support Circle (McLaughlin and McLaughlin, 1989).

To overcome these barriers, Terenzini (1993) identifies three tiers of intelligence that an institutional research professional needs in order to add value to his or her college or university. First, **Technical Intelligence** is needed. This type of intelligence is the ability to work with the basic building blocks of our profession. These include methodological skills and the ability to use tools like statistics, cost-benefit analyses, planning models, computers, and strategic management tools. This set of skills is similar to those that are frequently needed for entry-level institutional research positions. They are also the abilities that are needed to complete institutional research projects and the day-to-day operations of an institutional research office or function. The second level of intelligence is **Issues Intelligence** and involves dealing with problems that require the skill to use technical and analytical skills. This includes understanding the reasons for managerial activities and understanding decision-making processes. Issues Intelligence also includes general organizational skills, communication skills, and the more advanced skill of being able to apply what is known from various disciplines in tasks such as shaping an inquiry or studying complex issues like student retention or program evaluation. **Contextual Intelligence** is the third level of intelligence and represents knowledge of the culture of higher education, both at the institutional level and in general. It includes an understanding of how business is done at a specific institution, the key issues facing the institution, and how to most appropriately effect change. This level of intelligence makes the technical application of intelligence to locally meaningful versions of general issues possible.

It is interesting to note that these levels of knowing are very similar to those developed by the National Research Council in discussing fluency in information technology (1999). In their concept, the person who is fluent with information technology has contemporary skills to deal with the current set of computer packages. In addition, they understand the fundamental concepts of information technology so that they can readily grasp new skills as they become relevant, and they need skills in the use of information technology so they can understand the new concepts. (NRC, 1999)

Practicing across these three levels of intelligence also needs to be part of the management of the institutional research office, where it exists, as well as other institutional research functions at the institution. The management of institutional research activities and functions needs to continually pursue the values and concepts we have described above. The function needs to be positioned in a strategic niche where it can add value to the institution. In addition, where an office does exist, the institutional research function needs to be managed in an effective and efficient manner. Some of these concepts were discussed in the previous standards of the Southern Association of Colleges and Schools. (SACS, 1997) Other strategies involve building alliances with other offices across the institution and partnering in key projects. (McLaughlin and Snyder, 1993)

Central to efforts to sustain the practice of institutional research has been the development of a Code of Ethics, which includes a set of standards for conducting institutional research. (Schiltz, 1992) This Code came from the recognition by Mike Schiltz and others that the Association for Institutional Research and its members had gone through a transformation. Bringing together numerous diverse perspectives, a document was fashioned and approved by the membership that defined quality and stressed a focus on quality in the practice of institutional research. The Code is on the Web (www.fsu.edu/~air/ethics.htm), and is printed in the annual AIR *Members' Handbook/Annual Report*. The Code is summarized below for those who have not had the opportunity to read it. In *New Directions for Institutional Research*, vol. 73, Schiltz and his colleagues extends the explanation and provides a discussion that led to its creation.

Competency: Work within your skills and do not overstate them. Develop the skills of yourself and your subordinates.

Execution: Work within the boundaries of your methodologies. Use appropriate standards of practice and various analytical techniques. Identify assumptions, values and limitations.

Confidentiality: Work within agreements for security and confidentiality of the data. Permit no release of data that violates base agreements or the laws such as FERPA. Support and train others in the appropriate guidelines.

Community: Work with processes that support openness, participation, equity and diversity. Provide for archiving data for further use in research. Help interpret internal and external requests to prevent misunderstanding.

Craft: Work to strengthen the profession and do not falsely demean those who practice the profession. Support consistent practice and work to change those that are inconsistent with our standards of ethics.

It should be noted that this Code is a theory and a practice issue. It describes how we should apply our trade. As such, it now returns us to our roots of Suslow, Saupe, Russell, and others. While these individuals gave us information on the tasks we were to consider appropriate, they also focused much of their discussion on how we were to function within our institutions.

CLOSING THOUGHTS

A modest action agenda ... would include the following: ...

- Focus attention on the need for a common view of the practice of institutional research as a inclusive process of information collection, analysis, research, and utilization related to planning, management, resource allocation, and evaluation decisions....

- Promote a professional theme focused on the improvement of institutions of postsecondary education through institutional research that relates theory to practice and that responds to new rational methods. (Peterson and Corcoran, 1985, p. 111)

In general, the theoretical and conceptual models presented above define institutional research as a practice of adding value to facts within the context of a complex organization. As mentioned by Hubbard, we exist to add value to our institutions. Our institutions are complex organizations with multiple issues, multiple priorities, and multiple linkages among key individuals. They do tend to have a central purpose as stated in their mission, and there is a motivation to move toward that purpose. There need to be general rules that govern behavior and there needs to be an ability for such an organization to learn from activities and events. The activity of institutional research can add value to the organization by providing quality information and intelligence, thereby reducing uncertainty in decision-making processes. Institutional research can be looked at in the following terms: **function** which is becoming increasingly distributed across the campus; an **office** which needs to be relevant, but not buried in operational activities; and the **projects** of institutional research which give focus to our activities and are the visible manifestation of our function.

Through the Information Support Circle (Figure 6.1), we propose that institutional researchers can best approach the challenges they face in a systematic manner. Situations need to be analyzed in terms of the duties that need to be performed. We need to understand that these duties are typically clustered into three major roles — Custodian, Broker, and User. Institutional research professionals need to understand and work with individuals in all three roles, with the greatest part of their responsibilities in the role of Broker. In this role, the institutional researcher brings together the activities of the custodian of data and technology with the activities of the user, who is often required to make decisions and manage the institution. This role can be further understood by looking at our brokering as being part of a five-step process that results in the creation of information support. We also need to understand these activities and elements within the context of the institution, the decision processes, and the decision style of the user of the information.

In order to overcome the barriers that will limit our effectiveness and efficiency, we need to develop the technical ability to use a broad range of methodologies, the skill to use these abilities within the context of the decisions to be made, and the knowledge to use these skills to enhance organizational intelligence and support change within our institutions. The application of these abilities, skills, and knowledge should help our colleges and universities manage their institutional research resources. They should help identify a shared purpose for the institution. They should help the institution evaluate current programs and establish the need for new programs. They should help our institutions test beliefs of current realities with comparisons against time, other institutions, and ideal goals. They should help anticipate future events. They should help provide a history of lessons learned so that the process is heuristic. To continue the learning process, they should look at the policies, procedures, and even the culture that established the rules of interaction and learning.

How to Do Institutional Research Better

As noted above and elsewhere in this publication, the history of institutional research has been focused on doing things better and to do better things. From Suslow to current writers such as Chaffee, Ewell, Middaugh, Peterson, Saunders, Smart , and Terenzini, to name only a few, and from agencies such as NCES and NPEC (1999), numerous papers, articles, chapters, and books on the subject of improvement have regularly appeared. In looking at these works, a type of grounded theory has emerged on how we should do what we do and on opportunities to improve both the way we do things and the things we do. The challenge now is to think of this stream of improvement as a continuous process. Certainly the professional development process of the Association for Institutional Research is focused on the improvement of our profession and on the use of our profession to improve higher education. The Association's publications range from the scholarly Research in Higher Education to the very applied Professional File and include the thematic New Directions for Institutional Research, Higher Education Handbook of Theory and Research, the ASHE/ERIC Higher Education Reports, and the book series Resources in Institutional Research. The Association's collaboration includes support of the ASHE/ERIC monograph series and a broad range of electronic communications. Practicing institutional research professionals and academics serve on national boards for improving higher education-related data such as the NPEC with NCES. These ideas and concepts of improving the profession and its practice are taught through the Association's institutes, workshops, forums, and its numerous affiliated associations.

In line with the Association's many activities for improving both individuals' practice of institutional research and the profession, we feel the words of Sidney Suslow spoken some 30 years ago are still relevant.

> As a field of higher education, institutional research will be fruitful and gather strength if the individual researcher neither allows himself to be intimidated by those who wish to save our institutions through pervasive management untempered by social conscience nor permits himself to ignore the value to be derived from management tools when aptly applied....

> If we are pretentious in our pride for our achievements to date, then let us simply accept it; if we are satisfied to rest with this achievement we are foolish, and if we cannot accelerate and enlarge on our achievements then, I, for one, will be damned disappointed. (p. 3)

References

Billups, F. D. and DeLucia, L. A. (1990). Integrating institutional research into the organization. In J. B. Presley (Vol. Ed.), New Directions for Institutional Research: No. 66. Organizing effective institutional research offices. (pp. 93-102) San Francisco, CA: Jossey-Bass.

Brackett, G. B. (1983). Educational preparation opportunities for institutional research practitioners. Unpublished doctoral dissertation: Southern Illinois University at Carbondale.

Chen, H. T. (1990). Theory-driven evaluations. London: Sage Publications.

Dressel, P. L. & Associates. (1971). Institutional research in the university: A handbook. San Francisco, CA: Jossey-Bass.

Ewell, P. T. (1989). Putting it all together: four questions for practitioners. In P. T. Ewell (Vol. Ed.), New Directions for Institutional Research: No. 64. Enhancing information use in decision-making (pp. 85-90), San Francisco, CA: Jossey-Bass.

Guba, E. G. (1991). The alternative paradigm dialog. In E.G. Guba (Ed.), The paradigm dialog, (pp. 17-27). Newbury Park, CA: Sage Publications.

Hackman, J. (1989). The psychological contest: Seven maxims for institutional researchers. In P. Ewell (Vol. Ed.), New Directions for Institutional Research: No. 64. Enhancing information use in decision-making. (pp. 35-48). San Francisco, CA: Jossey-Bass.

Howard, R. D., McLaughlin, G. W., & McLaughlin, J. S. (1989). Bridging the gap between the data base and user in a distributed environment. CAUSE/EFFECT: Vol. 12 No. 2, 19-25.

Hubbard, R. W., Baskin, S., & Grout, S. (1964). A conceptual framework for institutional research: Three points of view. In C. H. Bagley (Ed.), A conceptual framework for institutional research. Proceedings of the fourth annual National Institutional Research Forum. 7-10.

Knight, W. R., Moore, M. E., & Coperthwaite, C. A. (1997). Institutional research: Knowledge, skills, and perspectives of effectiveness. Research in Higher Education: Vol. 38, No. 4.

Lyons, John M. (1976). A memorandum to a newcomer to the field of institutional research. Tallahassee, FL: Association for Institutional Research.

McLaughlin, G. W., & McLaughlin, J. S. (1989). Barriers to information use: The organizational context. In P. Ewell (Vol. Ed.), New Directions for Institutional Research: No. 64. Enhancing information use in decision-making. (pp. 21-33). San Francisco, CA: Jossey-Bass.

McLaughlin, G. W., Howard, R. D., Balkan, L. A., & Blythe, E. W. (1998). People, processes and data administration. Resources in Institutional Research: No. 11. Tallahassee FL: Association for Institutional Research.

McLaughlin, G. W., McLaughlin, J. S., & Howard, R. D. (1987). Decision support in the information age. In E. M. Stayman (Vol. Ed.), New Directions for Institutional Research: No. 55. Managing information in higher education. (pp. 81-91) San Francisco, CA: Jossey-Bass.

McLaughlin, G. W. & Snyder J. K. (1993). Plan-do-check-act and the management of institutional research. The AIR Professional File: No. 48. Tallahassee, FL: Association for Institutional Research.

Middaugh, M. F., Trusheim, D. W., & Bauer, K. W. (1994). Strategies for the practice of institutional research: Concepts, resources, and applications. In Resources in Institutional Research: No. 9. Tallahassee, FL: Association for Institutional Research and Northeast Association for Institutional Research.

Muffo, J. A., & McLaughlin, G. W. (Eds.). (1987). A primer on institutional research. Tallahassee, FL: Association for Institutional Research.

National Postsecondary Educational Cooperative. (1999). Best practices for data collectors and data providers. Washington DC: National Center for Educational Statistics. (http://nces.ed.gov/pubs99/1999191.pdf)

National Research Council. (1999). Fluency in information technology. Washington, DC: National Research Council.

Pascarella, E. T. & Terenzini, P. T. (1991). How college affects students: Findings and insights from twenty years of research. San Francisco, CA: Jossey-Bass.

Peterson, M. W. (1985). Institutional research: An evolutionary perspective. In M. W. Peterson, & M. Corcoran (Vol. Eds.), New Directions for Institutional Research: No. 46. Institutional research in transition. (pp. 5-16). San Francisco, CA: Jossey-Bass.

Peterson, M. W. (1985). Emerging developments in post-secondary organizations theory and research: Fragmentation or integration? Journal of Educational Research: Vol. 14, No. 3. 5-12.

Peterson, M. W., & Corcoran, M. (1985). Proliferation or professional integration: Transition or transformation. In M. W. Peterson, & M. Corcoran (Vol. Eds.), New Directions for Institutional Research: No. 46. Institutional research in transition. (pp. 99-112). San Francisco, CA: Jossey-Bass.

Peterson, M. W. (Ed.) (1999). ASHE reader on planning and institutional research, Needam Hts, MA: Pearson Custom Publishing.

Presley, J. B. (Ed.), (1990). New Directions for Institutional Research: No. 66. Organizing effective institutional research offices. San Francisco, CA: Jossey-Bass.

Russell, J. D. (1960). The purpose and organization of institutional research. In R. G. Axt & H. T. Sprague (Eds.), College self study lectures on institutional research. Boulder, CO: Western Interstate Commission for Higher Education.

Saunders, L. E., (1983). Politics within the institution. In J. W. Firnberg & W. F. Lasher (Vol. Eds.), New Directions for Institutional Research: No. 38. The politics and pragmatics of institutional research. (pp. 25-38). San Francisco, CA: Jossey-Bass.

Saupe, J. L., & Montgomery, J. R. (1970). The nature and role of institutional research—memo to a college or university president. Tallahassee, FL: The Association for Institutional Research.

Saupe, J. L. (1990). The functions of institutional research. 2nd edition. Tallahassee, FL: Association for Institutional Research.

Schiltz, M. (Ed.). (1992). New Directions for Institutional Research: No. 73. Ethics and standards and institutional research. San Francisco, CA: Jossey-Bass.

Sheehan, B. S. (1985). Telematics and the decision support intermediary. In M. W. Peterson, & M. Corcoran (Vol. Eds.), New Directions for Institutional Research: No. 46. Institutional research in transition. (pp. 81-98). San Francisco, CA: Jossey-Bass.   Southern Association of Colleges and Schools. (1997). Criteria for accreditation: Section 3.3. Atlanta, GA: Commission on Colleges: Southern Association of Schools and Colleges.

Southern Association of Colleges and Schools. (2000). Criteria for accreditation: Section 3.3. Atlanta, GA: Commission on Colleges: Southern Association of Schools and Colleges.

Stickler, W. H. (1967). The role of institutional research. In E. F. Schietinger (Ed.), The managerial revolution in higher education: An overview. In Introductory papers on institutional research. (pp 1-15). Atlanta, GA: Southern Regional Education Board.

Suslow, S. (1971). Present reality of institutional research. C. L. Stewart (Ed.), Presidential Address, 11th Annual Forum of the Association for Institutional Research. Tallahassee, FL: Association for Institutional Research.

Suslow, S. (1972). A declaration of institutional research. Tallahassee, FL: Association for Institutional Research.

Stecklein, J. E. (1970). Institutional research. In A. S. Knowles (Editor-in-Chief), Handbook of college and university administration: Section 4. (pp. 123-134). New York, NY: McGraw-Hill Book Co.

Terenzini P. T. (1993). On the nature of institutional research and the knowledge and skills it requires. The Journal of Research in Higher Education: Vol. 34, No. 1. 1-10.

Tetlow, W. L. (1983). The pragmatic imperative of institutional research. In J. W. Firnberg & W. F. Lasher (Vol. Eds.), New Directions for Institutional Research: No. 38. The politics and pragmatics of institutional research. (pp. 3-10). San Francisco, CA: Jossey-Bass.

Volkwein, J. F. (Ed.). (2000). New Directions for Institutional Research: No. 104. What is institutional research all about?: A critical and comprehensive assessment of the profession. San Francisco, CA: Jossey-Bass.

Whitney, M. A., Porter, J. D., & Fenske, R. H. (Eds.). (1992). The primer for institutional research. Resources for Institutional Research: No. 7. Tallahassee, FL: Association for Institutional Research.

CHAPTER 7: TECHNOLOGY AND TOOLS FOR INSTITUTIONAL RESEARCH

Authors: Victor Borden, Tod Massa, and John Milam

This chapter focuses on the development of tools and technologies in computer technology, information processing and reporting, telecommunications, statistics, and research design which could influence institutional research. Database design and management, electronic communications, and information analysis and reporting, which affect the effectiveness and efficiency of institutional research.

Introduction

There is no doubt that the explosive growth of information technologies has greatly impacted the practice of institutional research in higher education. The impact has been as much qualitative as it has been quantitative. Quantitatively, an information professional can bring together, analyze, and disseminate information more quickly than ever before. Qualitatively, the kinds of information one can access, and the ways one can analyze and disseminate information are fundamentally different than as recently as 10 years ago. Quantum advances in the speed of processing, connectivity, and storage capacity have made available inexpensive and highly sophisticated tools for information management, analysis and dissemination. Creative practitioners, scholars, and organizations have harnessed these technologies to create new methods for deriving intelligence from varying forms of information.

Through a cursory reading of the trade literature, though, it seems that advances in access to raw data and relatively unprocessed information have outpaced advances in our ability to screen and process this information into useable and timely form. This situation was characterized well by Nobel Laureate Herbert Simon (in Varian, 1995, p 200):

> What information consumes is rather obvious: it consumes the attention of its recipients. Hence a wealth of information creates a poverty of attention, and a need to allocate that attention efficiently among the overabundance of information sources that might consume it.

It is a challenge to put into print any discussion about the tools and technologies of institutional research. Changes over the years ahead will likely make obsolete references to specific products or even, in some cases, to a whole class of products. In the spirit of Herbert Simon's remarks, we seek in this chapter to put forth a framework for making decisions about how to allocate attention efficiently among the abundance of information sources regarding the use of information technologies and tools for conducting institutional research. Institutional researchers must be able to do so in order to help their institutional colleagues allocate attention effectively among the vast stores of information now available to support planning and management.

The first section of this chapter considers the processes and products of institutional research. What are we attempting to build with these tools and technologies? What routine processes are we attempting to facilitate? What kinds of tools best suit these various processes? This section construes the practice of institutional research broadly and generically.

In the second section of the chapter, we bring into consideration the variety of skill sets and professional roles that are brought to bear in the practice of institutional research and the use of its common tools. It is evident within large institutions that the practice of institutional research is distributed across a variety of staff and throughout the organization. But, even in the classic "one-person IR shop," the institutional researcher does not work in isolation to transform raw data into useable management information. By mapping tools and technologies to roles, and skill sets, we provide a backdrop for assessing the strategic position of an organization with regard to harnessing information for institutional planning, management, evaluation, and improvement.

In the final section of this chapter, we climb out boldly onto the proverbial limb. We follow some of the current paths of technology development to forecast some future scenarios. We acknowledge that the specific language may change in the coming years, but we believe the basic concepts of the forthcoming transformation are sound.

THE PROCESS AND PRODUCTS OF INSTITUTIONAL RESEARCH

When the only tool you own is a hammer, every problem begins to resemble a nail. – Abraham Maslow

Before turning our attention to specific technologies and tools, we must first consider what we are trying to build, and the processes we use to do so. The previous chapters of this book focus on the content of this work: the types of activities and analyses that the institutional research function supports across the diverse array of institutions of higher education in the United States and internationally. Our concern here is more with the method of institutional research, rather than the content.

In his seminal monograph on the functions of institutional research, Joe Saupe (1990) characterizes the basic function as one of "providing" information which supports institutional planning, policy formation and decision-making" (p. 1). With information as the primary output of institutional research function, the primary processes revolve around converting data into information and presenting that information in appropriate forms and formats for its use in decision-making processes. The particular content focus of an institutional research function,

196

whether on enrollment management, resource allocation, strategic planning, student outcomes assessment, and so on, depends on organizational culture, politics, and structures, as well as office resources. However, the core processes of turning data into usable information are fairly generic.

The process of transforming data into usable information is often characterized as part of a broader cycle. One example is the inductive-deductive cycle that characterizes scientific inquiry as a cycle of conceptualization, hypothesis formulation, data collection, and generalization. The practices of quality improvement revolve around a similar Plan-Do-Check-Act cycle. McLaughlin, et al. (1998) describe an "Information Support Circle," along similar lines, with five functions: identify concepts and measures; collect and store data; restructure and analyze facts; deliver and report information; and use and influence decisions (which connects back to identify concepts and measures, and so on).

Following McLaughlin, et al. but modifying the stages slightly to provide a context for characterizing the technologies and tools that support this work, we propose a "life cycle" of institutional research activity. We stipulate that the stages of development can be viewed for a specific task as well as for the general organizational structures and functions that generally support each stage. We follow the path of a prototypical IR project, from its inception to its completion, through stages of design, collection, preparation, analysis, and dissemination.

The IR Life Cycle

Design

The first stage of any IR task, whether it is conducting an analysis, evaluating a program, or forecasting enrollments, is to develop an overall design. The design is based on the goals and objectives of the project, as well as the audience for whom it is intended. At the macro level, an IR office is guided by its organizational design. It has a mission, goals, and primary clientele. Sometimes these statements are explicit but they may be based on informal dialogue among IR office staff and those to whom they report.

The design stage sets the context for institutional research work, whether on a specific project or more generally with regard to office goals and objectives. The technologies and tools related to design are those that help people communicate and to discover how others have approached similar problems. Word processing, e-mail, and telecommunications have all come to supplement face-to-face meetings as media for communication. Aside from e-mail, the Internet provides possibilities for telecommuting and virtual meetings that will gain in popularity as the bandwidth increases.

Already, the Internet has revolutionized research into best practice. Most major college and university library systems are now linked to, or completely based on the Internet, providing access to vast stores of literature. Beyond the published literature, the Internet provides access to organizational practice at the majority of higher education institutions internationally. Unfortunately, the increased quantity of information has made judgements of quality more difficult. However, the amount of available information for conducting just about any type of institutional research has expanded exponentially over the past decade.

Collection

When the design is complete, the generic IR project moves next to the stage of collection. This refers to both raw data and to more highly processed information, depending on the nature of the project. Generally speaking, the data and information may come from one of three sources: institutional information systems (e.g., student, human resource, and fiscal systems), surveys and other local data collection efforts (e.g., departmental databases, learning assessments), and external sources (IPEDS, Bureau of Census, other institutions, regional sources, etc.). At the macro level, the IR office must develop and maintain an information access and storage infrastructure to accommodate collection. Staff must be trained in local information systems, survey expertise may be necessary, testing and measurement capabilities would be warranted for learning assessment functions, and data and database administration would be necessary at least for managing secondary (decision support) data resources.

The tools and technologies for data collection include those that support data extraction and query (e.g., fourth generation languages), survey design and administration (e.g., word processing, scanning, Web-authoring, data entry, etc.), environmental scanning (general Internet skills and especially external data system manipulation), and database administration (database design tools and databases). Because much of the data and information used in institutional research is first collected by others, the IR practitioner must be well versed in dealing with various file and database formats to function effectively.

Preparation

Given the various sources of data and information used in IR work, there is often a range of activities involved in further preparing extracted data before it is ready for analysis. Error checking and validation are common, as well as merging files, creating derived data elements (using calculations and conditional logic), reconciling data from varying courses or points in time, and so on. Data scrubbing processes are required for data that are collected routinely as well as data that are unique to a specific analysis.

IR practitioners use a broad range of technologies for data scrubbing. Database software may seem the most obvious choice, but many of the software packages designed for analysis (the next stage) include data manipulation functions that support the preparation stages. For example, the statistical package SAS has long been known for its strength as a data preparation tool.

Although less rigorous in this area, the SPSS statistical package can be used for matching, merging, and error checking. Spreadsheet packages also provide some data scrubbing capabilities. The relatively recent addition to Microsoft Excel of data filtering and pivot tables provides a range of data manipulation functions, especially when combined with the database querying capabilities (which all of these packages now have).

Analysis

The next stage of the IR life cycle is data and information analysis. This can take many forms, depending on the nature of the design along with the data and information sources. Quantitative analyses still dominate most IR tasks, but more qualitative methods such as portfolio analysis, focus group research, and ethnographic studies, are gaining in popularity. Within the quantitative realm, the majority of work is in the "descriptive" domain. However, inferential methods are often more appropriate, especially when dealing with survey data.

The choice of tool follows closely with the method of analysis. However, most modern analytical tools can accommodate a range of methods. According to the most recent Association of Institutional Research member survey, the spreadsheet is the most popular tool for institutional researchers. This relates, in part, to the range of activities that a spreadsheet can support, from data preparation through analysis and dissemination. The popularity of the spreadsheet can also be attributed to the prevalence of descriptive analysis. That is, the most popular output of institutional research is a frequency table and simple bar or line chart. Although statistical packages can produce the same tables and charts, the spreadsheet is used more frequently as it is designed more specifically for these purposes and has better formatting capabilities. Spreadsheet packages also support several other popular IR methodologies, including scenario modeling (what-if analysis), projection models, and induced course load matrices.

Statistical packages are the second most widely used technology for the analysis stage. IR practitioners who have more experience with statistical packages are likely to use them for descriptive analysis. Anyone with the skill to conduct inferential analyses is likely to use a statistical package, as it is designed specifically for such tasks. Spreadsheet packages have limited inferential functions, but they are not as well suited to the task.

When it comes to creating graphs and charts, the choice between a spreadsheet and a statistical package (or for that matter, a more full-featured graphing package) is more idiosyncratic. Each type of package has its strengths and weaknesses. Again, spreadsheet packages have a wider range of formatting capabilities. Statistical packages include certain types of graphs not readily available in a spreadsheet (e.g., error bars and box and whisker plots). Stand-alone graphing software may have the widest range of graphing choices and formats. However, they present additional cost and learning requirements.

Dissemination

The final stage of the institutional research life cycle is dissemination. Traditionally, this takes one of two general forms: the preparation of a written report and presentation at a meeting. In practice, however, dissemination is ubiquitous. Telephone calls, speeches, and face-to-face dialogue have always supplemented the dissemination process. Electronic documents are now shared routinely by e-mail and through Web sites. Each form of media serves best a different manner of presentation.

The technologies of dissemination generally align themselves with the media just described. Written documents are generated in word processors and e-mail software, presentations in presentation software. The Internet plays an increasingly important role in dissemination through the transfer of electronic files, e-mail more generally, and Web sites. Although these technologies are the final conduits, several other technologies provide the pieces that are assembled into these. Reports, tables and charts from database spreadsheet and statistical packages are pasted or published into word processing, e-mail, and Web documents. Web sites tie directly to databases for accessing information through a dynamic and interactive interface. Dissemination processes integrate elements of the tools and technologies that support the entire range of activities involved in conducting institutional research.

Application and Feedback

Although not mentioned explicitly as stages of the information cycle, two activities that occur after information dissemination are the most critical determinants of the success and usefulness of the entire process. The use or application of the information product is the primary determinant of success. In addition, institutional research staff require feedback from users of their products to guide the design of future information support efforts.

One could argue that the quality of institutional research products should be gauged mostly, if not entirely, by how they impact institutional decisions and processes. Regardless of the quality of information collection, preparation, analysis, and dissemination, the entire process fails if the report or presentation is not clear, timely, or directly relevant to the audience or use for which it is intended.

For several reasons, it is often helpful for the person who produced the information to be involved in meetings and processes in which it is used. The information producer usually knows best the limitations of the data. Although all information should be accompanied by at least some interpretive comments, there are likely to be questions that arise which require additional interpretations.

It is also important to get feedback from the recipients of information as to how they interpreted and used the supplied information. It is not safe to assume that a lack of unsolicited feedback implies that the information was useful as presented. Dissemination is not the end of a sequential path, but rather the last part of a single revolution. As the cycle of work continues, the intelligence gained during the prior revolution must inform the next turn.

Application and feedback do not introduce additional technology and tool requirements to the information life cycle discussion. Some of the technologies and tools mentioned previously can facilitate these processes. For example, Web-based forms can be used to solicit user feedback or teleconferencing can facilitate participation in meetings during which the products of institutional research are used.

Figure 7.1 summarizes the stages of the institutional research life cycle and their attendant tools and technologies. This process view provides a simple map of tools and technologies to IR activities. In the next section, we consider in more detail the level of sophistication with which one can approach the use of these tools and technologies and the professional roles that are associated with a focus on different technology skill sets.

Figure 7.1
The Life Cycle of Institutional Research and its Associated Technologies

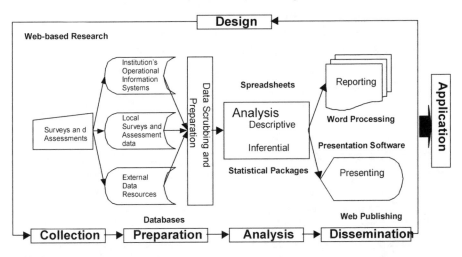

TECHNOLOGY SKILL SETS AND INSTITUTIONAL RESEARCH ROLES

Patrick Terenzini (1993) describes three tiers of intelligence defining the nature of institutional research and its prerequisite skills. Technological skills are delegated to the lowest of the three tiers. Tier 1 intelligence is based in substantive and methodological knowledge, essentially the ability to do things. In Terenzini's own words, "This form of intelligence is foundational: By itself, however, it is of little value." (p. 9). Given the current high demand and corresponding high salaries for technicians such as webmasters, database architects, and system administrators, it is arguable that such intelligence is highly valued in one sense, even if not of high value as described by Terenzini. This leaves us to question the level of involvement with information technology that is appropriate for the typical (or stereotypical) institutional researcher. Should Web-mastering be considered a staple skill for institutional researchers? Is there a limit to the type of programming skills that are appropriate for institutional research?

Information Technology Skills for Institutional Research Professionals

Through the electronic dialog of the Association for Institutional Research Task Force on Information Practices and Technology, a set of primary skills were identified as most relevant to the work of institutional research. As with the tasks of institutional research defined in the first section, we recognize that no one person is likely to embody the entire skill set. Rather, the following skills are identified as necessary for the information management responsibilities of the institutional research function throughout an organization. For a highly centralized IR function, it is probably desirable for office staff to represent the full range of these skills. To the degree that the IR function is distributed across an organization, so should be the relevant skills. In effect, these skills represent the basic abilities of a well-developed information professional.

In broad terms these skills can be grouped in the following categories, which will be considered, in turn:

1. Managing information flow
2. Operating system competency
3. Software application competency
4. Systems planning and management
5. Knowledge of administrative systems
6. Effective Reporting

These six categories focus specifically on activities related to information development, management, and processing. Because of our present focus on information tools and technologies, we are not focusing on skill sets related to such activities as policy analysis, budgeting, space management, and other activities various institutional research practitioners are called on to support.

<u>**Understanding and Managing Information Flow**</u>

This skill set relates to the contextual grasp of how data and information enter the realm of institutional research and flow through storage, analysis and processing, output (as in reports) and into new storage. It includes the following more specific skills:

- Understanding the "business rules" for a specific organization. How does (or should) information from the various institutional operational systems fit together? This relates closely to the "boundary spanning" role of institutional research (Saupe, 1990). Although the institutional researcher does not need to know the vast details of any one system, she or he should have an "enterprise view" of the institutional information across the various operational systems.

- Ability to locate stored information – whether on paper or electronic files. Paper-based information is referenced here mainly to reinforce the idea that information technology is still dependent on existing archives of data. However, the ability to locate data and information stored electronically is a very important skill. This skill represents abilities to intuit relations designed and unintended between elements as well as the more pedestrian abilities to incorporate a knowledge of data dictionaries and access application screens to locate data.

- Track the evolution of a unit record through multiple relationships with the institution (applicant to student to alumnus/ae) – probably the most important skill in data verification and validation.

- Deconstruct higher-level information (such as complex aggregations) to verify accuracy – at some point, critical analysis of another's work or the practitioner's own must be done.

- Develop and maintain contacts in "data custodian" offices that are responsible for the data with which the institutional research office deals. The typical institutional research practitioner cannot be an expert in all the administrative systems, nor should it be considered an option. It is essential to develop collegial relationships with those who maintain the institution's operational information systems instead.

Operating System Competency

This refers to basic computer operation practices and abilities including the following:

- Logging in and out of administrative systems
- Opening system and software applications
- Storing, finding, copying, moving, and deleting files
- Backing up system information and data
- Restoring files and programs from backup
- Formatting removable media (disks, tapes, CD-Rs)
- Installing a new application
- Creating a new password

- Restricting and enabling access to files on a single computer or network

These skills are simple enough that they do not require much explanation or elaboration. Perhaps because of their simplicity, their importance is often taken for granted, at least until a crisis is encountered. Among these skills, the importance of system backup and restoration is too often learned "the hard way."

Software Application Competency

In this realm we include the basic skills for using specific types of applications. This follows closely with the tasks and products development presented in the first section of this chapter. Rather than focusing on the appropriate choice of tool as we did earlier, we here list some desirable skills for effective use of the core IR applications: Word processors, spreadsheets, databases, statistical packages, presentation packages, and the Internet.

Word Processors

In one of the author's experience in converting submitted AIR Forum papers and presentations to HTML format, it was apparent that a number of presenters were still using modern word processing applications as if they were typewriters. It is becoming increasingly important for IR practitioners to master the formatting and style features of modern word processing as we move away from a simple text orientation and toward more highly formatted expectations among those who read our reports. We suggest the following minimum set of word processing competencies:

- Using appropriate formatting techniques, e.g. tables instead of tabs, block indents instead of new paragraphs for each line, tabs instead of spaces, etc.
- Creating a complex report using headings, columns, styles, headers and footers, and other available formatting techniques.
- Using mail merge in coordination with a database
- Creating and maintaining standard templates for reports, memoranda, form letters, etc.
- Embedding graphics and tables from other applications.
- Creating a camera-ready or publishable report

Spreadsheets

As mentioned previously, spreadsheets are one of the two most frequently used applications among institutional research practitioners (the other being e-mail). This is not surprising given that the primary function of spreadsheet software reflects the most common activity of the institutional researcher—preparing tables and charts. It is therefore important that the institutional research practitioner master spreadsheet technology at a relatively high level of sophistication. Toward that end, we list below some of the higher-level spreadsheet skills as essential to the IR application competency skill set:

- Using embedded functions for advanced calculations and descriptive statistics
- Creating appropriate links between cells and worksheets to automate changes and avoid data redundancy
- Performing "what-if?" analyses to monitor the effects of changes in parameters on desired outcomes.
- Creating macros to automate routine and repetitive functions.
- Creating a range of different types of graphs that explain relationships in data or trends.
- Using lookup and matching functions to retrieve information into cells from spreadsheet and external databases.
- Performing pivot table analyses to dynamically manipulate cross-tabulations.
- Creating camera-ready or publishable reports

Databases

Whether an institutional research office uses databases maintained by other offices or develops its own, the IR practitioner should have a core competency in database software. We define an adequate level of competency as including the following skills:

- Designing and creating database objects (tables, queries, forms, reports, and macros)
- Interpreting and writing (or at least editing) SQL queries.
- Manipulating data in complex analyses using multiple queries and reporting templates, etc.
- Sharing data directly between a database and other applications that have compatible data engines (e.g., ODBC)
- Importing and exporting data from and to administrative systems and other applications that do not have compatible data engines.

Statistical Packages

Statistics can be defined as "a collection of methods for planning experiments, obtaining data, and then analyzing, interpreting and drawing conclusions based on the data" (Triola 1992, p. 4). Although most institutional researchers do not conduct their studies within a controlled experimental environment, the relevance of statistical method to core institutional research functions cannot be disputed. Statistical packages are thus considered a core application for the institutional researcher, with the following benchmark skills:

- Selecting methods appropriate to the research design (which for most institutional research studies is generally within the domain of correlational and cross-tabulation analyses)
- Manipulating, recoding, and transforming data as necessary to create measurement scales appropriate to the design
- Merging and concatenating data from multiple files into a "flattened" dataset
- Importing and exporting data from and to administrative systems and other applications that do not have compatible data engines
- Interpreting statistical results appropriately
- Exporting statistical package output to spreadsheets and word processors for inclusion in written reports

Presentation Software

The products of institutional research often have the greatest impact when presented interactively to decision-making groups. Presentation software provides a mechanism for communicating effectively the results of research and analysis. We offer the following minimum set of benchmark skills and best practice guidelines:

- Creating a focused and clear presentation, avoiding the use of "entertaining" graphics and animations that distract the observer
- Embedding table and graphic displays from spreadsheets, word processors and statistical packages
- Using slides as a complement to the spoken word, not an exact copy
- A basic understanding of graphic design and style standards, such as font selection, and color and pattern contrasts

Internet

As mentioned in the first section of this chapter, the Internet has become an increasingly important platform for collecting, analyzing and disseminating information. It is also the platform across which most practitioners communicate within their own institutions and with colleagues throughout the world. Consequently, Internet skills have quickly become part of the core competencies for institutional researchers. These skills include:

- Using the full range of features of a Web browser, including such things as setting preferences and altering standard font sizes

- Downloading and uploading files using FTP software or Web browser
- Selecting and using a search engine effectively to find a relevant Web sites
- Using Web-based data extract systems, such as WebCaspar, Census Bureau and the National Center for Education Statistics data access tools.
- Creating a Web page with an authoring tool or raw HTML
- Incorporating data and information from other applications (spreadsheets, database, word processing reports) into Web pages
- Working knowledge of the Web page "Internet Resources for Institutional Researchers" (http://airweb.org/) and the key information resources linked to that page (e.g., AIR and regional sites, SCUP, NACUBO, CHE Academe Today and Archives, Department of Education, etc.)
- Ability to work with various file formats (compressed files, e-mail attachments, etc.)
- Understanding and using the etiquette of e-mail discussion lists and newsgroups

Systems Planning and Management

This skill set is less about hardware and software and more about the ability to design new and map existing relationships between data and information. For example, designing a longitudinal student tracking system database is more about the relationships between students, the institution, and sequential events than it is about the types and sizes of fields to use within the database. Core skills in this area include:

- Ability to state IR needs in IT language. Administrative programmers and systems support staff often do not understand the decision support information needs of institutional research. It is incumbent upon the institutional researcher to learn to work with IT people and communicate effectively. Doing so also improves the IR practitioner's understanding of the IT systems in place.
- Understanding the tradeoffs between efficiency of storage vs. efficiencies of access and analysis – this is simply the struggle between levels of data normalization. How should data be structured for maximum efficiency – whether for the software's efficiency or the user's efficiency?
- Ability to differentiate between accurate and inaccurate data (including out-of-range and inconsistent data). An institutional researcher needs to be able to verify unit record data using the operational systems and error-checking algorithms. To do this effectively the practitioner must be equipped with significant knowledge of the institution's operational information systems.
- Ability to operationalize a research question into a program or set of

queries and tests. Although more of a "research" skill than an "IT" skill, it is included here because of the wide variety of tools utilized, including applications that are designed particularly for statistical analysis and research.

Knowledge of Administrative Systems

Institutional researchers employ data and information from a variety of sources. However, an institution's mission-critical operational information systems represent a critical data resource with special skill requirements:

- Familiarity with data-entry processes and data lookups
- Ability to extract data for analysis
- Familiarity with user groups and support sites
- Awareness of available data access and analysis tools on-campus and generally

Competency for Effective Reporting

These core skills relate to reporting, displaying, and publishing data and information, including:

- Displaying data aggregations with clarity and purpose. Aggregations should be obvious in placement and intent.
- Making the most important pieces the most obvious. Short of drawing circles and arrows, the eye of the reader should be drawn to the data that are most important.
- Creating maintainable and portable report procedures. Treat every new report as a new standard report. Use standard procedures for commenting code and storing queries and database objects to allow ad hoc queries and reports to be used again later.
- Finding a contextually appropriate level of detail for the audience.

A more complete elaboration of guidelines for best practice in this area can be found in the writings of Edward Tufte including his books, *The Visual Display of Quantitative Information* (1983) and *Envisioning Information* (1990).

The Information Professional Roles of Institutional Researchers

A given institutional research practitioner is likely to possess strengths and weaknesses in the various skills elaborated above. In addition, unless one individual is called on to conduct a full range of institutional research functions, it is probably best to staff an institutional research office with a range of skill sets to "cover the technical bases." In this section, we describe three information professional roles that map the range of technology skills to the range of

208

institutional research tasks described in the first section of the chapter. We do not intend to imply that these roles <u>should</u> be used as guidelines for defining staff positions (although they <u>can</u> be). Rather, we offer these as a framework for evaluating how well-positioned an institutional research office or function is for taking advantage of the full range of tools of the trade.

Information Executive

The Information Executive does her job at the beginning and end stages of an institutional research project. At the beginning, she coordinates the design of the task, including the specification of research design, necessary resources, timelines, and division of labor among other staff. At the end, she coordinates the interpretation, packaging, and presentation of results to decision-makers. This role is often associated with the institutional research director position, but may well be distributed to others within the organization, such as associate deans, administrative directors, and other assistants to top-level administrators.

The Information Executive should be well-versed in the technologies of presentation: Word processors, presentation packages, and spreadsheets. She will likely also be well-versed in the tools of analysis, because knowledge of research design and interpretation generally follow from hands-on experience with analysis. Moreover, if in the director position, she will likely be familiar with the tools of data extraction and maintenance, in order to effectively supervise staff who support these efforts. Finally, the Information Executive should be well-versed in the Internet resources that are most relevant to conceptualizing and operationalizing an institutional research project.

Information Architect

The Information Architect uses data extracted from various sources. With this, he builds secondary databases for use in analysis. He also conducts the analysis and prepares summaries for the Information Executive. The Information Architect knows enough about primary data sources to successfully identify appropriate sources. However, he does not necessarily know the detailed nuances of these data sources, and may not even know how to extract the data. The information role is prototypically associated with a research analyst position.

The technology and tools most important to the Information Architect Role include desktop database systems, statistical packages, and spreadsheets. That is, the tools most relevant to the "middle range" of institutional research tasks as depicted in Table 7.1 on page 210.

Information Engineer

The Information Engineer supports the design, development and maintenance of the core data infrastructure for institutional research tasks. She will need to be well-versed in the administrative information systems of her organization, and the tools needed to extract data for institutional research and decision support analysis. The position titles associated with this role vary. Traditionally, the role might have been classified as a programmer or technician. More recently, titles such as webmaster have appeared. In small institutional research shops, a research analyst position may span both the Information Engineer and Architect roles. In the smallest of shops—the one-person shop—the institutional researcher must span elements of all three roles, or have staff in other areas that serve in the necessary capacities.

In today's information environment, the Information Engineer will likely be involved in the creation and maintenance of data warehouses or other forms of decision support database development and maintenance. She will still likely need to rely on fourth generation languages (4GLs) to extract data from legacy systems. The Information Engineer's skill set should therefore include strong administrative information system competencies, database design and maintenance systems. SQL and other algorithmic programming tools (e.g., Visual Basic, C+, or Java) and Web-authoring tools with focus on database connectivity are becoming increasingly important to this role.

The three information roles and their associated tasks and tools are summarized in Table 7.1. We reiterate that these are not prescriptive roles, nor are they guidelines for defining positions. Moreover, the organizational climate and information access policies of an institution influence the range of information roles available to an institutional research practitioner. For example, some institutions may place the Information Engineer role outside the IR office, in the information technology (IT) organization. This can be an effective arrangement if the IT organization is responsive to institutional research staff and fully understands their needs. Furthermore, placing the entire Information Engineer role within the IR office can work well only if it is provided sufficient resources and unhampered access to institutional data.

MAPPING THE FUTURE: WHERE CURRENT PATHS LEAD

In this section, we consider how several emerging technologies will help shape higher education and the nature of institutional research work in the years to come. Clearly the development of spreadsheets, databases, word processing, and graphics packages changed IR dramatically beginning in the early to mid 1980s. There was much excitement then over using SuperCalc on an Apple IIe to build enrollment projections and ask "What if?" questions. For the first time, IR practitioners could graphically display pie, bar, and line charts using Harvard Graphics with DOS on an 8086 processor. The emergence of the World Wide Web since 1993 is at least a comparable transformation, and probably greater. The advent of the Web, and the expanded use of an Internet which has itself evolved over 30 years, represent more of a paradigmatic shift than the introduction of spreadsheets.

The constellation of Web servers, database application middleware, and

Table 7.1

Information Professional Roles and the Associated Tasks and Tools

Role	Tasks	Tools
Information Executives	Specifies formats and requests data/ information; interprets, packages and presents information; typically works with data at a high level of abstraction	Primary-word processors, spreadsheets, presentation software, Internet Secondary-Statistical packages, Databases
Information Architects	Requests flat-files of data to specifications; designs and builds structures to hold the data and create new levels of information and abstraction. Analyzes data and prepares preliminary tables and charts	Primary-databases, spreadsheets, statistical packages Secondary-data query and manipulation tools
Information Engineers	Typified by direct access to the administrative system; develops queries to extract data and port it to self-designed structures for archiving, analysis and reporting.	Administrative information systems, 4GLs, desktop databases, programming and scripting languages, web/database development systems

HTML editors gives institutional research practitioners the opportunity to gather and present information in ways never imagined before. These developments allow us to become the knowledge brokers rather than just "number crunchers." With hypertext, Web database applications, and highly sophisticated analysis software, we are free to see new kinds of patterns in the data and to present and disseminate ideas instantaneously, unhampered by the technology and perhaps even our own limitations.

Changing Tools

The theory and essential work of institutional researchers are not changing as much as the tools. The literature base is the same, growing cumulatively. There are still a relatively finite number of data elements for each type of administrative system, but the possibilities for collecting, analyzing, and disseminating data, information, and knowledge are now much more sophisticated.

Clearly, we are benefiting from years of software development and the evolution of data extraction systems. Database environments such as Microsoft's SQL Server provide online analytical processing (OLAP) tools for data mining that are relatively inexpensive, enterprise-wide solutions. From Visual C++ to

Visual J, new and easier programming language packages are available. These will continue to evolve into tools that require less technical training and experience.

The development of Open Database Connectivity (ODBC) and Object Linking and Embedding (OLE) drivers allow us to query any database (including live data) using Structured Query Language (SQL), which is itself a major innovation for IR work. SAS, SPSS, Microsoft Access, and most every database and statistical tool we now use allow us to write programs against data in any format, from AASCII to Oracle. Microsoft Windows and Macintosh operating systems continue to evolve as well.

Internet Development

Dynamic HTML and interactive Web sites have become the expectation of Internet users. Although much of the commercial implementation of Javascript, cascading style sheets, and plug-in software such as Shockwave and RealPlayer is exciting, it does not add nearly as much value to the institutional research function as do Web database applications. Products such as Cold Fusion, IBM Lotus Notes, SPSS SmartViewer Web Server, and Microsoft's technology of Active Server Pages (ASP) will continue to evolve in ways that allow an exciting new level of application development. Essentially, IR offices will be able to collect and disseminate data in myriad ways, simply painting the online screens they want. With ODBC/OLE and SQL, any dataset can be used for drilling down and up on data and querying at any level of aggregation. Java applets and products such as Chart FX allow for dynamic creation of graphs on the fly, using any combination of fields and color schemes. While these require limited knowledge of Java and data element parameters, software such as Cold Fusion Studio, Drumbeat 2000, Visual InterDev, and Tango allow users with relatively little knowledge of programming to build complex Web database applications.

New Transaction Systems

All of the major administrative system vendors—SCT, PeopleSoft, Datatel, and Oracle—have, or are in the process of developing online, Web versions of admissions, registration, student, course, financial aid, human resources, research, financial, and space information systems. The vendors have moved in this direction to keep pace with Web expectations. Sometimes the innovations are only on the surface, for example using "screen scraper" software to design a Web interface to an existing mainframe application. This limited approach gives the appearance of being more user friendly without requiring the reinvention of business rules and data element dictionaries. Other implementations require a complete conversion, with many issues of data integrity, new ways to build extracts, screen and report design, and database administration.

With either of these divergent paths to building online systems, IR offices must be prepared to continue their typical tasks of extracting datasets for census and operational reporting. IR staff must be prepared to learn new extraction tools to meet required reporting needs. Many schools had to learn this the hard way, rewriting old Cobol programs to extract data from legacy systems as part of year 2000 compliance problems.

Too often, the transaction-based approach of the vendors' administrative systems fails to anticipate the higher level needs of management and it is IR's responsibility to ensure that these needs are addressed in any conversion or upgrade. This process, while onerous, is an opportunity to help senior administration think through difficult data issues, such as organizational mapping. Sometimes different levels of mapping are used in financial and human resource systems than in student information systems. A department for academic purposes is not always a department for finance purposes. With 4GL tools, IR can map these relationships, model them, and bring different systems together for analyses such as program review, and complex modeling such as cost of instruction.

Faster Product Cycles

The development of PC, Macintosh, and PDA hardware has been unparalleled. Development cycles for new products are much faster than they used to be before the Web, with many more iterations. Motherboards, bus designs, processor chips, memory, hard disks, read-write optical storage (CD/CD-R/CD-WR/DVD), floppy disks, networking cards and routers, monitors (flat and touch screen), pointing devices, keyboards, handheld devices such as the Palm Pilot and PocketPC, cameras, microphones, surround sound speakers, projectors, and printers are changing so rapidly that planned obsolescence is no longer a joke but a necessity. Equipment upgrades must become part of base budget planning.

Small portable computers (laptop, notebook, and pocket) are gaining in popularity and can often be used as a desktop substitute, not just for those on the road or wanting to work at home. Current notebooks and pocket PCs meet a variety of needs and become a useful tool in any office or conference room. With wireless networking and modems, notebook users are free to roam, to go wherever they need to for collecting and presenting data. New Web "clipping" standards help convert HTML Web sites for wireless PDA access to IR information.

Bandwidth

Changes in bandwidth may well represent the most influential shift in hardware capability. The Internet 2 and Next Generation Internet initiatives, and the increasing installation of cable modems, ADSL over standard telephone lines, and satellite downloading will practically eliminate the current limitations in Web that are related to limited bandwidth. From viewing HDTV-quality video to downloading, installing, and running software on demand, there is no limit to what is possible with existing technology once the solution to bandwidth is fully implemented.

With ubiquitous Internet access, increased bandwidth, and firewall protection, the Virtual Private Network (VPN) replaces the client server model of the early 1990s as the emerging networking approach. It no longer matters where someone works. Data can be shared across platforms. With the lowest computing prices ever, the vision for the Java Virtual Machine and thin clients will be within reach of everyone. PCs with minimal configurations will load a version of software such as Windows Pocket PC or Java, then serve up software on demand as needed.

New Skills and Roles

The process of keeping up with all of these technological changes may seem daunting. However, an institutional researcher need only be an average user, not a power user or developer, to take advantage of these new technologies. Notebook configurations, Web servers, HTML, and Web-enabled database applications are not arcane or occult. These existing tools are being used by hundreds of thousands of companies. Institutional research practitioners do need to keep up with technology changes, however, so this task needs to be given a high value among competing priorities.

Perhaps this is one of the more difficult issues to raise among readers from a variety of institutional types with different missions. The point is that there is no way, regardless of staffing, to keep up with the changing tasks of IR without technology, and there is no way to use technology without making time to stay current with existing tools. One doesn't need to become a beta tester, but to install the latest version of software and to stay alert to new trends. It doesn't matter whether one works in a single-person office or as part of a team with seven people, technology may be used to transform the work of IR and the institution, if the vision is there and if this becomes part of the mission of the office.

Those who use a wide variety of software and hardware find that it becomes easier, not harder, the more we try new technology. It is a little like learning a language. The first new language requires great effort, especially for adults. Once a few languages are learned well, such as Spanish and French, it is less of an effort to learn to read a half-dozen more. One becomes acutely aware of the patterns involved, of the intuitive nature of learning and the structures of knowledge. Many software packages do work alike, and understanding new programs is a cumulative, sequential, and linear, albeit also intuitive, process.

Seeing Patterns in the Data

Much as in learning to use any software package well, there is a need for IR practitioners to learn to understand datasets. Once one grasps the possible structures of data for a given type of system, whether student or space, it is

214

easy to see patterns in how the data may be used for aggregate decision-making. This ability to see patterns in the data is the heart of the skill set required for providing leadership in the information infrastructure of institutions.

In Web-enabled institutional research, it is important to know about best practices for disseminating data electronically. More importantly, what are the critical analytical conventions for sharing data? How should the data be aggregated, grouped, sorted, and mapped? How might one drill down or up on the data to summarize results at different levels? Which variables need to be included for meaningful comparisons at each level?

After users experience this kind of approach to a dataset, they will be able to make use of many kinds of data, from space to financial aid to human resource. Tools such as Cold Fusion and Drumbeat 2000, along with SQL and HTML, can be learned by anyone who takes the time and is willing to experiment. What it is impossible to get from these tools, and what IR offices are most prepared to offer, is the insight into how data can be meaningfully arrayed for Web-enabled institutional research. This approach is the same whether the data are quantitative or qualitative. Even in ethnographic studies and data collection efforts, there is reliance on the development of patterns in the data. In student portfolios and open-ended, unstructured interview protocols for outcomes assessment, the key is finding, analyzing, and reporting on patterns, however the data are arrayed.

Merging Roles with IT and Library Systems

Natural confusion sets in when trying to overlay this new role for institutional research with those traditionally associated with information technology (IT) and library systems. It is IT that runs the mainframes, keeps the network running, manages the conversion to administrative systems, supports Internet access and bandwidth, makes standards for buying PCs and Macs, and maintains and supports computers on campus. It is the library that first developed gopher menu systems and then Web sites for the institution. Librarians play a tremendously important role in helping users find the information resources they need, whether these are online documents or data.

The IR role is blurring by necessity with those of IT and library systems, and IR offices are working alongside these units in building database applications and university-wide Web sites. However, there is an important distinction. Neither IT nor the library is responsible for the aggregate use of data for decision-making. Neither is tasked with meeting the immediate and long-range needs at the executive level for producing and interpreting policy data, or for producing factbooks, unit record reporting, or federal IPEDS reports.

IR is the key player in making sense of the data, and this function needs to adopt something of the other two. From IT, it needs to share the task of keeping up with and supporting current technology and not reinvent the wheel in the appropriate use of Web server and database technology, given natural constraints of cost, staffing, maintenance, and security. From library systems,

IR must rethink the best ways to present information in a system which users can effectively navigate. This role is one of Knowledge Management (or KM), in which institutional researchers begin to see themselves as critical knowledge workers in the higher education industry.

Building the New Infrastructure

Moving to less abstract ideas about incorporating technology, it is helpful to focus on some critical implementations of software and hardware tools which will help shape the information infrastructure or landscape. Examined here will be IR projects for environmental scanning, performance indicators, data marts/ data warehouses, online surveys, executive information systems, and intranets/ extranets.

Environmental Scanning

With the World Wide Web, institutional researchers have the best possible tool for conducting what Jim Morrison and others have defined as the important task of environmental scanning. Information about everything from competitor institutions to feeder schools to business and industry in the region is available for free with the click of a mouse. To facilitate the use of these links, IR offices are building value-added homepages which categorize links by topical area. The Web site "Internet Resources for Institutional Research" (http://airweb.org/links) may be considered an environmental scanning portal, with thousands of links on a hundred different topics.

Many IR offices provide links to their peers and to critical data sources. This is a good start. Building the new infrastructure demands that IR offices go the next step, that they spend the time to find all types of quality Web sites that might be of use in management and decision-making. With these links, they need to build mini-reviews. One idea tried by the authors, is recording mini briefs of one to two minutes to talk about each link. Users can click on an icon and get the audio briefing. No Web server software is required, only a media player that recognizes the Mime type audio file, usually installed in the browser. The bottom line is that IR staff must be proactive in searching and using the Internet for data and information and developing innovative ways to share what they find.

Performance Indicators

This hot topic of the accountability and quality movements is also well served by the Web. There are dozens of key datasets available for use, everything from IPEDS files to admissions guide data. While the selection of indicators is unique to each institution's mission, climate, and governance structure, gathering data to support the broad themes of indicators that are chosen is a basic Internet task.

The NCES and NSF Web sites have the most utility and so are a basic starting point. If users don't want to download and analyze the raw datasets, they have many choices, among them: (1) the IPEDS Peer Analysis System; (2) the IPEDS College Opportunities On-Line (COOL); (3) the WebCASPAR site, with various NSF, NCES, and NRC data; (4) the NSF SESTAT online database with SDR, NSCG, and NSRCG data; (5) Census data; and (6) DAS on the Web with NCES survey data such as NSOPF and NPSFAS. The NPEC ANSWERS Web site, Accessing National Surveys with Electronic Research Sources, is another new online tool sponsored by NCES, offering a portal of information about institutional datasets.

Each of these sites will continue to evolve, and users should check them regularly for the most recent datasets, best practices and analytical conventions about how they should be used. Once specific indicators are chosen, there are many ways to display the results over time. In spreadsheets or in simple database tables, these can be saved readily in HTML format. With hundreds of potential indicators, some IR offices build database-driven Web applications to list the current choices by category, source, or date.

One of the most fruitful ways to share performance indicators via existing technology is with a digital dashboard of indicators. There is no reason to expect a standard list of indicators to meet all needs. Why not list two hundred and let the user pick the top ones that she or he wishes to keep track of? These data don't have to be just institutional peer comparison data, but can be internal data queried through a data mart or data warehouse and made available daily, monthly, or annually over the Web. Use Java to display each choice graphically in a "dashboard" effect for useful monitoring. The key here is flexibility, allowing many choices and many paths to getting critical data for decision-making and accountability. This blurs the distinction between data mart and Web database application, but these are artificial barriers. What matters is that the Web allows timely and useful display of complex data in a secure and user-friendly, graphical environment.

Data Marts/Data Warehouses

The indicator example above illustrates a single dimension of a possible data mart approach. There is a specific report structure, the indicator, and there is a dataset from which the results are taken. The data can be refreshed on any schedule, and can be operational or census. Many times, the utility of census data is low after the 10th class day for student information. For financial, human resource, and space data, many administrators are only interested in the most current data.

In getting to know executive users, over time IR staffers begin to sense which types of reports and levels of aggregation are most appropriate. Building a data mart is relatively simple, as knowing the data is key. Setting up a Web server and a database application is secondary. While perceived as complicated because it is new, this kind of Web-enabled institutional research is relatively easy. Many offices can hire a freshman engineering student to help them get started. Once running, Web servers require little maintenance. Again, the hard part is determining useful data and establishing the appropriate level of aggregation and possible ways to drill down or up on the data.

Data warehouses require data to be normalized with tables that permit only appropriate one-to-many and many-to-one relationships. Mapping issues are always present, as they are in any complex report. Issues of referential integrity and bad or missing data are data administration tasks that IR offices routinely face as part of preparing unit record reports for statewide reporting.

Building a data mart or warehouse involves the same basic building blocks mentioned above: (1) a computer running an operating system such as Unix, Linux, Windows, or Mac; (2) Web server software such as Internet Information Server for "serving the data;" (3) a database middleware technology, such as Cold Fusion software or Active Server Pages; (4) ODBC/OLE drivers for accessing a specific type of database; (5) SQL for manipulating the data; (6) HTML forms for selecting data; and (7) HTML tables and other features for presenting the results.

The only limitations of this approach are in the imagination of the IR staff. Some versions of the software will still run on a PC with at least 32 MB of RAM. The Web server is usually free or low cost. While some of the middleware products have increased in cost, academic pricing is still very competitive. IR offices need to be using SQL anyway to think about how they are manipulating their data. The rest is simple HTML and knowing how to present effective aggregate information.

IR Office Web Sites

Most IR offices have at least a few static homepages available on some campus Web server which describe the work they do and present some simple forms of data. A growing number have gone the next step and built electronic factbooks and data marts. This has occurred because of many efforts to share good practice and justify the existence of the IR function. IR offices have to build Web sites if they are going to remain viable players in the information infrastructure. Every entity with which institutions interact, from federal/state/ local government to financial aid agencies to professional associations to online admissions services, has an evolving presence on the Web.

Many of the electronic factbooks which are currently available are simply online mirrors of the print version, but there is so much more that can be done. The print model should not guide the development of online data. It is just a starting point for looking at the data and at appropriate analytical conventions and means for their display. For example, graphs that are printed in black and white can be displayed in color. Graphs can be made interactive so that different data are displayed by clicking on the legend and on different bars or slices of a pie.

In addition to various types of data marts for sharing all aspects of institutional data, IR offices are building other data-driven applications, such as

218

for enrollment targets. The classic induced course load matrix (ICLM) of departmental consumption and contribution is an unwieldy product in spreadsheet format, much less in print. On the Web, the ICLM is a manageable tool that allows thousands of permutations in viewing these complex and important data.

With online feedback forms and pages that detail the office mission, staff, and reports, IR can ensure a level of continuous quality feedback necessary for improvement. The IR Web site is critical to the office becoming a leader in facilitating the use of information. Data are made available anytime/anywhere to executives and, depending upon the level of security, the public to meet many levels and types of data needs.

Online Surveys

Many IR offices have responsibility conducting surveys for assessment, enrollment management, or other decision support purposes. Existing Web tools make the development and analysis of online surveys a real jewel in the arsenal of IR tools. Radio buttons are perfect for Likert scales. Where it was often too expensive to record comments when doing data entry, online surveys shift the data entry role to the respondent. Also, value-based security can ensure that only valid responses to a survey item are allowed to be submitted.

The National Center for Education Statistics (NCES) began in August 1999 to make all of its IPEDS surveys Web-based. Another NCES-sponsored project is the Voluntary Institutional On-Line Information Network (VIOLIN), a new type of voluntary data collection effort that will supplement IPEDS and be linked to the Peer Analysis System.

One does not need a Web server and an understanding of Web database applications to conduct an online survey. The basics of HTML forms may be mastered by studying other examples and the results may be submitted via e-mail with the use of the mailto function in http. The resulting data become a single record in a dataset, marked by specific delimiters. Software such as Web Forms may be used to read these e-mails and save them in database format. Free Perl scripts exist as well for saving the results into a dataset format.

It is not just assessment surveys of graduating seniors and returning students that are being moved to the Web. Student ratings of instruction and faculty/staff surveys are also being conducted online. It is important to recognize that both tasks of the survey effort, data collection and data dissemination, can be accommodated on the Web. Just as forms are used to collect data, tables are use to display the results. In some cases, form data are used for polling and results are immediately displayed against the data collected to date. This value-added feedback to respondents allows them to know how they compared to the rest of the survey population. This technique also increases response rates. If online surveys are going to do any better than their print counterparts, there must be some increased rewards for participating, either in comparing responses or in giveaways such as free phone cards or printable coupons.

A next step in thinking about data collection via the Web is the emergence of online workflow processes. At some schools, Web data about budget requests, requests for space, and even online ordering of supplies are collected and processed. The results are passed to the next approval level for action and then forwarded as appropriate for purchase or decision-making. All aspects of the workflow diagram of many such tasks can be emulated and enhanced via the Web.

Executive Information Systems

Assembled together, the environmental scanning links, dashboard of performance indicators, IR Web site, online workflow, and data mart/warehouse comprise the bulk of many models for an executive information system (EIS). As IR offices facilitate ways in which their administrators may use the Web, it may be useful to present a vision of the EIS to executives.

Like the data warehouse, the EIS is often perceived as a complex application only attainable at the most sophisticated university. The truth is that size of institution and IR office are not the best predictors of success. Rather it is the recognition by senior executives that the Web is a critical way to disseminate data and information and that an alliance can be formed between IR and IT in providing this solution.

As discussed earlier, the Web server and Web database technologies involved are easily grasped if time is spent experimenting with them and if they are given a high priority among competing tasks. IR staff already know and understand the most important ways to use aggregate data for decision-making. The key to success is individualizing the process, for there are many expectations about what an EIS should offer and there are many levels of expertise and interest in using the Web. Administrators who are reluctant to check e-mail on a regular basis and who do not maintain a personal list of bookmarks will not be likely candidates for EIS adoption. IR must make assumptions about the change process which most executives will undergo when adopting a new technology. Again, these are larger questions about the infrastructure of information at an institution which IR staff can facilitate and help in providing leadership.

Given assumptions about the campus climate for using Web technology, all of the best Web applications will be of little utility if they are not used. For this reason, personalized homepages are important, with individually chosen dashboards of performance indicators. The VP for student affairs will want different indicators than the VP for finance. Student affairs may want specialized queries of the data mart, while the finance VP may rely on the administrative system for financial reporting. Both may want access to an environmental scanning page, though both will follow different links of interest. Both may want some kind of project or topic tracking application, which allows them to be kept current on topics of high interest to their roles.

Though many schools are developing their online presence as a kind of Web portal, with navigation designed for different audiences such as students and alumni, few concentrate on meeting the needs of major administrators. The building blocks of this system move from basic, static IR pages to interactive electronic factbooks to specialized data warehouse queries. In each case, the definition and use of the EIS is different, tailored to the audience. It is this personalized version of the use of technology that is most critical to its success.

Intranets and Extranets

On a broader level, various Web applications are often strung together in a single Web site to foster the appearance of an intranet for internal audiences, whether administrators or students. The extranet goes beyond internal needs to provide a user interface that addresses larger constituent groups, such as the media, potential students, peer institutions, and the general public. Intranet content varies so widely, even in a specific industry, that assumptions about what it should or should not offer topically are misplaced. For example, some intranets feature the daily menu of student dining and others provide the interface to online admissions and registration.

In place of specific content, there are certain features to look for in thinking about facilitating online communication and coordination at an institution. These are the panoply of Web applications and include static pages, chat rooms, listservs, threaded discussion groups, whiteboards, guest books, myriad database applications, audio broadcasts, video, Java applets for simulations, virtual tours/images (with 3D and panorama), and numerous document and data collection and dissemination efforts.

While many other offices besides IR are addressing Web site needs for students and faculty, there is often less emphasis on administrative needs. It is here that IR offices will find substantial support for their ideas. Do not duplicate the obvious pockets of intranet offerings wherever they spring up. Some will be done well and others will duplicate your own attempts. Innovation is key, and there is a delicate balance between duplication of effort and creating new paths for sharing information. This is an evolving process, and it is more important to facilitate the use of the Web for various needs than to control or ration it.

A Vision of the Virtual IR Office

The virtual IR office is not necessarily found in a specific room or building. With a notebook, projector, and wireless Internet connection, IR staff can be found working anywhere and everywhere, from the library to the boardroom. Existing, cutting-edge tools are used to share data and information in myriad formats, with Web sites as the primary method of navigation and dissemination.

There are no data, from space to sponsored research to continuing education, to which IR staff cannot get extracts in some format to manipulate and analyze. Because they are part of a larger dialogue about data administration, organizational mapping, and entity relationships, IR staff are prepared to see patterns in any dataset and to develop aggregate reports for decision-making on any topic critical to the mission of the institution.

Assessment surveys and continuous quality improvement feedback are collected online. Online workflow processes are developed to implement best practices and improve operational efficiency. With links to all types of institutional documents and Internet resources, environmental scanning is an ongoing process serving the current and future hot topics of executives. Data marts are built for a variety of purposes with operational, census, and historical data. Over time, these evolve into data warehouses and these into the base of an executive information system. Each administrator's data needs are personalized with Web-based dashboards of performance indicators, relevant links, document warehouses, and specialized queries.

Working as part of a larger team with IT and library systems, it is the IR staff who are looked to by administrators and external constituencies as the knowledge brokers of the institution. There is no question or need for data which IR cannot address. With technology support as a high priority of the office, staff members are prepared to use whatever tools necessary to solve a problem, build an application, or research a policy issue. This blurring of operational and staff support roles is recognized as a symbol of the emerging knowledge economy and the roles necessary to be leaders in the knowledge management of complex and increasingly virtual higher education institutions.

References

McLaughlin, G. W., Howard, R. D., Balkan, L. A., & Blythe, E. W. (1998). People, processes, and managing data. Resources in Institutional Research; No. 11. Tallahassee, FL: Association for Institutional Research.

Saupe, J. L. (1990). The functions of institutional research, (2nd Ed.). Tallahassee, FL: Association for Institutional Research.

Terenzini, P. T. (1993). On the nature of institutional research and the knowledge and skills it requires. Research in Higher Education, 34 (1), 1-10.

Triola, M. F. (1992). Elementary statistics. Reading, MA : Addison-Wesley.

Tufte, E. R. (1983). The visual display of quantitative information. Cheshire, CT: Graphics Press.

Tufte, E. R. (1990). Envisioning information Cheshire, CT: Graphics Press.

Varian, H. (1995). The information economy. Scientific American, 273 (3), 200.